Descendants

Descendants

The Divided Lineage of a Louisiana Creole Family

John W. Durel

University of Louisiana at Lafayette Press
2025

ISBN 13 (paper): 978-1-959569-21-3

http://ulpress.org
University of Louisiana at Lafayette Press
P.O. Box 43558
Lafayette, LA 70504-3558

Library of Congress Cataloging-in-Publication Data

Names: Durel, John W. (John Walter), 1945- author.
Title: Descendants : the divided lineage of a Louisiana Creole family / John W. Durel.
Other titles: Divided lineage of a Louisiana Creole family
Description: Lafayette, LA : University of Louisiana at Lafayette Press, 2025. | Includes bibliographical references.
Identifiers: LCCN 2024060653 | ISBN 9781959569213 (paperback)
Subjects: LCSH: Dorrell family. | Durel, Jean Baptiste, 1727-1790--Family. | Multiracial families--Louisiana--New Orleans. | Creoles--Louisiana--New Orleans--Biography. | Creoles--Louisiana--New Orleans--Genealogy. | New Orleans (La.)--Race relations--History. | New Orleans (La.)--Genealogy.
Classification: LCC F379.N553 A224 2025 | DDC
305.8009763092/2--dcundefined
LC record available at https://lccn.loc.gov/2024060653

Cover image: (Top) *Edmond Gustave Fortier* (1822–1862). Historical Archives of the Supreme Court of Louisiana. Public Domain. (Bottom) *Clara DeJan,* née *Abat* by Adolphe Rinck, 1841. Courtesy of the Louisiana State Museum.

CONTENTS

Prologue vii

Chapter 1. *The Founding Generation* 1

Jean Baptiste Durel and Cécile LeBrun

Marie Jeanne, old Marie, and the girl Marie

Ester Durel and Other Free Persons of Color

Chapter 2. *The First Creole Generation* 29

Rose Durel and Michel Fortier

Victoire Durel and Florent Basile

Manette and Françoise Durel, *née* Dejan

Clarisse Durel, *née* Andry

Chapter 3. *The Second Creole Generation* 59

Jean Michel Fortier and Henriette Milon, *Free Woman of Color*

Michel, Aimée and Félicité Durel, *Mestizos*

Jean Florent Durel and Idalise Manadé, *Free Woman of Color*

Jean Baptiste Durel, *Free Man of Color*

Chapter 4. *The Civil War and Reconstruction Generation* 87

Henry Durel and Félicité Knoll

J. B. Numa Durel and Louise Brulard, *Free Persons of Color*

Forester Durel and Caroline Duchamp

Chapter 5. *The Divided Generation* 115

Professor Alcée Fortier, *White*

Delphine Fortier, *Black*

Chapter 6. *The Jim Crow Generations* 135

Two Durel Families, One Black, One White

Edward, *Black*, and Walter, *White*

Milton, *Black*, and Mederic, *White*

Chapter 7. The Civil Rights Generation 157
Stafford, *Black,* and John, *White*

Epilogue 173

Acknowledgments 177

Abbreviations 179

Appendix 181

Endnotes 201

Bibliography 231

Index 237

Prologue

Felix was a wigmaker, Cuspin a personal servant, Ursin a ship's captain. All three men were in their twenties when they met in the French colony of Saint-Domingue in the year 1790.[1] Their encounter changed the lives of two of them forever. The third thought nothing of it.

Eighteenth-century France was a showy age. Gentlemen and ladies dressed in satins and ruffles, powdered their faces and adorned wigs à la mode, following styles set by royalty. Men showed off their calves, women their bosoms. As if on stage, they dressed to be noticed and admired. At a fancy ball or at the theater, at Sunday Mass or on a Sunday afternoon promenade, or simply at home receiving guests, they sought to stand out, to attract attention, to rise above the crowd. In a society defined by hierarchy, people used appearance to signify status. Walking down a street one could see where one fit relative to another, whom to look in the eye, and whom to step aside for. Consciousness of status was ingrained in everyday life.

Behind the scenes, certain men and women made it all possible. Tailors and seamstresses, wigmakers and lacemakers, laundresses and ironers, barbers and personal servants toiled away, largely invisible, so that gentlemen and ladies could look their best. Polished shoes, powdered wigs, starched collars, a touch of rouge on the cheek—all due to the skills and attention of individuals who, by virtue of ancestry, worked in service to those considered "well born." Felix and Cuspin were two such men living in Saint-Domingue. Felix had learned the skills of barbering and wig-making; Cuspin was a personal servant. Documents describe Felix as *negro,* a Spanish word meaning black and implying African ancestry; Cuspin was described as *grif,* a term that suggests a mixed ancestry of the indigenous Taíno people and African. Each lived as the property of a man who was considered *blanco,* or White.

Planters had established vast sugar and coffee plantations in the French colony, bringing great fortunes to themselves and prosperity to their home country. The display of status and wealth was in full force, with planters living in grand houses, their sons educated in France, and their wives and daughters entertaining and being entertained in lavish style. To keep their lifestyle going, a European population of thirty thousand to forty thousand held in captivity almost a half million African men and women. The enslaved[2] people labored in brutal conditions; on average their lives working in the cane fields lasted little more than ten years. When they died, planters simply purchased more captured Africans.[3]

Yet in 1790, things in Saint-Domingue were about to change. Revolution had erupted in France two years earlier, in part prompted by the excessive displays of status, and in another year the enslaved people in Saint-Domingue would begin their own revolution that would last thirteen years. For the enslavers, the times were fraught with fear and uncertainty. That year, the merchant who held Felix the wigmaker captive sold him to the ship captain, Ursin, who had sailed from New Orleans on a trading voyage, likely exchanging lumber for sugar and rum. In New Orleans, wigmakers were highly valued; "every gentleman with means had one."[4] Ursin purchased Felix as an investment, paying 1,782 French *livres*, the equivalent of about 340 Spanish *piastres* (approximately $11,382 in 2024). Upon returning home, he sold Felix for 700 piastres, more than doubling his money.[5] He also bought Cuspin, the merchant's personal servant. The record does not show what he paid, but once back in New Orleans, he sold Cuspin for 525 piastres.

Ursin's full name was Jean Ursin Durel. He was my fourth great-grandfather. The exchange above is revealed in surviving records of the sales of Felix and Cuspin and in a court case where Ursin was called upon to prove his ownership of Felix. The sources reveal only this brief glimpse into an event that was life-altering for Felix and Cuspin and very profitable for Ursin. Like traders of his era, Ursin did this as a matter of course, apparently without a second thought. For Felix and Cuspin, who had no choice in the matter, it was fateful. Ursin separated them from their families, carried them to a new colony, and sold them to new owners. From that point, they disappeared from the historical record.

As a descendant of Ursin, what am I to make of this? As a historian, how can I understand it?

I grew up in a small, racially segregated city in Louisiana in the 1940s and '50s. As children do, I learned about the world around me by observing and mirroring the adults in my life. While I was taught to be polite and respectful of others, I also came to understand that some people were different from us. They had skin that was darker than ours, lived in another part of town, came to the back door when they needed to see my mother, and always addressed her as "Miss Nette." My mother, who was widowed when I was very young, often hired Black men to cut the grass or do handyman's work. I remember one time when she was given a live turkey to cook for Thanksgiving dinner and she hired a Black man to come and wring its neck. My brothers and I watched, and, needless to say, we refused to eat turkey that year.

I learned to refer to Black people as either "colored" or "Negro" and to think of myself as "White." This was the terminology of the period. I was also taught not to use what is now called the N-word, which was considered impolite and insulting to Black people. Although most Black people were tangential to my childhood, encountered only occasionally, there was one exception. Eva Thomas walked to our house almost every day except Sunday to help my mother with cleaning, cooking our meals, and washing and ironing our clothes. She was an almost daily presence and yet somehow even she was on the periphery. She cooked for us but did not sit down to eat with us. She ate alone after we were done. At the end of the day, she went back to her own home and family.

Of course, as a child I did not comprehend that I was embedded in a racial system that had evolved over two centuries from the theories of educated Europeans, mostly men, as they sought to define differences among people from various parts of the world. Most notable was Johann Friedrich Blumenbach, who in 1795 coined the label "Caucasian" for light-skinned people of European descent. He measured skulls, added skin color, mixed in a heavy dose of European chauvinism, and produced a ranked order of human "varieties." In descending order, using skin color as the primary indicator, he listed the types: white, yellow, olive-tinged, copper (bronze), tawny, and last, tawny black. At the very top were "white" Europeans, the most beautiful of whom, he asserted, came from the Caucasus region on the Black Sea. Hence the word *Caucasian*. At the very bottom, the "tawny black" people from Africa, he deemed brutish and ugly.[6]

In addition to skin color and facial features, Europeans invented the notion of blood purity as an indicator of character. Spanish authorities in the fifteenth century, reacting to the growing number and influence of Jews and Muslims in their country, enacted laws to prevent these "infidels" from gaining office or marrying into Christian families. The laws applied even if a Jew or Muslim converted to Christianity, and it extended to their descendants. Ancestry, not religious belief, became the determinant. It was a small step to apply the same thinking to Africans. The result was "a socio-racial order based on the concept of whiteness that held that only those of pure European ancestry possessed honor, legitimacy, respectability and rank."[7]

By my day, these early notions of White European superiority and Black African inferiority had taken firm hold and had been simplified and codified. Louisiana law simply identified each person as either "Caucasian" or "White" on one hand and as "colored" or "Negro" on the other. Although the United States Supreme Court allowed this division based on a doctrine of "separate but equal" accommodations, the state always provided greater services and privileges to those identified as White. Thus, I grew up believing that Black people were by nature inferior to White people. I took racial separation and inequality as the natural order of things. It never occurred to me to question why they were poor, why they lived in impoverished neighborhoods away from the main streets of town, or why they attended their own schools and churches.

The message of Black inferiority and of my own White superiority was reinforced in subtle ways throughout my childhood. For example, one summer when I was in high school a friend and I got jobs working on a horse ranch. My friend's father knew the owner. The work was primarily gathering bales of hay from the fields and stacking them in the barn. I loved it. I loved the oppressive summer heat, the sweat on my young body, the roar of the afternoon thunderstorm on the barn roof—the very idea of being a ranch hand. It was the year the movie *Hud* came out, and I imagined myself a version of young Paul Newman.[8]

One morning the ranch foreman told us to get into the pickup truck; we were going to get additional help. We turned down a gravel road where poor Black families lived, and boys about my age began to come out of the houses. The foreman selected five or six and told them to climb into the back. When we returned to the ranch, we drove out to the fields where the baling machine had left hay bales lying in rows. I jumped out of the cab and headed into the field, eager to work. But the foreman called me back. My job was to get up on the wagon and stack the bales. The Black kids were to haul the bales from the field and throw them up to me. The next day the foreman praised me for the way I had stacked the bales so that they did not tumble when he towed the wagon out of the field and into the barn. As a reward he let me drive the truck, with a stick shift.

I felt good about myself that summer. Without any self-reflection, I saw myself as talented and accomplished, ready to go off to college and out into the larger world. What of the other kids? The question never entered my mind. Nor did I recognize that I only got the job in the first place because of my friend's father.

It would take me many years to begin to comprehend this system that divided people into two groups based simply on ancestry and skin color. Watching the Civil Rights Movement unfold on television, going away to college where I met people from other parts of the country, and joining the navy, which took me to Asia and Europe, enabled me to see what I could not see as a boy. I had to leave the South in order to understand the South. Eventually, I came to realize that the concept of race I grew up with was just an idea fabricated by men and not a fact of nature.

Nevertheless, as a concept, race has been formative in my life. It has always been with me, from the prejudices of my childhood to an affirmed belief in racial equality that I embraced as an adult, and now, in my seventies, to an earnest desire to understand how race shaped my story and the story of my family.

The story of the Durel family in Louisiana begins with Ursin's parents. Jean Baptiste Durel and Cécile LeBrun arrived as a young, newly married couple from Bordeaux, France, in 1753 or 1754. They were the progenitors of what is now ten or more generations of people who carry the Durel surname as well as thousands of others who descend from a Durel daughter. I am of the eighth generation. The first generation numbered two individuals, the second ten, the third at least sixty-nine, and after that I stopped counting. There were and are a lot of us. And these numbers include only children considered "legitimate" by the laws of the day and do not include children of Durel men with women of African or American Indian descent, of whom I have identified some but certainly not all.

Genealogy is not my primary interest. My aim has been to write stories about selected family members in each generation, stories that reveal something about race and are based on historical evidence. However, to do so, I first needed to identify and distinguish among the numerous references I found to people with the Durel name in Louisiana historical records from the eighteenth and early nineteenth centuries. As the daughters in the second generation married, I added more names to the search: Andry, Basile, Beauregard, Dejan, and Fortier.

My starting point was a three-page published genealogy titled "The Durel Family" that appeared in 1982 in *New Orleans Genesis,* the journal of the Genealogical Research Society of New Orleans.[9] The author, Charles R. Maduell Jr., was a Durel descendant and very active in genealogical circles at that time. Yet I could not simply accept his work. Maduell rarely indicated the sources he used, and I wanted historical accuracy. It turned out that although he did get many things right, that was not always the case. For example, he stated that Jean Baptiste's father was a wine merchant in Bordeaux who owned his own boats and traded along the Garonne River between Bordeaux and Toulouse. Another article, published in the *National Genealogy Quarterly* (2000), includes footnotes that identify sources.[10] The author, Robert de Berardinis, another Durel descendant, used both sacramental and civil records created at the time of the marriage of Jean Baptiste and Cécile to show clearly that Jean Baptiste's father was not a wine merchant but a master *tapissier* (upholstery maker). He also corrected information about Cécile, whom Maduell described as being from Blois, a city 250 miles distant from Bordeaux, whereas in fact she was from Blaye, only thirty miles away. She was the daughter of a master joiner (maker of fine furniture) who died when she was young.

It took me several years researching sacramental records (baptisms, marriages, funerals), notarial records (property transactions, including transactions for the sale and purchase of enslaved people), probate records (wills and estate inventories), and numerous other sources. Most of the early documents are handwritten in French or Spanish and many are in poor condition. It was slow work. Eventually, however, I was able to create a genealogical reference document for the first three generations, containing all (or mostly all) family members of wholly European descent, as well as some people with African and American Indian ancestry who used the Durel surname. (This reference document is included as an Appendix to help readers keep track of the individuals mentioned throughout the book.)

Obviously, I could not write about every family member. I have chosen individuals from each generation, down to my own. Some descendants may be disappointed that I did not select their ancestor. I invite them to pick up a pen and have a go. It is very rewarding work.

Like the Sirens of Greek mythology, whose beautiful music drew sailors to shipwreck on rocky shoals, history is alluring but can be dangerous. We want to know the past, but if we are not careful, we will get things wrong. Still, the lure is strong. My brother Justin puts it this way:

In moments of quiet reflection
Distant voices can be heard
Across the wide expanse
Of the relentless fourth dimension
- - - -
Long forgotten ancestral links
Seven times removed
Between the Alpha and the Omega
Each hyphen remains unproved

If only it were a portal
Not just a simple line
To view the life in total
A personality to assign

Belief systems, daily concerns
Personal preferences, physical traits
All now possible to discern
Through those linear gates[11]

Yes, if only one could enter the past and fully know what people believed, felt, and worried about. I would know what Felix, Cuspin, and Ursin each thought and felt when Ursin forcibly took the two men from their families. Instead of a door, however, there is at best a spy hole, a glimpse of a life as it moves briefly into view. A clear danger when writing about race through the lens of genealogy is to fill out the picture in ways that present one's forebears in the best possible light. For decades, for example, Thomas Jefferson's White descendants, bolstered by White scholars studying his life, refused to believe that he could possibly have had sexual relations with Sally Hemings because, according to them, doing so would have been contrary to his character and against his own standards of decency.[12] Similarly, for well over a century following the Civil War, volunteer guides at historic antebellum plantations routinely referred to enslaved people as "servants" and to White plantation owners as good "masters." Even recently, I read a piece that implied that most White enslavers were compassionate, although the author admitted that some committed "unkindnesses." This inclination on the part of some White people to deny or gloss over the cruelty of slavery was on my mind as I began to research my family.

Whether one's ancestors were kind is really beside the point. Slavery, like the Jim Crow world in which I grew up, was a racist system that permeated life and advantaged White people. In the stories that follow I attempt to show the advantages White descendants of Jean Baptiste and Cécile enjoyed, generation by generation, as the system evolved. At times, some behaved in ways that were considerate of Black people; at other times, they were callous. All benefited from the system. Only one descendant, as far as I have been able to discern, ever took a stand against it. He was a Black man.

Le Cap Français. This port in Saint-Domingue, called Cap Français by the French and Guarico by the local Taíno Indians, was where Ursin Durel purchased two enslaved Black men, carried them to New Orleans, and sold them, more than doubling his money. Courtesy of the Historic New Orleans Collection.

Table I.
Parents and Children of Jean Baptiste Durel and Cécile LeBrun

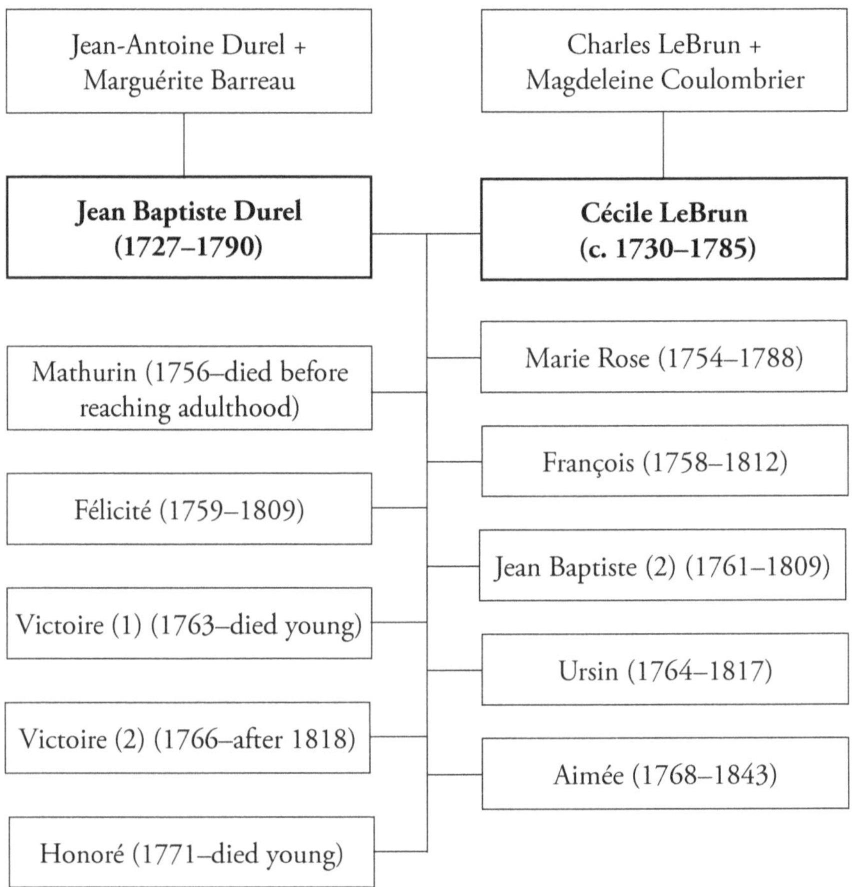

Chapter 1

The Founding Generation

=== Jean Baptiste Durel and Cécile LeBrun ===

My quest to learn about the story of race in my family took me first, figuratively, to the port city of Bordeaux in southwestern France. On September 14, 1752, in the parish church of Saint-Projet, a young *tapissier* (upholstery or carpet maker) named Jean Baptiste Durel, age twenty-five, married a young woman named Cécile LeBrun, whose father, then deceased, had been a master joiner (maker of fine furniture).[1] This was not yet a time when romantic love and individual choice determined marriage partners. Although their wedding probably followed a period of courtship during which they came to know one another and determined that they were compatible, their union was essentially an alliance between families, designed to ensure that each family's standing and wealth would be maintained into the next generation.[2]

French society at the time was highly stratified and one's social standing meant everything. The higher up the chain, the more privileges one received: tax exemptions, political appointments, higher education, greater leisure, and more plentiful nourishment. The nobility, aristocracy, and church hierarchy controlled vast estates and lived in grand houses, as they had for centuries. The bourgeoisie, comprising wealthy merchants and financiers, were a growing force and some had built houses to rival the nobility. Next in line came artisans and shopkeepers, who often lived and worked in the same dwelling, with a shop and large common room on the ground floor for cooking, eating, and sleeping, and several additional sleeping rooms upstairs. Next were laborers and their families, crowded into structures of one or two rooms. At the very bottom were vagabonds and homeless men and women, who had no standing at all in the social structure.[3]

The Durel and LeBrun families were not quite bourgeois but were of the highest rank of the artisan class. Jean Baptiste learned to make upholstery from his father, Jean-Antoine Durel, who was also a master *tapissier* and was addressed as *Sieur* Durel. (Had he been an aristocrat, he would have been called *Monsieur* Durel.) Jean Baptiste's mother died when he was not yet two years old, and he was raised by his stepmother as the eldest child in a household of many children. By the time he was in his early twenties, he too had become a master of the trade and had set up a shop of his own. He was well-suited for marriage.

Cécile's family was from Blaye, an ancient, fortified city about thirty miles downriver from Bordeaux. After her father's death, her mother arranged for her to move to the port city and live in the home of an aristocratic gentleman named Monsieur de Fauquier, there "to be educated or 'ladyfied.'"[4] She would have learned the needle arts, read literature, and practiced proper deportment. When it came time for her to marry, her mother granted power of attorney to look after her interests to another gentleman, Monsieur Jean Borie de Pomarède. These associations with aristocratic gentlemen suggest that Cécile had inherited considerable wealth.

Thus, Cécile and Jean Baptiste began their life together with ample resources and the promise of even more wealth. The merchants and financiers of the growing bourgeoisie were making money, and Jean Baptiste was well positioned to furnish their grand houses with finely upholstered furniture. The money came from a burgeoning triangular trade in which Bordeaux merchants sent their ships to the coast of Africa to take on Black men and women who had been captured and imprisoned. From there the ships sailed to French colonies in the West Indies, where the merchants sold their human cargo (those who had survived) to the owners of plantations in exchange for barrels of sugar and coffee. To complete the triangle, the ships returned to Bordeaux and the sugar and coffee made their way to the kitchens and dining tables of the wealthy throughout France. This trade in humans brought immense wealth to merchants and to the city treasury, enabling the creation of grand public buildings, boulevards, and squares. The latter half of the eighteenth century was Bordeaux's golden age; its population grew from 60,000 to more than 110,000, making it the third-largest city in France.[5]

In spite of the promise of a good life in Bordeaux, Jean Baptiste and Cécile opted to emigrate to the French colony of Louisiana. It is not clear why they made this choice. It was certainly not religious or political persecution or poverty that caused them to leave, as was so often the case for people leaving an old world for the new. More likely it was a sense of adventure or an ambition to rise above the artisan ranks into the merchant class. They may well have had connections with others of their class from Bordeaux who had earlier made the same decision and who could aid them in establishing themselves in a new community. There is also the possibility that they wanted to escape family tensions. Cécile had not lived with her mother for several years and when she married her mother did not attend the ceremony. Jean Baptiste had already moved out of his father's crowded home and had set up his own upholstery shop, in competition with his father.

Whatever the reason, four months after their wedding Cécile and Jean Baptiste boarded *Le Jeune André,* a vessel bound for the French colony of Martinique. Every passenger had to provide information, including proof of their religion. The ship's clerk identified Jean Baptiste as being of the "*ancienne catholique*" faith, of average height, and accompanied by his spouse. The purpose of the voyage was *les affaires* (business).[6]

Growing up in France, it is unlikely that they had ever seen a *noir* (Black person). A few merchants had brought Africans directly to Bordeaux, and some colonists had returned to the city with enslaved men and women, but they were rare. The government sought to discourage the practice by limiting both the number of Africans that could be brought in and the duration of their stay, although the regulations seem to have been largely ignored. The total number of Black people in the region was never large; as late as 1777, only 302 lived there (208 enslaved and 94 free), at a time when the local population exceeded 60,000.[7] If Cécile or Jean Baptiste had by chance seen a *noir,* it would have been highly unusual.

Yet when they disembarked in Martinique, they found themselves in the midst of people of various shades of darkened skin. For the first time they were acutely aware that skin color made a difference. An island in the West Indies, Martinique had been a French colony for more than a century. It was a fully developed sugar plantation society with a population of some 50,000, the majority enslaved people of African descent. The Durels were accustomed to social hierarchy and to the cues of dress and demeanor that revealed someone's status. Now they would add skin color and facial features to their understanding of the other person.

At this time, French merchants had more or less given up on Louisiana. Early plans for tobacco to become the territory's major export were dashed when the soil and climate proved unsuitable. Planters also tried exporting indigo, but they never managed to grow it with sufficient quality to compete with other colonies. Furthermore, Louisiana gained a reputation for disorder and smuggling, so that merchants in France increasingly sent their ships only as far as the West Indies. Any passengers or merchandise going to New Orleans had to transfer to another ship.[8]

While in Martinique, the Durel couple may have stayed with a relative. Twenty-four years earlier, a gentleman named Michel Durel had departed Bordeaux "on business," traveling on *Le Patriarche Abraham* bound for Martinique.[9] It is possible that a branch of the family was present in that colony. Regardless, their time in Martinique was brief; by July 1754, the young couple had established themselves in New Orleans, when their first child was baptized in St. Louis parish church.[10]

Upon arrival, Cécile and Jean Baptiste entered a social and cultural milieu thirty-five years in the making and well into its second generation of residents. New Orleans had a population of about 2,000 individuals, a decent size for a port town on the frontier of European settlement.[11] Figure 1 shows the extent of the settled area at the time the Durels arrived. Most of the inhabitants were *Creole*, a

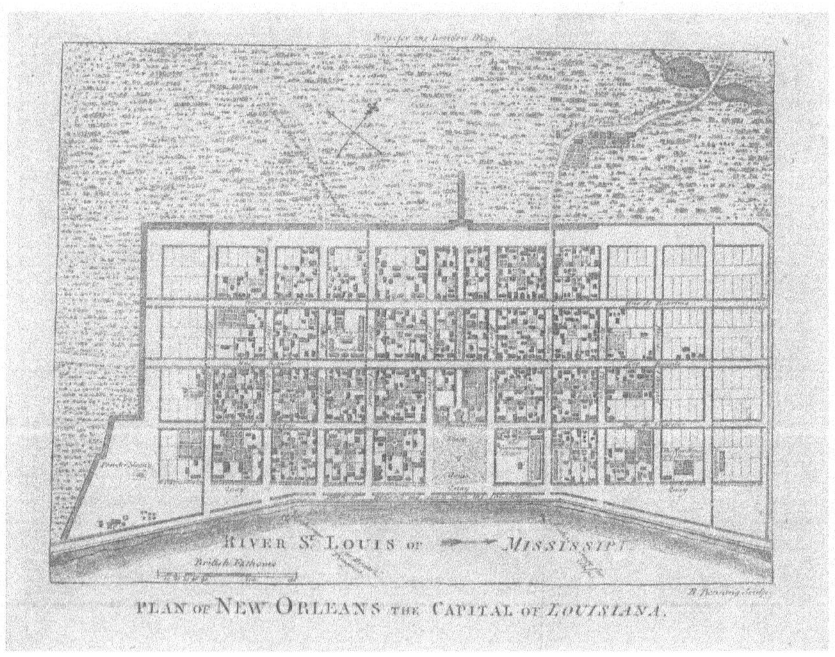

Fig. 1: *Plan of New Orleans the Capital of Louisiana, 1761.*
Courtesy of the Historic New Orleans Collection.

term that at the time applied to anyone, regardless of ancestry, born in the colony, as distinguished from those who had come from Europe or Africa. The meaning of *Creole* would change over time and take on important cultural and racial connotations (discussed in greater detail later). For now, it is important to note that Jean Baptiste and Cécile were newcomers in a community made up mostly of locals who had never been to France. This gave the place a distinctive character, recognizable as French, but different in subtle and not-so-subtle ways.

The biggest differences were due to the significant number of residents from Africa or of African descent, who made up about a quarter of the population.[12] During the first decade of settlement, thousands of captives from Senegal, Bambara, Gambia, and other African nations arrived against their will despite a high death rate and several attempted revolts at sea. The influx of captives ended in 1731 when the colony failed to grow as expected and the colony's leaders discovered they had more enslaved people than they could use. For the next three decades, the enslaved population grew only through natural increase, as enslaved women gave birth. Government ministers in France intended that all Africans and their children live on plantations outside the town's walls. In practice, however, local enslavers kept some of their captives in town, using them for heavy work like digging ditches, building structures, hauling goods, and caring for livestock. They put enslaved women to work growing food, preparing meals, laundering clothes, cleaning houses, and having babies. By the 1750s, people of African heritage could be seen everywhere, selling produce in the market, loading boats on the riverfront, drinking in taverns, praying in church, and gathering on Sunday afternoons to dance and socialize. They gave the emerging city an African subculture, expressed through music, dance, food, language, and spiritual beliefs.[13]

Most of these African-descended people were held in slavery, but not all. In the first decade of settlement there are references to free Black people in New Orleans.[14] A handful of Africans arrived as free individuals and others gained freedom in various ways. African men who exhibited loyalty and bravery in the fight against the Natchez nation in 1729 received freedom from the colonial government. So did Louis Congo, who negotiated his freedom with the Superior Council in exchange for serving as the colony's executioner. For enslaved women, gaining manumission often involved intimate relationships with a European man. The *Code Noir* (Black Code) of 1724, in an attempt to keep Europeans and Africans separated, forbade White people from living in concubinage with Black people. However, in a system that gave White enslavers enormous power over the people they enslaved, and in a population that had an extreme gender imbalance with twice as many males as females, enslaved women frequently endured sex with a White enslaver. Although the vast majority remained in bondage, a few were able to turn these intimate relationships to their advantage, negotiating freedom for themselves and their children. By the 1750s New Orleans had a small but growing population of *gens de couleur libres* (free people of color).[15]

Indigenous people also maintained a presence in the city. The French called the tribes in the vicinity of New Orleans *les petites nations* (the little nations), which included the Acolapissa, the Ouma (Houma), and the Ouacha or Tchouacha.[16] Although French settlers sometimes enslaved them, many Indigenous people continued to live in nearby villages and came to New Orleans to trade. Children of mixed Indigenous and European or African ancestry came to be called *mestizos*. For some purposes, the French treated them as a distinct racial group and at other times lumped them together with people of African descent. Their presence added further cultural diversity to the city encountered by the Durel newcomers.

Another element of society, one of greater familiarity for the Durels, was an elite class of wealthy families—although here, too, there were differences. In France, the long-established aristocracy owned vast properties and held government positions by virtue of birth. In New Orleans, the elite were not wellborn but rather well-to-do. That is, wealth replaced lineage as the means to prestige and privilege. To be sure, things were changing in France at the time, and wealthy merchants and financiers began buying their way into the aristocracy, but in the absence of an aristocracy in Louisiana, being wealthy became the primary determinant.

The first generation of leaders were Canadian frontiersmen and French adventurers who received both land grants to start plantations and loans to purchase African captives to work the land. Some took on aristocratic-sounding names, so that, for example, a frontiersman from Montreal by the name of Nicholas Chauvin became known as Nicholas Chauvin *de La Frénière*.[17] The frontier shaped the lives of these early leaders; they lacked European refinement. Then, in the 1740s, a new colonial governor arrived, Canadian-born but well connected in Paris and with true noble rank. Pierre de Rigaud, Marquis de Vaudreuil, came with smartly dressed troops and officers and added pomp and circumstance to military ceremonies. He invited locals to formal dinners and dances, and they turned up in fancy dress, eager to adopt or adapt the latest Parisian styles and customs.[18] Thus, by midcentury, the children of the founding leaders had begun to coalesce into a kind of self-fashioned aristocracy where birth and marriage, as well as wealth, determined membership. It was this class that Jean Baptiste and Cécile would soon join.

It was an inauspicious time to arrive for someone intending to set up business. In 1754, a new royal governor, Louis Billouart, Chevalier de Kerlérec, sent local soldiers and Indigenous allies up the Mississippi and Ohio Rivers to attack British forces under the command of a young Virginian named George Washington. The battle near present-day Pittsburgh sparked what is known in the United States as the French and Indian War and in Europe as the Seven Years' War. The next seven years brought economic disruption and hardship to Louisiana. The British blockaded the Gulf of Mexico, cutting off supplies and preventing local merchants from sending produce to France. Paper money lost value as prices rose. By 1759, the army survived on half-rations and the inhabitants of New Orleans were hurting.[19]

Still, in times like these, there are opportunities. The Durels likely arrived from France with money in silver coin rather than colonial paper. This would have given them an advantage. By 1758, Jean Baptiste starts to appear in records, identified not as an upholsterer but as an upholstery merchant. The fluidity of the local economy made it possible for him to self-identify as a merchant, not an artisan. In March of that year, he leased a brick house at the corner of Royal and Toulouse Streets, moved his family in, and set up a store.[20] Three months later, he attended an estate sale and spent 1,820 *livres*, presumably to furnish the house and stock his business.[21]

Court records reveal Jean Baptiste's growing relationships with inhabitants of means. In November of 1758, he attended a court-ordered meeting of the Songy family, following the death of the father, to decide whether two surviving sons, ages twenty and twenty-two, were old enough to manage their own affairs. Jean Baptiste is listed as a friend of the family.[22] In another instance, also in 1758, he witnessed the marriage of Nicolas Logis, widower, and Marie Louise Lormoir, widow.[23] In 1759, he attended another wedding, that of Vanetin Jautare and Magdelaine Fourneau.[24] After five years in New Orleans, he had begun to form a network.

As the Seven Years' War came to an end in 1763 and trade began to improve in the city, Jean Baptiste took advantage of the growing wealth and aspirations of New Orleans society to build a dry goods business, specializing in imported cloth. Based on an inventory taken at the time of his death, in his store customers could find material to furnish their fine houses and clothe themselves and the people they enslaved.[25] He carried both heavy textiles for drapery and upholstery and lighter fabrics for clothing and household use. He had rough and sturdy cotton and wool for laborers and fine silks and satins for fancy dress. His stock reflected a European trading network: "Flanders" cloth, a heavy, tightly woven wool from the Netherlands; "Silesia" a lightweight, finely twilled cotton from Prussia; "Ruan," a lightweight woolen textile produced in Rouen, France, often with wool fleece from Spain; Chinese painted taffeta and colorful printed cottons originating in India.[26] He also sold dishes, painted and plain; coffee cups and coffee makers; wine glasses, bowls, and other crockery; and large quantities of candles, a necessity for any household of substance in the eighteenth century. As the population and sophistication of New Orleans grew, so did his business.

As further indication of his growing prominence, Jean Baptiste's name began to occur in church and civic records. By 1768, he was the senior warden of St. Louis parish church, overseeing building maintenance and repairs, and representing the church in a legal dispute over the bequest of a deceased parishioner.[27] He served as secretary and then as treasurer of the almshouse board of directors, which was charged with providing housing and support for the poor.[28] Through these positions, his reputation grew and he came into contact with some of the most powerful men in the colony, including Charles Philippe Aubry, Knight of the Royal and Military Order of St. Louis, Commandant of the Province; Denis-Nicolas Foucault, acting intendant and first judge of the Superior Council; and Nicolas Chauvin de La Frénière (son of the Montreal frontiersman), whose title was procurator general for the king of France.[29]

In the treaty that ended the Seven Years' War, France ceded Louisiana to Spain. Spanish authorities were not eager to take on the challenge of governing the unruly colonials and did not send Don Antonio de Ulloa to take charge until 1765. Ulloa arrived with only a small force, and the Superior Council refused to recognize his authority. The locals, who had grown accustomed to acting independently, remained loyal to the French king and sent Ulloa packing.[30]

The next year was a remarkable one for Louisiana and for Jean Baptiste as well. In July 1769, he attended a meeting of the almshouse directors.[31] Also in attendance were Aubry, Foucault, and La Frénière. The previous year,

Foucault had joined La Frénière in the rebellion against Ulloa; Aubry had not. Now, as the men met on a rather mundane matter involving a payment to the almshouse, a new Spanish governor was on his way to Louisiana with a force of twenty-three ships and more than two thousand troops. This time there would be no resistance. General Alejandro O'Reilly arrived in August and with Aubry's assistance had Foucault, La Frénière, and other conspirators arrested. By the end of October, Foucault was in exile and La Frénière was dead, executed for treason.

Jean Baptiste, on the other hand, found himself among the majority of citizens who signed an oath of allegiance to the Spanish king. In December, O'Reilly established the Cabildo, a new governing body comprised of wealthy planters and merchants who had not resisted. At their first meeting the new councilors elected Jean Baptiste the first city treasurer.[32] In this role, he not only accounted for city revenues and expenses but also served as city syndic, representing New Orleans in business transactions and was called "major domo" of the city's goods.[33] He had positioned himself well, demonstrating competence in handling finances and getting things done for both the church and the almshouse. He had been noticed, and now he was moving up.

Office holding was a path to greater wealth. Not only did he receive a salary, but he also expanded his network of friends and acquaintances and found opportunities for investments. In 1775, he purchased a property on Chartres Street, halfway between St. Louis Church and the Ursuline Convent, with a house, a kitchen, a yard fenced with pickets, and a store built of brick.[34] He made this property his home and business. Subsequently, he bought and sold numerous other properties, making money in the process.

In an era when marriage continued to be primarily an alliance of two families of the same social class, husbands were expected to work hard, support the family financially, and keep a good reputation. Wives were to bear children, see to their education, and manage the household economy. Over the course of seventeen years, from her early twenties to her late thirties, Cécile gave birth to ten children, in order: Rose, Mathurin, François, Félicité, Jean Baptiste (2), Victoire (1), Ursin, Victoire (2), Aimée, Honoré (Table I). Three children died young. The first male child, Mathurin, born in 1756, lived until at least age fifteen, for a Durel son of that age was tallied in a militia census dated 1770.[35] Thereafter, there is no further reference to him. A daughter named Victoire was born in 1763 but lived no more than three years, for the next girl, born in 1766, was given the same name.[36] Finally, Honoré, the last born, in 1771, appears in only one record, that of his baptism.[37] Childhood death was common. That Cécile named her next daughter Victoire after the one who died reveals a mother's love for a child. Indeed, Cécile seems to have had a special affection for the second Victoire throughout her life (elaborated further in Chapter 2).

With the exception of mention in sacramental records, Cécile is largely invisible to history. She was present at the baptisms and weddings of her children and her own funeral was recorded in January 1785.[38] Nevertheless, historians provide a general understanding of the lives of women like Cécile in colonial New Orleans. Like her husband, she was of the "*ancienne catholique*" religion and responsible for raising her children in the faith. This was a requirement of French citizens as part of what was called the Counter-Reformation, designed to curtail the rise of Protestantism.

An important strategy of the Counter-Reformation was the founding of new religious orders in France, including the Company of St. Ursula, with a focus on the education of women. In the words of historian Emily Clark, "No country in Europe knew anything like the sweeping Ursuline campaign to educate women, which involved hundreds of convents and thousands of nuns in France at the end of the seventeenth century and made an Ursuline school a common feature of town life."[39] The sisters took in boarders as well as day students, and there were at least seven Ursuline schools in the Bordeaux region, including one in Bourg-sur-Mer, just ten miles from Blaye where Cécile grew up. It is very possible that she was taught by the Ursulines herself and that she chose to send her daughters to the Ursuline school in New Orleans.[40]

The Ursuline curriculum consisted of reading, writing, spelling, arithmetic, needlework, catechism, and religious practice. Boarding students had full days: up and dressed by 6:45 a.m., Mass at 7:00, recitation of prayers at intervals throughout the day, evening prayers, and to bed by 8:00 p.m. The routine taught discipline and prepared them for life as pious Catholic women. Such education was free and open to all, and over the years hundreds of New Orleans girls learned to read and write and to attend Mass regularly.[41]

The student body included not only girls of European but also African descent. That the Ursulines educated Black girls as well as White, enslaved as well as free, does not mean they believed in social equality. They paid deference to families of higher status and they themselves enslaved people of African descent at the convent in town as well as on two plantations they owned on the outskirts. They did, however, follow Catholic doctrine that held that Black people had souls. They ensured that the people they held captive were baptized and schooled in the faith and were encouraged to marry in the church.[42]

There was no comparable school for Cécile's sons.[43] She had the option of hiring a tutor to come to the house or sending them to one of the private schools set up by entrepreneurial educators. As they grew, the boys also learned at the side of their father, gaining experience in keeping accounts and understanding contracts. In the militia, which they joined when they reached their teens, they learned discipline and leadership. Wealthy families often sent sons to receive an education in France, but that was not the case with the Durels. Nevertheless, the three males who lived to be adults were all literate and had successful careers, two as merchants and one as a ship's captain.

=== Marie Jeanne, old Marie, and the girl, Marie ===

Cécile was in St. Louis church[44] on Saturday, April 14, 1770, attending one of the periodic group baptisms the parish priests held in order to ensure that all enslaved adults were baptized. Although the Church taught that Black people had souls and needed to be baptized, White enslavers did not always take the time to do so. Group baptisms, common in the 1770s and '80s, provided an efficient way to baptize numerous individuals at a single ceremony.

On this day, the church was crowded with fifty-eight enslaved Black men and women who would receive the sacrament, each accompanied by the White person who held them in slavery and by the people who would serve as their godparents. One of the recipients was Louis, identified as belonging to "Madame Durel."[45] Louis's godparents were François, a man enslaved by Madame Beauregard, and Marguerite, a woman enslaved by Madame Voye. The practice of enslaved people from different households serving as godparents hints at relationships among the enslaved that existed beyond the bounds of a White family. That is, just as Madame Durel, Madame Beauregard, and Madame Voye saw themselves as part of a distinct group, so too did people like Louis, François, and Marguerite. They had opportunities to see and talk to one another, briefly when passing on a street, in church on Sundays, across a neighboring fence, and at one of the social gatherings for Black people permitted by the White authorities.

Louis was one of twenty individuals I have found in sacramental and notarial records who were enslaved by Cécile or Jean Baptiste at one time or another. Almost certainly there were more, for many records have not survived, and of those that have, some are in very poor condition and difficult to decipher. The names of the men and women enslaved by the Durels, along with identifying information and source citations, appear in Table II.

Table II.
Men and Women of African Descent enslaved by Jean Baptiste Durel and Cécile LeBrun

Names	Description
1. Marie Jeanne 2. Jean, *père* 3. Félicité, *fille* 4. Jean, *fils*	1768: Marie Jeanne and her husband, Jean, described as *négres ésclaves*, were enslaved by the Durels as early as 1768, when their daughter Félicité was born.[1] Marie Jeanne also gave birth to a son named Jean around 1776.[2] She and her son appear in the inventory of Jean Baptiste's estate taken in 1790, at which time she is estimated to be sixty years old.[3]
5. Marie 6. Barthelemie, *fils*	1769: Marie was described as a *mulâtress* by the priest when he baptized her son, Barthelemie, in 1769.[4] Her name also appears in the estate inventory, where she is described as forty-two years old, making her twenty-one when her son was born.[5] She may have been a daughter of Marie (see no. 10 below).

1. Baptisms, Marriages, Funerals, 1764–1774, 11, SLC.
2. Baptisms Register 1772–1776, part 2, 128, SLC.
3. "Proceedings for the Settlement of the Estate of Juan Bautista Durel," Royal Court records, file 1802, June 4, 1790. The people who were enslaved to Jean Baptiste at the end of his life are described on page 43 of the estate inventory and appraisal.
4. Sacramental Records, Sixth Register of Blancs and Couleur, Baptisms of Persons of Color Slaves, 47, SLC.
5. "Proceedings for the Settlement of the Estate of Juan Bautista Durel," Royal Court records 1802.

7. Marechal	1770: A man named "Marechal Durelle" appears as a freedman serving in the militia in New Orleans in 1770.[6] He likely was formerly enslaved by Jean Baptiste and granted freedom because of his military service.
8. Petre	1781: Jean Baptiste purchased Petre in 1781. Petre is described as a *negro*, age forty-five.[7] Five years later, Petre was still enslaved to Jean Baptiste when he served as godfather for someone enslaved to another White family.[8]
9. Ester	1782: Jean Baptiste purchased Ester, described as a twenty-year-old *negra*, in 1782. Within two years she obtained her freedom.[9]
10. Maria	1783: Maria was emancipated by Jean Baptiste on January 17, 1783, when she was about sixty years old.[10] She would have been about thirty when the Durels first arrived in New Orleans and may have been the first person enslaved by them.
11. Issabel 12. Therese	1784: Issabel was baptized April 11, 1784, at which time she was described as being from Guinea and having been enslaved by the Durels for fifteen years.[11] She may have been the mother of Therese, who was baptized December 1, 1786.[12]
13. Louis	1784: Louis was baptized as an adult in a group of fifty-eight on April 14, 1774. He is identified as an enslaved person held by Madame Durel.[13]

6. "Marechal Durelle" appears in a list of freedmen and free mulattoes settled in the city of New Orleans compiled by Nicolas Bacus, Captain Moraine, undated but appended to a document dated 1770.
7. Leonardo Mazange, v. 3, folio 135 (back), February 22, 1781, NONA.
8. Book of Baptisms, Negros and Mulattos, from 17 June 1783, 178, SLC.
9. Leonardo Mazange, v. 1, folio 218, Mar 16, 1780, NONA.
10. Leonardo Mazange, v. 7, folio 28 (back), Jan 12, 1783, NONA.
11. Book of Baptisms, Negros and Mulattos, from 17 June 1783, 44, SLC.
12. Baptisms Book Four, Colored free and slave, from 12 December 1786 to 30 September 1792, 1.
13. Sacramental Records, Sixth Register, Baptisms, Marriages, Funerals, 80–81, SLC.

14. Amarante	1783: Amarante was acquired by Jean Baptiste on November 17, 1783, when she was seventeen years old.[14] This was related to a real estate transaction, where the buyer used Amarante to pay for a house lot on Royal Street.
15. Azor	1784: Azor was identified as enslaved by Jean Baptiste on February 3, 1784, when he served as the godfather of a child enslaved by Maxent.[15] Jean Baptiste sold Azor on May 23,1790, at which time he was described as a twenty-eight-year-old cook whom Jean Baptiste had acquired fifteen years earlier.[16]
16. Isabel 17. Victoria	1784: Both Isabel and Victoria were baptized in a group of seventy enslaved individuals on April 10, 1784. Victoria was number 47, Isabel number 54.[17]
18. Rose	1785: Rose is identified on August 7, 1785, as enslaved by Jean Baptiste when she served as godmother of a child born to Marie Louise, who was enslaved by another person.[18]
19. Magdalena	1786: Magdalena was sold by Jean Baptiste in May 1786, at which time he stated that he had purchased her the previous July. She was seventeen years old.[19]
20. Joseph	1788: Joseph, described as a *negro esclava* belonging to Jean Baptiste Durel, was baptized in 1788.[20] He also appears in the inventory of Jean Baptiste's estate in 1790, where his name is spelled Josef and he is described as being age fifty, unskilled and infirmed.[21]

14. Fernando Rodriguez, v. 6, folio 921, Oct 18, 1785, NONA.
15. Book of Baptisms, Negros and Mulattos, from 17 June 1783, 34, SLC.
16. Pedro Pedesclaux, v.10, folio 239 back, NONA.
17. Book of Baptisms, Negros and Mulattos, from 17 June 1783, 42-43, SLC.
18. Book of Baptisms, Negros and Mulattos, from 17 June 1783, 137, SLC.
19. Fernando Rodriguez, v. 8, folio 600, May 11, 1786, NONA.
20. Baptisms Book Four, Colored Free and Slave, from 12 December 1786 to 30 September 1792, 68, SLC.
21. "Proceedings for the Settlement of the Estate of Juan Bautista Durel," Royal Court records1802, June 4, 1790.

Many of those held captive by the Durels, including Louis, appear only once in the records. For them, one brief moment of their existence was noted on paper. For others, however, it is possible to construe a plausible picture of their lives. The earliest evidence of Jean Baptiste and Cécile enslaving Black people comes from a census taken in September of 1763, about nine years after they first arrived in New Orleans.[46] The census gives the name of only the head of a household, followed by the number of individuals by category. The Durel household consisted of Jean Baptiste and one adult female (Cécile), three male children under age fourteen (Mathurin, François, and Jean Baptiste Jr.), two females under twelve (Rose and Félicité),[47] two enslaved women, and one enslaved female child. Although the names of the enslaved are not given, based on later records I have deduced that they were:

- Marie Jeanne (Table II, number 1): She and her husband, Jean, appear at the baptism of their daughter, Félicité, in 1768. In the record they are described by the priest as *nègres,* indicating that they had dark skin and were probably of wholly African descent. Marie Jeanne gave birth to another child, a son named Jean, around 1776. In the eight-year span between the two births, she was probably pregnant two or three more times and may have had more children whose baptismal records are missing. She was still enslaved to Jean Baptiste at the time of his death in 1790, when she was described in the estate inventory as being about sixty years old, making her about thirty-three in 1763. The ages given in these records are approximations for often no one, not even the individual in question, knew the precise age of an enslaved person. Marie Jeanne's son, Jean, was also in the estate inventory but her husband and daughter were not, indicating they had either died or been sold away by that time.

- Marie (Table II, number 5): Marie appears in the baptismal record of her son, Barthelemie, in 1769. She is described using the term *mulâtress*, indicating brown skin color and a mixed African and European ancestry. Like Marie Jeanne, she is in Jean Baptist's estate inventory, where she is described as being forty-two years old. That this is not a rounded number suggests that someone knew her actual age. She would have been fifteen at the time of the 1763 census, making her a good candidate for the enslaved girl listed in that document.

- Marie (Table II, number 10): This woman named Marie appears in a 1783 document in which Jean Baptiste emancipates her "for the many services that I have received from her." At the time she was estimated to be sixty years old, making her about forty years old in 1763. I refer to her as "old Marie" to distinguish her from the fifteen-year-old girl of the same name.

Assuming these details are correct, by 1763, just nine years after their arrival in New Orleans, Cécile and Jean Baptiste had enslaved three females of African descent: old Marie, close to age forty; Marie Jeanne, thirty-three years old; and a girl also named Marie, age fifteen. Cécile made use of their skills and labor to keep house and assist with raising her children.

An important aspect of domestic life in the eighteenth century was sociability. Friends and neighbors visited one another frequently, and the house had to be kept neat and presentable. The quality of dress of a lady and her children and the display of her household linen were especially important to building a family's reputation.[48] Just as Jean Baptiste used strategies to build his reputation and strengthen relationships with wealthy and prominent men, Cécile did the same with their wives. Under her direction, old Marie, Marie Jeanne, and the girl Marie swept and dusted, scrubbed and cleaned, polished and arranged. They laundered and ironed clothes and table linen, arduous and time-consuming work for the growing White family. They went to the market for produce, cooked the meals, set the table, washed the dishes, and chopped wood to keep the fire going. They planted and weeded the garden (and perhaps in the process taught Cécile about okra and gumbo and other foods foreign to her). They made beds, straightened rooms, and emptied chamber pots. They picked up after Cécile's children and cared for them when they were sick. Theirs was a life of labor, giving the White Durel family time for relaxation, entertainment, and education.

As they helped Cécile raise her children, they gave birth and raised children of their own. And like Cécile, they mourned the loss of children who died young. There was one difference, though, for enslaved women lost children not only through death but also through sale. For Cécile and Jean Baptiste, the enslavement of women was foremost a financial investment in their own comfort and advancement. They anticipated a return not only in service but also in offspring. Although the girl Marie, who may have been a daughter of one of the older women, stayed with the family for decades, her own child, Barthelemie, disappears in the records and may well have been sold when he reached an age where he was strong enough to bring a good price. The same was the case with Marie Jeanne's Félicité. The mothers had little, if any, say in the matter, living with both the hope that their children would be sold to a nearby family and the fear that they would end up with an unscrupulous enslaver and subjected to physical and sexual abuse.

A similar view of slavery is evident in the following episode. On January 17, 1783, Jean Baptiste went to a notary and signed a document, freeing from "*cautiverio y servidumbre*" (captivity and servitude) old Marie, who by then had been enslaved by the family for more than two decades. He (or the notary) estimated her age at around sixty. The document states that Jean Baptiste took this action "*por el mucho amor y cariño que le tengo*" ("for the great love and affection that I have for her") and "*por los muchos servicios que he recivido de ella*" ("for the many services that I have received from her").[49]

At the time, manumission was not uncommon in New Orleans. Under Spanish law, enslavers did not need official permission to free a person from enslavement, as had been the case under the French. They simply went to a notary and enacted the transaction. In a study of more than fifteen hundred such transactions, slightly more than half of the enslavers cited services rendered as a reason for granting freedom, suggesting that these enslavers saw manumission in economic terms. In about a quarter of the cases, enslavers stated affection for the enslaved person as a motivation. (In other cases, either no reason was given, or the enslaver had an intimate or biological relationship with the enslaved.)[50] Jean Baptiste's use of both "services rendered" and "great love and affection" as his motivations reveals a view of slavery, seemingly paradoxical, in which he could hold someone in bondage and at the same time profess "great" love for them.

Regardless of whether his love for old Marie was genuine, considering that she was sixty years old and could no longer do the strenuous work she had once done, giving her freedom was no financial sacrifice for Jean Baptiste. He had long since received his return on investment. For her, this act was at best a symbolic gesture. She received freedom in her declining years rather than earlier in life when she might have benefitted from a degree of independence and self-determination. Being free and elderly could be a mixed blessing. Unaccustomed to being on her own, she may have feared facing an uncertain future. Fortunately for her, by law and custom, enslavers could not simply free an old or infirmed person in order to avoid the expense of caring for them.[51] It is likely that Jean Baptiste ensured she had some means of support. Although I have not been able to trace old Marie's life as a free woman of color, it is possible that she stayed in the Durel household, relieved of work responsibilities and cared for by the remaining enslaved women. Or it may be that the social network among enslaved and free people of color came to her aid, and she moved in with a free neighbor or relative.

Jean Baptiste's use of the word *cautiverio* (captivity) suggests that he understood slavery was a condition he had imposed on old Marie against her will. That he eventually freed her further shows that he understood freedom was a more desirable state. However, for him and other enslavers at the time, freedom was a reward for service, not a human right. Although European men of letters and even English colonists in North America had begun to profess a belief that all men have an inalienable right to liberty, they continued to live in a world defined by hierarchy, in which some people, by right, had power over others. In the study of manumissions cited above, only 3 percent of the enslavers expressed any moral misgivings about slavery.

=== Ester Durel and Other Free Persons of Color ===

When I first encountered Ester Durel in the early months of my research, she was a mystery to me. Her name appears in a survey of French Quarter properties available online. On November 16, 1782, Jean Baptiste transferred property on Royal Street to her. A second entry indicates that she, in turn, transferred this property to a woman named Marie Claire Andry in 1810. I did not yet have access to the original records and was unable to locate any other information about her. At the time, I assumed that she was a relative, perhaps a sister or cousin of Jean Baptiste, and he had sold or given the property to her. Showing my naïveté about race in eighteenth-century Louisiana, it never occurred to me that she could be a Black woman.

Eventually I traveled to New Orleans and visited the notarial archives, where I was able to read the original property transactions and much more. On March 16, 1780, Jean Baptiste purchased Ester, described by her then owner as "my Black slave named Ester age twenty years." Jean Baptiste paid

400 piastres ($9,100 in 2024).[52] Less than two years later, on January 26, 1782, he emancipated her "for the many services she has provided to me and for the cash payment of three hundred piastres."[53] In another ten months, on November 26, 1782, she purchased a lot of land on Royal Street from him, with a mortgage for 200 piastres to be paid over two years.[54] Then, on November 5, 1784, he signed a document stating that she had paid the mortgage in full.[55] Other sources reveal that she lived in a small house on the property for nearly three decades, adopted the Durel surname at some point, and maintained a relationship with the family, for the woman who bought the property from her in 1810 was in fact Clarisse Andry Durel, the recently widowed wife of Jean Baptiste's son, Jean Baptiste (2). Ester herself died the next year.[56]

To decipher this remarkable chain of events, I had to give it historical context. As I wrote earlier, for decades under French rule enslaved people had gained freedom through various means. Spain, when it took control, introduced a new method called *coartación,* which gave captives the right to purchase their own freedom for an appraised price. The Spanish monarch saw this as a way to counter the power of wealthy planters and encourage the loyalty of Black people to the crown. Although Louisiana planters resisted, by one estimate 1,330 enslaved people purchased freedom in the colony during the three decades of Spanish rule.[57]

Evidence from her manumission shows that Ester took advantage of *coartación* and paid 300 piastres in cash and provided other services to Jean Baptiste in exchange for her freedom. A plausible scenario is that Ester grew up enslaved to a different White man and when he died an appraisal of his estate pegged her value at 400 piastres. She had managed to put away some money. By law, enslaved people had Sundays off, and if they were required to work, they were to be paid.[58] She also may have sold produce from her own garden at the market or provided a domestic service (mending clothes, laundering, etc.) on her own time to someone outside the household. That said, it is clear that she did not have enough money to purchase her freedom directly from her owner's estate. Rather, she reached out by some means to Jean Baptiste, possibly through Cécile or after church on a Sunday morning, and struck a deal whereby he purchased her and kept her enslaved until she had accumulated sufficient funds.

Ester was the first but not the only Black person to buy land from Jean Baptiste. In March 1782, he purchased a large tract of land on the fringe of the built-up area, running from Chartres Street back to Royal Street, up against the city wall (present-day Canal Street).[59] The section closest to the river, along Chartres, contained a kiln for fabricating bricks or earthenware and a 12-foot by 80-foot warehouse divided into seven rooms, with double chimneys at either end. Jean Baptiste sold this portion to a White man named Joseph Collette. The back of the property, along Royal Street, was undeveloped. He subdivided this land into 30-foot house lots, two up against the wall at 180 feet deep; and five along Royal, staked out at a depth of 118 feet, 6 inches. Over the next fourteen months, he sold these seven lots to *gens de couleur libres* for 250 piastres each ($7,240 in 2024). Ester was the first. The others were, by date of purchase:

Elisabet *alias* Mandeville, *mulata libre*, January 11, 1783.[60]
Margarita, *mulata libre,* January 12, 1783.[61]
Theresa Dufaut, *negra libre*, November 18, 1783.[62]
Françoise Riché *mulata libre*, January 2, 1784.[63]
Pedro Clavert, *negro libre*, January 2, 1784.[64]
Martonne, *negra libre*, January 2, 1784.[65]

Last, on May 3, 1784, Jean Baptiste sold a slightly larger lot that had been staked out to form a corner of the intersection of Royal and Iberville Streets. Because of its location and size, he priced it at 325 piastres. The buyer was William Quays, a White man.[66] This series of property transactions occurred amid numerous other property sales by Jean Baptiste, who now had sufficient capital to invest in real estate.

These transactions were turning points for the freed people who purchased the house lots. With freedom, they were eager to establish themselves as residents of the city with a place of their own to live. Home ownership was one of several strategies that *gens de couleur libres* used to gain respectability and protect themselves and their families. Their freedom was limited and precarious. They had to be careful not to offend a White person, for if accused and convicted of certain crimes in a system of justice that favored White people, they could lose their freedom and be sold back into slavery.

That Jean Baptiste's buyers bought property at the edge of town does not indicate the sort of enforced residential segregation that became common in many US cities in the twentieth century. It was simply a matter of what was available and what one could afford. During the 1780s and '90s the built-up area expanded beyond Bourbon Street to the city wall, and both White and free Black people purchased properties, often side by side.[67] By my own count, in 1800 *gens de couleur libres* owned 26 percent of the properties within the city walls.[68] Above Bourbon Street, this figure was 34 percent, below only 16 percent, reflecting the fact that lots closer to the river were settled first and were generally larger and more expensive. While this residential mixing offered opportunities for frequent interaction and possible relationships to develop, it did not erase the social and legal differentiation between Black people and White.

Women made up 60 to 65 percent of all manumissions during the three decades of Spanish rule, so it is not surprising that six of the seven freed people who purchased house lots from Jean Baptiste were women.[69] The sole male buyer was a man identified as Pedro "Clavert" by the notary who recorded the transaction. This was an error, for it is clear from other documents that his name in French was Pierre Claver, with no "t" at the end of the surname. The Ursuline sisters had enslaved Pierre's parents, and when he was quite young a nun accused one of them—father, mother, or son—of theft. The sisters resolved the matter by selling the family to the Capuchin fathers.[70] Pierre thus grew up enslaved to the priests of St. Louis parish at the very time that Jean Baptiste served as church warden. Called simply Pierre at birth, at some point he adopted, or the priests gave him, the surname Claver after a famous Spanish missionary, Padre Pedro Claver y Cobreró, who was revered for having ministered to enslaved Africans in seventeenth-century Columbia.[71]

Pierre, the enslaved man in New Orleans, went on to serve in the "colored" militia, which may be how he earned his freedom. During the late 1770s and early 1780s, the Spanish regiment stationed in New Orleans battled the English for control of territory east of the Mississippi River all the way to Florida. Local militia, both White and men of color, fought alongside the Spanish army. In 1794 Pierre married Celeste Hugon, *mulata* daughter of a "colored" militia officer. Other militiamen attended the wedding in uniform, lending pomp and dignity to the ceremony. Among them was Marechal Durelle who, judging from his name, may have been enslaved and freed by Jean Baptiste at some point.[72] Over the next two decades, Pierre stood in uniform as a witness to eighteen marriages between free men and women of color.[73] Like home ownership, solemn marriage in the church accompanied by men in uniform was a strategy that freed Black people employed to secure their freedom and standing in a White-dominated society.

Pierre and Celeste raised a family in their house on Royal Street, where they resided for forty-five years.[74] Late in life he sold the property, taking advantage of rising prices for real estate in that area, and moved to a smaller, less expensive house on Burgundy Street. He died in 1831, close to the age of eighty.

Pierre Claver and Ester Durel were neighbors on Royal Street for nearly three decades. They had successfully escaped lives in slavery and lived as freed people, albeit with limitations to their freedom. However, telling only their stories obscures the lived reality of the majority of African-descended people in eighteenth-century New Orleans. The fact is that far more Black people remained enslaved than were freed. The story of another buyer gives a more balanced view.

When the notary documented Theresa Dufaut's purchase of property from Jean Baptiste, he actually recorded two transactions. In the first, she purchased the house lot for 250 piastres; in the second, she sold to Jean Baptiste, for 500 piastres ($14,487 in 2024), a seventeen-year-old girl named Amarante, whom she stated had been "born in my house, daughter of a Black female named Françoise."[75] In other words, in a society and economy based on the enslavement of others, Theresa sold the daughter of an enslaved Black woman in order to purchase property and make her own precarious position more secure.

Amarante's presence in this transaction reveals the other side of the story. I am unable to relate her experience specifically, for like so many she appears only once in the records. What is certain is that she was in a potentially dangerous situation. Enslavers placed high value on young enslaved female bodies, not only because they would provide labor and offspring for years to come, but also because men found them sexually attractive. The practice of displaying an enslaved woman nearly naked, ostensibly to show that she had no deformity or disease, served to arouse potential buyers, who were free to feel between her legs and to fondle her breasts.[76] In a city with a population that had twice as many White men as White women, young Black women were in demand. An unscrupulous enslaver could sexually exploit her with impunity, either by raping her himself or by charging a fee and making her available to other men, perhaps a transient seaman or resident soldier, or even a neighbor. Any woman who resisted would be whipped, as was the enslaver's right. An enslaver might be reprimanded for malicious cruelty, if discovered, but not for what was considered ordinary punishment.[77]

White men developed a myth of Black carnality, a belief that African women and women of African descent were by nature wanton and lascivious, that it was they and not the man who initiated sexual intercourse. In this view, enslaved women, who by law had no control over their own lives, somehow had full control when it came to sex. Widely believed, the myth relieved the White man of all responsibility for his actions.[78]

Countless young, enslaved women in Amarante's situation endured rape by White men, not only in New Orleans but anywhere that slavery existed. While a fortunate few were able to turn intimate relationships to their advantage, securing safety and freedom for themselves and their kin, most suffered silently, or to paraphrase one historian, they screamed through the silence of the archives.[79] Their stories have gone unheard because the men who decided what records to keep deemed their stories unimportant. In property transactions one can discover when they were sold, their estimated age, and the value placed on them, but little else. When they are mentioned in court cases, the only concern is the impact of their behavior on their value as property. In New Orleans, when they appear in sacramental records for the baptism of a child, their full story is denied, for the priest invariably entered *padre incognito* (father unknown) unless the father wished to acknowledge the child.

Amarante's full story remains untold. There is no way of knowing if she suffered sexual exploitation at the hands of Jean Baptiste or a subsequent owner. What is clear is that Jean Baptiste's willingness to do business with freed Black women like Ester and Theresa in no way signifies opposition to slavery or a regard for their safety. In July 1785, a year after he had finished selling the lots on Royal Street, he purchased an enslaved woman named Magdalena and sold her the following May.[80] Like Amarante, Magdalena was seventeen years old. For Jean Baptiste, the buying and selling of property, whether real estate or human, was simply a means to greater wealth. The vulnerability of young women like Amarante and Magdalena was not his concern.

The story of Ester and her neighbors revealed to me an unexpected dimension of life for people of African descent in Louisiana. That a free Black woman had the name Durel within twenty-five years of the family's arrival was a surprise. My thinking about race in the eighteenth century began to change, no longer seeing it as solely a matter of enslaved Black people and White enslavers, but as something more complex and complicated.

Cécile died in January 1785, in her early fifties. Four of her living children had already married, one more would marry that March, and the final two would do so within a few years. One generation was giving way to the next. Although Jean Baptiste continued to run his dry goods business, over his remaining years he began to liquidate his property. He no longer needed a large house and sold the property on Chartres Street to his son-in-law, Michel Fortier, husband of his eldest daughter, Rose.[81] He also had no need for the number of enslaved persons as previously held. Judging from Table II, at the time of Cécile's death, he and his wife held in captivity an estimated twelve individuals. At the time of his own death five years later, only four remained. Let me name the eight individuals that he sold before he died: Petre, Louis, Azor, Isabel, Victoria, Rose, another Issabel, and her daughter, Therese.

Jean Baptiste died on June 4, 1790, just shy of his sixty-third birthday.[82] For enslaved people, the days following the death of their enslaver was a time fraught with uncertainty. They worried about what would happen to them. Jean Baptiste dictated his last will and testament shortly before his death, leaving everything to be divided equally among the seven children he had with Cécile.[83] He did not choose to emancipate any of the enslaved, as was sometimes done. An appraisal of his estate was made a few days later so that everything could be sold and the money equally divided. This included the four remaining enslaved people:

- Marie, age forty-two, cook and laundress, valued at 600 pesos. She was the adolescent girl mentioned in the 1763 census and thus had been enslaved to the Durels her entire adult life.

- Marie Jeanne, age sixty, maid, valued at 100 pesos. She was enslaved by the Durels when she was in her twenties and worked as a cook or laundress. Her designation here as a sixty-year-old maid indicates that she was no longer able to perform those functions, hence her lower valuation.

- Jean, age fifteen, personal servant, valued at 500 pesos. Jean was Marie Jeanne's son, and his valuation reflects his youth and potential.

- Josef, age fifty, unskilled and infirm, valued at 100 pesos. Josef had spent his life as an unskilled laborer, perhaps working in Jean Baptiste's warehouse, hoisting and carrying heavy bolts of cloth and crates of earthenware. By age fifty, his body had given out and he could no longer perform those functions, hence his low valuation.

As it turned out, all four of them stayed with the Durel family. Ursin, the youngest son, had recently married and was setting up a household of his own. He purchased Marie from the estate. He had known her his entire life, and her maturity and experience would be a great benefit to his young and pregnant wife.

Given Marie Jeanne's age and Josef's infirmity, it is unlikely that anyone would want to purchase them, so Aimée, the youngest of the siblings, took them to the upriver plantation where she and her husband, Jacques, lived. On the plantation, other enslaved people would be able to care for them in their waning years. They would be given light tasks, she perhaps watching the enslaved toddlers while their mothers went to work in the fields, he sweeping a porch or weeding a garden.

Aimée also purchased fifteen-year-old Jean. He was fresh and fit, already had the skills of a personal servant, and had many years of labor ahead of him. Aimée's decision may have been touched by sentiment, for when Aimée was an impressionable seven-year-old she had served as Jean's godmother.[84] Nevertheless, Jean remained enslaved, the strength of his body and the skill of his hands to be used for the sole purpose of generating comfort and more wealth for Aimée and her offspring.

The end of a life; the end of an era. Less than a year before the death of Jean Baptiste, Frenchmen stormed the Bastille in Paris, marking the beginning of the French Revolution and the end of the ancien régime. The aristocratic world that shaped and limited the early lives of Cécile and Jean Baptiste—she, the daughter of a wealthy joiner, sent to live in the home of an aristocrat to learn the proper ways of a lady, perhaps in the hope of marrying into that class; he, following in the footsteps of his father, becoming a master upholsterer and quickly reaching the top of the artisan class—was drawing to a close. They had long since escaped the limitations of that world to find new opportunities in a distant colony. In so doing, their lives became closely entwined with people of African descent.

As I wrote their story, I was struck by how easily, seemingly without misgiving, they adopted the practice of enslaving and holding captive other humans in order to advance their own position in a society that measured status by wealth and appearance. Had they stayed in France, it is likely that they would have had no direct involvement with slavery, although they would have benefited indirectly since much of Bordeaux's wealth was due to its role in the slave trade. In New Orleans, they enslaved at least twenty people, more than I expected to find. Some labored for the family for decades; others came and went, casually bought and sold, as Jean Baptiste went about his business. The ability to enslave others was not simply a matter of personal power. It depended on the authority of White men in France and in Louisiana who passed and enforced laws that deprived people of African descent the right to control their own lives. There is no denying that the Durels were complicit in this offense.

Some White people, myself included at times, downplay the cruelty of slavery. My first attempts to write this chapter produced a depiction of race relations more benign than what I have written here. I emphasized the freedom attained by Ester and other people of color, without writing about Amarante, the vulnerable seventeen-year-old girl whom Jean Baptiste took as payment for one of his properties. I wrote about how the four enslaved people at the end of Jean Baptiste's life remained with the family, taking that as a sign of caring, without mentioning the others whom he sold before he died or the fact that the four, nonetheless, remained enslaved. It was not until I learned to consider the full context in which records were created and began to think about what was not being said that I realized I was telling only half of a story.

Evidently, there was never a question of the morality of slavery for Cécile and Jean Baptiste. The Catholic Church, through its priests and nuns, supported the practice, so long as the people held captive were baptized and instructed in the Catholic faith. The hypocrisy of saving the soul while enslaving the body did not bother them, as it does me. For me, the racial segregation of the Catholic Church and parochial schools during my own childhood became a moral issue that I took to heart. As I write in the final chapter of this book, it took an archbishop from New York, who as a young priest had once served in an integrated parish in Harlem, to challenge segregation in New Orleans on moral grounds.

In another connection to my time, from the moment I learned the story of Ester Durel, I kept my eyes open for Durels of African descent living today. As I progressed through the generations, I tracked several possibilities that led to dead ends. It was not until I reached my grandparents' generation that I discovered a Black Durel family living less than two blocks from them, at a time when my father was only nine years old.

Table III.
Marriages of the Children of Jean Baptiste Durel and Cécile LeBrun

Child	Age at Marriage	Spouse	Marriage Date
Marie Cécile Rose Durel 1754–1788	About 20	Michel Fortier 1750–1819	Before November 24, 1774, when first child was born
Jean François Durel 1758–1812	25	Marie "Manette" Dejan c. 1768–1833	December 9, 1783
Marie Félicité Durel 1759–1809	Under 23	Elias Toutant Beauregard c. 1750–1809	Before April 8, 1783, when first child was baptized
Jean Baptiste Durel (2) (called Baptiste in the text) 1761–1809	24	Marie Claire "Clarisse" Andry 1767–1842	March 31, 1785
Jean Ursin Durel 1764–1817	24	Marie Françoise Dejan c. 1772–1844	July 1, 1789
Félicité Victoire (2) Durel 1766–after 1818	15	Marie Louis Florent Basile 1760–1816	December 10, 1781
Aimée Marie Victoire Durel 1768–1844	19	Jacques Fortier 1759–1820	October 1787

Note: Three children died young and did not marry: Mathurin, Victoire (1), and François Honoré.

Chapter 2

The First Creole Generation

The children of Jean Baptiste Durel and Cécile LeBrun were the first Creole generation of the family. That is, they were born in the colony and had not immigrated from Europe. They were raised in the 1750s and '60s and came of age and married in the '70s and '80s. Their lives as adults encompassed the last decades of Spanish rule and, beginning in 1803, the initial period when Louisiana was a territory of the United States. Most died by 1820, with the exception of four women (one daughter and three daughters-in-law) who lived into the 1830s and '40s.

Unlike their parents, who as newcomers adopted the practice of enslaving others, the second generation of White Durels were born into it. As adults, every one of them held in captivity people from Africa or of African descent, and they all benefited from enslaved labor. For them, the enslavement of others seemed part of a natural order, the way in which the maker had ordained the world.

The siblings and their spouses remained close as they started families of their own. They often served as godparents for one another's children. Nevertheless, seeds were already sown for very different futures for their descendants. Some became very wealthy landowners, others worked as tradesmen and clerks. The four stories that follow shed differing light on the family's ongoing engagement with people of African descent.

== Rose Durel and Michel Fortier ==

As the Durels became known and especially as Jean Baptiste took on public roles as church warden, almshouse treasurer, and city treasurer, they made the acquaintance of other parents who were also looking for suitable partners for their children. At dances and other gatherings, parents observed the youngsters, and when two seemed compatible and showed affection for one another, they began to discuss a possible union. If the parents had someone in mind but the child strenuously objected, the parents thought better of it and looked elsewhere. If the child favored someone that the parents found unsuitable, the child generally acquiesced. It was in everyone's interest that the marriage be successful.

In New Orleans at this time, White men outnumbered White women by nearly two to one, which gave the Durels, with four daughters, an advantage.[1] A common strategy was to secure the best possible alliance with a wealthy family by selecting one daughter, often the eldest, and providing a large dowry. The investment was protected from an unscrupulous husband because the wife retained legal ownership of the property she brought into the marriage.[2]

Thus, when the eldest Durel child, Rose, came of age, Jean Baptiste made a deal with Michel Fortier, a master gunsmith who had held the title of "Armourer to the King" under the French monarch. By the 1770s, Fortier was a well-established merchant-planter with property in New Orleans and a plantation upriver. Fortier chose his eldest son, also named Michel, to marry Rose. The young couple courted and wed in 1773 or early 1774. Their first child was born November 11, 1774, named Jean Michel after the two grandfathers.[3]

Rose's dowry amounted to 40 percent of their joint property, which included both a house in the city and the upriver plantation that Michel, the son, eventually inherited from his father.[4] As a young man in his midtwenties, Michel started a successful trading partnership with Alex Reaud, and in time their ships carried goods to and from the Caribbean and across the Atlantic. At least on one occasion, they brought African captives to New Orleans from Saint-Domingue.[5] To add prestige to his growing wealth, Michel received a commission from the king of Spain as "Captain of the Artillery of the Militia," a title given because of his service under Governor Galvez in conquering the English forts on the Mississippi River.[6] As the firstborn and first to marry, Rose and Michel began their married life with advantages.

Rose gave birth to six children over the course of thirteen years (see Appendix to track the children). Much like her mother, her life revolved around managing the household, seeing to the education of the children, and socializing with families of similar status. One difference, however, was that she enjoyed far greater wealth and status than Cécile. Her elite social standing is reflected in a portrait by Josef Francisco Xavier de Salazar y Mendoza, the first artist of note to spend time in New Orleans (Figure 2). Few could afford to have a portrait done, so the painting's very existence demonstrates wealth. The artist depicts Rose in a *chemise à la reine*, a style made fashionable by

Fig. 2: *Marie Cécile Rose Durel with her daughter, Marie Félicité Julie Fortier* by Josef Francisco Xavier de Salazar y Mendoza, c. 1784–1788. Courtesy of Peter Patout.

Queen Marie Antoinette. Her eldest daughter, Julie, stands beside her, dressed similarly. Rose holds an apple in her hand, a traditional symbol of fertility, underscoring the centrality of motherhood in her life. This portrayal of mother and daughter together, dressed in aristocratic fashion, places them at the forefront of an idealized colonial elite.[7]

A sure sign of affluence was the number of people of African descent that a family enslaved. Unlike her parents, who enslaved an estimated twenty individuals over the course of their lifetimes, Rose and Michel held captive fifty-two at one time—thirty-two on their plantation and twenty in the city. Their names and ages appear in Table IV. Among them were some who were Creole, born in Louisiana or Saint-Domingue, and some who had been captured in Africa. The appraised value placed on these men, women, and children was 64 percent of the total property valuation.[8] That is, the enslaved were worth more than all of the inventoried land, buildings, livestock, farm tools, and household furnishings together. Slavery was the real generator of wealth.

Table IV.
Enslaved people in the estate inventory of Rose Durel, 1790

Inventory Item #	Name	Description	Age	Value in pesos
		Day 1: At the city house		
2	Juan Bautista	*negro, criollo*	50	400
3	Lendos	*mulato de Santo Domingo*	28	350
4	Guime	*negro, criollo*	23	400
5	Lebelle	*criollo*	-	350
6	-	*de nacion Auzar* [Azores]	28	600
7	Maria	*negra, criolla de Guarico*	70	250
8	Rosa	*criolla*	58	250
9	Francisca	*de nacion Carata* [?]	25	350
10	Marianna	*de nacion Hibo* [Ibo]	28	650
	Maria Louisa*	*hija* [daughter] *de Marianna*	6	
11	Rosa*	*de nacion Vrima*	19	400
	Luis	*hijo* [son] *de Rosa, mulato*	2	
-	Margarita*	*de nacion Conga*	24	350
		Day 2: At the plantation		
1	Carlos	*negro, criolo*	50	400
2	Pedro	-	50	360
3	Cueré	*un poco carpintero* [carpenter]	27	400
4	Romia	*un poco carpintero*	30	450
5	Juan Bautista	-	20	450
6	Isodoro	*mulato, prima de carpintero*	19	450
7	Luis	-	27	400
8	Antonio	*negro, de oficio labrador* [farmer by trade]	32	360

Inventory Item #	Name	Description	Age	Value in pesos
9	Josef	*labrador*	32	340
10	Neptuno	*labrador*	30	350
11	Augustin	*labrador*	27	350
	Thomson	*labrador*	31	350
	Principe	*labrador*	29	350
Day 3: At the plantation				
1	Luis	*negro, labrador*	30	350
2	Manuel	-	22	360
3	Jupiter	-	25	360
4	Same	*labrador*	29	350
5	Dominica	-	45	320
6	J - - -	*labrador*	50	280
Missing page containing four individuals				
11	Christoval	*labrador*	28	350
12	Figuero	-	20	370
13	Telemac	-	35	320
14	Valentino	*labrador*	18	370
15	Juan	*labrador*	29	350
16	Juan Pedro	-	30	345
17	Pedro	-	27	350
18	Jacobo	-	27	350
	Ramon	-	25	360
Day 4: In New Orleans				
1	Juan Luis	*poco carpintero*	18	360
2	Ector		17	370
3	Margarita*	*negra*	20	320
4	Cress		20	300
5	Rosa*		35	280
6	Maria Luisa*		7	150
7	Flor		6	120

* Three individuals, Margarita, Rosa, and Maria Luisa, may have been counted twice. These names appear on both the first and fourth days of the inventory, although the ages given are different.

The thirty-two enslaved on the plantation were all male, ranging in age from nineteen to fifty. Carlos, a fifty-year-old *negro criolo*, was listed first in the inventory and may have been the leader of the entire force. Several men were singled out as *carpenterios* (carpenters) and valued highly because of their skill. Most of the others were identified as *labradores* (farmers), including Antonio, *de oficio labrador* (farmer by trade), who may have been the leader of the agricultural workers. These men labored from dawn to dusk, organized into work groups, planting and harvesting sugar and perhaps indigo for export, and corn and vegetables for the local market. The carpenters not only built and maintained farm buildings, but also felled timber and produced lumber for use in the city and for export to the Caribbean. These were the staples that fed Michel's mercantile enterprise.

Daily life was different for the enslaved workers in the city. Six or seven men attended to the needs of the family, but just as likely they worked at Michel's business. The enslaved women, ranging in age from nineteen to fifty-eight, handled the domestic duties of cooking, cleaning, laundering, and waiting table. Two women were listed with a child each, and another child appears without reference to her mother. Rose's household appears to have functioned much like her mother's, but larger to accommodate her higher status and more active social calendar.

It was customary for the wealthy to spend the winter social season, roughly December to March, at their city residences. They were in town for both Christmas and carnival, a time of parties, dances, and family gatherings. In warmer weather, which can come to south Louisiana as early as March, the family moved to the country, where it was relatively cooler, less humid, and certainly less crowded. The list in Table IV was taken from a tally made during the month of January; hence, the sexual imbalance between an all-male plantation and a city house that was mostly women and children. Family relationships among the enslaved are not evident but almost certainly existed. That said, the overall ratio was thirty-nine males to nine females, leaving a large number of young men in search of female companionship either in town or on neighboring plantations.

Rose's life took a tragic turn in 1788. Her infant daughter, Marie Isabel, whom she gave birth to the previous September, grew sickly and died.[9] The personal loss was compounded by a great fire that swept through the city in

March, destroying many homes, including that of Rose and her five remaining children. Michel was away on a voyage to Europe at the time and Rose may have taken refuge in her father's house, which had been spared, or she may have fled with the children to the country.[10] Then, in late summer, with Michel still away, Rose fell ill herself and died. No cause was given. She had just turned thirty-four.[11]

Upon Michel's return from Europe, things began to change quickly for the family. Rose's youngest sister, Aimée, had married Michel's younger brother, Jacques, a year earlier.[12] The young couple soon began to play a larger role. By the terms of her dowry, Rose's children were entitled to her share of the estate. The probate court had an inventory taken (which is the source of the data in Table IV). It ordered Michel to place sufficient money in a trust to be distributed to the children as they came of age. Not having ready cash, Michel sold a number of enslaved individuals for 5,750 pesos and, for a similar price, an undivided share of his plantation to Jacques, thus making his brother a junior partner in the enterprise. Jacques and Aimée soon took up residence on the plantation, where Jacques served as the on-site manager.

Michel stayed in the city and saw to the upbringing of the children. He sent his oldest child, Jean Michel, to France to be educated. The second daughter, Victoire, succumbed to disease at age ten in 1792, leaving Julie as his only surviving daughter. A son, Zenon, died five years later, at age eighteen.[13] Thus, only three of the children—Jean Michel, Julie, and Edmond, the youngest—reached adulthood. To assist with running the household, Michel retained some of his wife's enslaved women. He never remarried.

As rich as Michel was, after 1795 he became even richer. That year another planter, Étienne de Boré, following the guidance of a sugar chemist, a free man of color from Saint-Domingue, succeeded in producing granulated sugar suitable for shipping. Planters up and down the river quickly followed and expanded sugar production, ushering in a form of agriculture and a source of wealth that would shape south Louisiana into the twentieth century.[14] The increase in cultivation meant a corresponding increase in the enslaved population. At the Fortier plantation, where thirty-two captive laborers had been sufficient to work the land in 1790, eighty-five were needed twenty years later.[15] By then, the family had also acquired another property farther upriver in St. Charles Parish, where sixty-five captives toiled, managed by Michel's son Edmond.

The number of enslaved men and women on sugar plantations in Louisiana continued to grow as the new century progressed and methods of production improved. In the 1830s and '40s, planters adopted steam power to run the sugar mill and increased the pace at which the cane growing in the fields could be converted into granulated sugar. Production rose from 70,000 hogshead of sugar processed in 1832 to nearly 237,000 in 1851. Over roughly the same period, United States domestic annual consumption of sugar increased from thirteen pounds of sugar per person to thirty pounds, and the number of enslaved people in Louisiana producing sugar swelled to 125,000.[16]

I have not made an extensive study of the plantations owned by the children and grandchildren of Rose and Michel. However, scholars have written about what it took to manage a large, captive workforce in order to produce a profit from the manufacture and export of sugar. As is true with slavery wherever and whenever it exists, all practices rest on the use or threat of violence. Some methods may pass for kindness or generosity, but ultimately whenever an enslaved person goes against the interests or will of their enslaver, the enslaver inflicts pain, sometimes to the point of death.[17]

In antebellum Louisiana, the most obvious instrument of violence was the whip. The regular beating of enslaved people, in the open where others could see, was central to a well-disciplined operation. A White "owner" whipping an enslaved woman or man was so routine as to hardly bear mentioning. It is important to emphasize here that ownership is a legal concept. That is, the dominance of White people over Black people was only possible because of the law—the law, created by White enslavers, was in itself an act of violence.

For example, Article 167 of the Louisiana Civil Code (1825–1853) states that a "master" could correct a White servant or apprentice for laxity or carelessness, so long as he did so "with moderation" and provided he did not use a whip.[18] No such concern was shown for enslaved Black workers. The law placed no restriction on the means of correcting or punishing them, although it did admonish enslavers not to use "unusual rigor," which meant not to "maim or mutilate" them or cause their death. The pain inflicted using a rawhide whip was acceptable and customary, reserved for Black bodies and work animals.[19]

The sting of the whip, supported by the law, whether applied or simply threatened, undergirded other routine forms of oppression. Beyond long days of toil in the heat and cold, there was the enslaver's right to sell an enslaved child, the splitting-up of enslaved families, the sexual exploitation of enslaved women (and men), and the constant reminder of subordinate status in the required bended back and downcast eyes when being addressed by *any* White person. According to the law, a captive could not leave the plantation without written permission and, if caught doing so, was beaten. A captive who defended himself against the insults or blows of *any* White person, not just his enslaver, was presumed guilty and subjected to the whip. The only exception was when a captive acted to prevent another White man from harming his enslaver.[20]

This is not to say that enslaved people were completely powerless. In addition to docility, sugar planters needed a disciplined and productive workforce in order to turn a profit. The process of making sugar and getting it to market involved many steps, from planting cane in January and February to harvesting and grinding from mid-October to late December.[21] In the process of grinding, laborers would take stalks of cane, which had been trimmed and cut near the base in the fields, and feed them onto a conveyor belt where they were squeezed between rollers to produce juice. Next, the juice was heated in a series of open kettles, each time evaporating more water and leaving the juice thicker, to the point where it eventually granulated. Grinding season was a time of intense labor for the enslaved and high anxiety for the enslaver. The year's profit rested on the ability to harvest and process the entire crop within a brief timeframe of roughly two months. The planter had to calculate when to begin, leaving the cane in the ground long enough for it to mature and reach a high sucrose level, but not so long as to risk freezing temperatures before all of it could be cut and taken to the mill.

The pressure of getting the work done quickly gave the enslaved leverage to improve their situation. They could easily slow the process: a dulled cane knife making it harder to trim and cut the cane stalks; a loosened bolt causing a cart to tip over when transporting the cane to the mill; a stone mixed in with the cane on the conveyor belt, jamming the rollers; a fire too hot under a kettle and scorching the sugar.[22] Such acts of defiance could be met with more violence. However, planters soon found that incentives worked better than the whip in getting their captive workers to labor extra-long hours at a rapid pace. The whip worked best for repetitive, low-skilled work, but for the care, precision, and speed required during harvest, the cooperation of the workers proved essential. To achieve this, many planters chose to negotiate.

Incentives took many forms. During grinding season, planters typically required their enslaved workers to labor on Sundays, for which the workers received payment, as was their due in accordance with state law.[23] Planters paid premiums to talented and skilled workers who manned key positions in the sugar-making process: drivers of work gangs in the fields who kept a steady flow of cane arriving at the mill; operators of the steam-powered conveyor belt and rollers that kept the juice flowing; and those who kept the fires going at the correct temperature under the kettles, transforming the juice into granulated sugar at just the right moment. All workers got better rations and sometimes new work clothes and shoes at harvest time, and if the harvest was successful, they often received a financial bonus and extra days off at Christmas, when the work was done. Of course, if at any point the incentives did not work, there was always the whip. That said, because the harvest bonus affected everyone collectively, the enslaved usually policed themselves, putting pressure on slackers to keep up the pace. [24]

Enslaved workers generally did not have to work added hours for their slaveholders at other times of year. Still, they found and negotiated opportunities to earn a modicum of money. For example, the use of steam power at the mill required enormous amounts of fuel in the form of wood. A planter could purchase cords of wood on the open market, but most often he found that his workers were willing to do the work on their own time. Although this cut into their time to rest their weary bodies after a day's work, they spent spring and summer evenings in twilight and moonlight, cutting and hauling wood from plantation woodlands and stacking it near the mill. Here, too, it was a negotiated arrangement, with the enslaver benefiting from a lower price and the workers paid a modest sum for their labor.[25]

Enslaved men and women used the money they earned to purchase items at the plantation store. They were able to buy colorful ribbons and fabrics, kitchen utensils and dishes, and perhaps something special, like a pendant or even a silver watch. These items made their lives a little easier and more enjoyable, but the real benefit was that through possession they asserted their self-identity and self-worth. For example, in contrast to the drab work garments they were forced to wear the rest of the week, they gathered on Sundays in colorful clothes and adorned themselves with ribbons and scarves. After attending church services, as was required by some planters, they gathered to dance, sing, and tell stories of their people. By making wise use of the free time allotted to them, they built communities of kinship and friendship, united in their shared experience of oppression and pain at the hands of their enslavers.[26]

Planters preferred to cast their financial dealings with the enslaved as paternal benevolence. The enslaved understood that any payments they received were compensation for laboring extra hours on their own time as well as, for some, their sugar production skills. However, planters preferred to describe the payment as a gift, given freely, as a father might reward a child for being obedient or for doing well in school. Whether a charade or sincerely believed, Creole planters considered themselves compassionate Christians who were obliged to care for those entrusted to them in slavery. They thought of the enslaved as childlike people who benefited from discipline and hard work and who appreciated the guidance they received from their "masters."[27]

Paternalism, a belief in a God-given right and obligation to rule over other people, ensnared planters and their families. Solomon Northup, a free Black man from New York who was duped into traveling to Washington, DC, where he was placed in chains, carried to New Orleans, and sold into slavery, later wrote of one of his enslavers: "There never was a more kind, noble, candid, Christian man." But then he added: "The influences and associations that had always surrounded him, blinded him to the inherent wrong at the bottom of the system of slavery. He never doubted the moral right of one man holding another in subjection."[28] Like Northup's enslaver, the children and grandchildren of Rose and Michel saw nothing wrong and plenty right in the practice of holding other humans in captivity. They embraced both their Catholic faith and paternalism, believing that God had anointed them rulers of their estates, not unlike feudal lords. As their profits from sugar rose, their houses became grander and their lifestyle more luxurious. They believed their growing affluence and lives of comfort were their just reward for living as good Christians.

Among the grandchildren of Rose and Michel who owned plantations along the river above the city, one stands out. Valcour Aime was known among the Creole landed aristocracy as the wealthiest man in Louisiana. His mother was Julie, the girl depicted in the Salazar painting with her mother, Rose (Figure 2). He inherited enormous wealth from both his father, François-Gabriel Aime, a planter in St. Charles Parish, and from his grandfather, Michel. Valcour married Josephine Roman, daughter of another wealthy planter family. Combining their resources enabled them to expand her parent's plantation in St. James Parish, just downriver from her brother, who built the now famous Oak Alley plantation. At the time, Valcour's estate was deemed the more impressive of the two properties.

Beyond the advantages that came to him through inheritance, Valcour took a scientific approach to running his plantation. He experimented and recorded the results of various techniques used in the cultivation of cane and the production of sugar. He was one of the first to adopt steam power for the grinding process. He kept track of the purchase price, age, and assignments made to the men and women he held in bondage, looking for ways to improve productivity. He spent time in Cuba observing methods there and tried various strains of cane to improve yield. His innovations gave him a competitive advantage over other planters, and his wealth grew.[29] As was typical of other planters, Valcour no doubt recognized his dependence on the cooperation of these enslaved workers for his success and calculated with care how much he would have to pay to earn a profit. On the eve of the Civil War, Valcour and Josephine held, with their grown daughters and sons-in-law on neighboring plantations, more than 280 men, women, and children in slavery.[30]

One of Valcour Aime's grandsons recalled his grandfather's plantation on the river, describing it in glowing terms with its "grand and stately house with large white pillars and wide balconies," and its elaborate pleasure garden replete with an artificial lake and a Chinese pagoda. In keeping with the principles of Christian paternalism, he praised his grandfather as "exceedingly charitable," "very pious," and "always ready to help the needy," and that "his kindness extended to the blacks as well as the whites." He went on to claim that Valcour treated the men and women he held in captivity with compassion, by assigning the elderly and frail light work in the garden, never giving delicate women and children more work than they could handle, ensuring that all were well fed and clothed, and permitting them to have a "little patch of ground where they grew vegetables and corn." In the end, the grandson concludes that "the negroes in Louisiana . . . were not unhappy. They had games of their own, and dances which they enjoyed immensely."[31]

It is easy to see paternalism at play in this remembrance. Belief in a God-given right to rule over people of African descent was handed down from generation to generation, just as White family wealth descended, and did not die with the end of slavery. On the contrary, paternalism served as a justification for the continued subjugation of Black people following the Civil War and Reconstruction, leading directly to the imposition of the racial segregation in the twentieth century that I knew growing up.

=== Victoire Durel (2) and Florent Basile ===

Although six of the Durel children married within a circle of friends and business acquaintances of their parents, Victoire, the third daughter, was different. On November 29, 1781, she married Louis Florent Basile, called Florent, who had only recently arrived in the city.[32] He apparently came from Port-au-Prince in Saint-Domingue, in charge of a cargo of merchandise. He met local merchants and had occasion to socialize with their families. At some point he made the acquaintance of Victoire. He was twenty-one years old; she was only fifteen.

Marriage of a girl at age fifteen was not unheard of at the time, but it was unusual for the Durels (refer to Table III). Victoire's older sisters married in their twenties, and her younger sister was nineteen on her wedding day. Also, although Victoire was the sixth child, she married second. Victoire's youth and quick courtship raise the possibility that she was pregnant. However, there is no record of a child born within nine months of the wedding, and the first child came eleven months later, leaving little time for Victoire to miscarry and become pregnant again.[33]

Florent, too, was young for marriage. Although twenty-one, he wrote in the marriage register the word *jeune* under his name, indicating that he was legally underage. Spanish law required children under twenty-five to obtain permission to marry.[34] It appears that he received permission from his mother, who traveled from Saint-Domingue to attend the wedding. Indeed, it seems the mothers rather than the fathers took the lead in arranging this marriage.

It may be a stretch, but it is an intriguing possibility that this union reflects a new conception of marriage that was just emerging in literature at the time, one in which individual choice played a greater role than parental authority. Historians have traced this view in French novels and theatrical works, such as *The Barber of Seville* by Pierre-Augustin Caron de Beaumarchais, a satirical work written in 1773 and first performed in 1775. In the play, Count Almaviva falls in love with the beautiful young Rosine, but fearing that she may marry him simply because of his money he disguises himself as a poor university student and attempts to woo her. He succeeds, and they marry out of love.[35]

An inventory of books in the library of the Ursuline Convent, taken at a much later date, includes eighteenth-century editions of the works of Beaumarchais.[36] It is conceivable that Victoire read the story and as an impressionable and willful girl opted for love, rather than wait for her father to find a suitable partner.

A comparison of marriage records reinforces this interpretation. Such records were created by the priest who performed the ceremony and signed by the parents who had arranged the marriage, as well as the married couple, followed by family members and witnesses in attendance. This was the case for Victoire's three brothers, where Jean Baptiste's signature appears on the first or second line, either before or just after the bride and groom. In Victoire's record, however, his is the eighth signature, preceded by two of his sons-in-law, and others. The first to sign was Cécile, followed by Florent's mother. They, not the fathers, stepped up first to affirm this marriage.

Victoire's relationship with her mother remained important. She and Florent stayed in New Orleans and enslaved at least three people of African descent: Philipe, Angelica, and a girl named Maria.[37] The couple's first child came on October 19, 1782, and was named Victoire Cécile, after the baby's mother and grandmother. At the baptism the following April, Cécile stood as the child's godmother.[38] Victoire gave birth to a second child, whom they named Jean Florent, in July 1784. Life seemed pleasant for the young family, and they gave every indication that they planned to stay in the city. However, in January 1785, Cécile died, at which time things gradually began to change.

Victoire gave birth to another son (François Edward) that summer. They held a christening for both sons on September 10. It was a big family affair. Victoire's sister Rose and brother-in-law Michel were present for the baptisms of a son and a Fortier niece, and her brother François and his wife were there for the baptism of a son.[39] Following the ceremonies, Florent and Michel went to see a notary, who recorded a transaction in which Florent gave special power of attorney to Michel to handle his affairs in New Orleans.[40] Over the next six months or so, Florent and Victoire made plans for their young family to leave the city, including the sale of two remaining people they held enslaved.[41] They had decided to move to Port-au-Prince, presumably to be close to his family, perhaps because Victoire's mother had passed.

Merchant ships traveled regularly between New Orleans and Saint-Domingue, so they were not entirely cut off from the Durel family. Victoire could send and receive letters, and it is possible that Florent used his connections in both places to build a business, serving as an agent and arranging shipments in both directions. Victoire made the trip home at least once, in 1800, to serve as godmother for a child named after her, a daughter of her sister, Aimée.[42] She had no more children after the three born in New Orleans. The oldest, Victoire Cécile, married Louis-Hector de Mons d'Orbigny, a planter born in Saint-Domingue and descended from French nobility.[43] The middle child, Jean Florent, grew to manhood in Port-au-Prince. The youngest died early.

Five years after Florent and Victoire made the move, enslaved workers in Saint-Domingue rose up against their oppressors, pushing thousands of Whites to the sea and causing them to flee to Philadelphia, Baltimore, and other American ports along the Eastern Seaboard. By the spring of 1792 the self-liberating people of African descent were in command of the northern third of the colony. Port-au-Prince, farther to the south, remained in French hands, and Florent took up arms to defend against the uprising, serving as colonel in a regiment of *chasseurs* (light cavalry). Fighting continued off and on for the next twelve years as France, England, Spain, and the freedom fighters vied for control.

Ultimately, the revolutionaries claimed victory and established the Republic of Haiti in January 1804. Toward the end of the fighting, the island witnessed another mass exodus of Whites, who took enslaved people with them, as well as free people of color who chose not to side with the revolution. As many as thirty thousand refugees resettled in Cuba. Florent and his family made their escape to San Julian de los Güines in western Cuba in time for their daughter to give birth to a child named Mathilde in 1801. They reestablished a life there for eight years, until 1809, when the Cuban government expelled all French nationals.[44] Twice displaced, the next stop for many refugees, including Florent and Victoire, was Louisiana. This time their family split. Their daughter Victoire Cécile evidently died during their time in Cuba, and her widowed husband, Louis-Hector, took young Mathilde (their only grandchild) to Philadelphia and eventually to France. Victoire and Florent's son, Jean Florent, by then in his early twenties, appears to have remained in Cuba.

After twenty-five years living abroad, Florent and Victoire returned to live among her siblings and their nephews and nieces. They chose to live in St. Charles Parish, on a modest farm not far from the plantation of their nephew Edmond Fortier, youngest son of Rose and Michel. Once again Florent set up business. He maintained contacts with merchants in Havana and imported wine and household goods, which he sold to his neighbors.[45]

Judging from a property inventory taken after his death in 1816, he and Victoire lived a very comfortable life. Parlor furnishings included a large mahogany table; a sofa and fourteen chairs with seats upholstered in golden fabric; a Sèvres porcelain coffee service with twenty-four cups and saucers, a creamer, and sugar bowl, all with gold decoration; a grand mirror hanging on the wall; and copper andirons in the fireplace. For formal dining they had nineteen place settings of silverware, a large silver coffee maker, and various silver serving utensils. In the bedrooms they had four-poster beds of either mahogany or cherry, with bed curtains and feather mattresses, and sundry armoires, side tables, and armchairs. There were commodes for nighttime relief, and a *petit miroir de toilette* for Victoire to apply her makeup.

They also had a library that contained numerous volumes of poetry, plays, novels, travel accounts, and philosophy. They owned a history of France and a history of Saint-Domingue. There were several multivolume dictionaries, a reminder that they lived in a multilingual world. Notably, the library included works by Voltaire, the French philosopher whose writings inspired both Jefferson and the French revolutionaries. Also, two volumes titled *Liberté de Pensée* (*Freedom of Thought*), a phrase taken from France's Declaration of the Rights of Man, referring to freedom of religion. Clearly, though they lived in rural Louisiana, they remained very much a part of the larger European world.

The possessions of Florent and Victoire offer a glimpse into the lives of Louisiana's landed elite. They enjoyed elegant and expensive furnishings, on display for guests to admire, silver place settings for large dinner parties, and gilded mirrors to reflect candlelight and the features of attractive ladies and men.

To create and sustain this world, Victoire and Florent enslaved five people: Babet, Betsy, Jean, Pierre, and Bill. Thirty-year-old Babet was captured in Congo. She may have come with Victoire and Florent from Cuba or they may have acquired her at the market in New Orleans. She was both the cook and the head housekeeper. She prepared all meals, whether for two people or a dozen, and ensured that the household furnishings were cleaned, polished, and properly arranged. Betsy, a twenty-year-old *mulata* described as a talented chambermaid, assisted Babet. It was her job to empty and clean the chamber pots, make the beds, and be on hand to assist Victoire with her dressing.

Among the enslaved men, Jean was described as a strong and intelligent twenty-five-year-old, with a knack for baking. He also did farm work and knew how to handle a horse and wagon. Like Babet, he had been taken from Congo. Another man, Pierre, although only eighteen, was the butler; he bowed to guests as they arrived, took their coats and shawls, and brought them drinks. He was described as Creole and could have been born in Louisiana, Cuba, or Saint-Domingue.

Finally, the enslaved fifteen-year-old boy named Bill tells a different story. He came from Baltimore. In 1807, as the demand for enslaved workers grew in Louisiana, the United States government outlawed the importation of captives directly from Africa or other countries.[46] Enslavers on the Eastern Seaboard seized the opportunity to meet the demand. After two hundred years of growing tobacco, land there was not as productive as it had been, and states like Virginia and Maryland had a surfeit of enslaved people. To get Bill to Louisiana, his enslaver in Maryland most likely sold him to a trader offering "Cash for Negroes."[47] Maryland was known for producing healthy and skilled farm workers, and Bill would have commanded a premium price. The trader would have taken him to a building near the Baltimore waterfront and confined him, with others, in chains. If Bill resisted, the trader would have beat him with a whip, perhaps severely.[48] Once the trader had gathered a sufficient number, he loaded his human cargo onto a ship bound for New Orleans. Frederick Douglass, a young, enslaved dockworker in Baltimore around this time, recalled "the dead heavy footsteps, and the piteous cries of the chained gangs" as they were driven down the street to the ship in the darkness of night.[49]

New Orleans was the largest market for enslaved people in the Deep South. Captured Africans had been sold there for a century and with the closing of the African trade, focus shifted to the East Coast. Solomon Northup, who, like Bill, was transported to New Orleans by ship, described his experience being sold in New Orleans:

> We were required to wash thoroughly, and those with beards, to shave. We were then furnished with a new suit each, cheap but clean. . . . The women [received] frocks of calico, and handkerchiefs

> to bind about their heads. . . . After being fed, in the afternoon, we were again paraded and made to dance.[50]

The trader required his captives to appear clean and healthy. Northup goes on:

> He would make us hold up our heads, walk briskly back and forth, while customers would feel of our hands and arms and bodies, turn us about, ask us what we could do, make us open our mouths and show our teeth, precisely as a jockey examines a horse. . . . Sometimes a man or woman was taken back to the small house in the yard, stripped, and inspected more minutely. Scars upon a slave's back were considered evidence of a rebellious or unruly spirit, and hurt his sale.[51]

Most wrenching of all is Northup's description of the separation of a mother and her daughter. Emily "was seven or eight years old, of light complexion, with a face of admirable beauty." A buyer purchased the mother, who begged not to be separated from her child. Emily screamed, "Don't leave me, mama—don't leave me," as her mother was taken away. Although the buyer was sympathetic and offered to purchase the child as well, the trader refused, stating that he would keep her until she was a few years older, for "there were men enough in New Orleans who would give five thousand dollars for such an extra, handsome, fancy piece as Emily would be."[52]

Bill had been separated from his mother years earlier. He survived the brutal journey from Baltimore and the humiliation of the sale in New Orleans, ending up on the Basile farm in St. Charles Parish. He had only one good eye, a reminder of the violence that was ever-present in the lives of the enslaved. On the farm, Florent assigned him to caring for the livestock. He also drove the cabriolet for Victoire when she visited her sisters and in-laws along the river and in the city.

The financial value of Bill and the other four captives underscores how integral they were to the privileged life enjoyed by Victoire and Florent. At an estate sale in October 1816, the household furnishings and farm equipment—fine porcelain and silver, gilded mirrors and mahogany furniture, bottles of wine and olive oil, the cabriolet and horse—brought in a total of 2,282 piastres ($50,394 in 2024). The five captives sold for more than twice that, a sum of 4,635 piastres ($102,340 in 2024).

Florent died in 1816. A neighbor purchased the farm along with the men and women who had made his life of luxury possible. Victoire, widowed at age fifty-one, lived on. The willful fifteen-year-old girl who had married a handsome young man against her father's wishes, who had only three children (whereas the norm for her sisters was six or more), who had lived her adult life abroad and was twice forced to flee, seems unlikely to simply fade away into widowhood. Yet, she disappears from local records. I surmise that she either returned to Cuba to live near her son or went to Philadelphia and eventually to France to be close to her granddaughter. If the latter, she might have lived on her son-in-law's estate south of Tours in the Loire Valley, where he possessed the fiefdom of la Roche d'Enchaille, and she would have witnessed her granddaughter's marriage to Louis-Felix le Blanc de la Combe, a lieutenant colonel in the French army and also of aristocratic descent.[53] (Earlier genealogists wanted desperately for the Durel family to have French aristocratic or even noble origins. For those who harbor such sentiments, this is the best I can offer.)

== Manette and Françoise Durel *née* Dejan ==

Just as two Durel daughters married Fortier brothers, two Durel sons married sisters, daughters of Antoine Dejan and his wife, Angelique Monget. Antoine was a master blacksmith who had come from Bordeaux as a child with his parents, not long before Jean Baptiste and Cécile arrived. It is conceivable that the two men were acquainted in France, although I have found no direct evidence for that. They certainly knew each other by 1769 when Jean Baptiste hired Antoine to construct a new communion rail for the church, and again in 1771 when he paid him for making iron dogs, a shovel, and tongs for the fireplace in the Cabildo Council chamber.[54] The wedding of François Durel and Marie Dejan, called Manette, occurred on December 10, 1783. Ursin Durel and Françoise Dejan wed on July 1, 1789.[55]

The Dejan sisters lived their entire lives in New Orleans. Unlike their sister-in-law, Victoire, who lived at various times in Saint-Domingue, Cuba, and perhaps in France, and unlike their more affluent Fortier in-laws, who divided their time between plantation homes and city mansions, the Dejan sisters were strictly urban dwellers. Their daily existence followed the tempo of city living, going to the market, visiting friends, raising children, and managing the household. Manette's husband, François, made his living as a minor merchant and never reached the stature of his father. Françoise's husband, Ursin, was a sea captain who was often away on trading voyages in the Caribbean.[56] They were by no means poor, but of all the family lines descending from Jean Baptiste and Cécile, theirs were the least wealthy.

Manette was married for twenty-nine years, until François's death in 1812. She then lived as a widow for another twenty years, until her own death in 1833 at age sixty-five. Similarly, Françoise lived twenty-eight years as a wife and another twenty-seven years as a widow, dying at age seventy-two in 1844. Over the span of their long lives, they witnessed the transformation of New Orleans from a remote colonial city on the northwestern edge of the Caribbean world to a major American *entrepôt* for the sale of grain, cotton, sugar, and human captives. The population grew from seven thousand inhabitants when they were children to more than one hundred thousand in 1840 as newcomers arrived, many speaking English and not French.[57] They saw the bounds of the city expand so that the original city they knew from childhood and where they continued to live as adults became known as the Old or French Quarter, one of several distinct city districts. Through it all, their own lives changed as they transitioned from wives and mothers to widows and grandmothers.

Manette gave birth to her first child in 1785, followed by thirteen more over the next twenty-five years.[58] Françoise's firstborn came in 1791, followed by eight more over twenty-three years. Childhood survival was always a concern and became even more precarious in 1796, when the growing city experienced its first epidemic of yellow fever.[59] That September, Françoise gave birth to her fourth child, named Edmond. A month later the third child, Michel, died at age two. In another month François, the oldest child, died; he was five. The newborn Edmond, who perhaps provided some solace when his older brothers died, did not make it to his third birthday. Of the first five children, the only to survive was a boy named Ursin (2) after his father. In total, five of Françoise's nine children did not survive childhood. Manette's experience was much the same. Of her fourteen children, she buried six. Motherhood for these two women, as it was for many in their generation, was a sequence of childbearing and child death.

As wives, the sisters managed their households with the help of enslaved people of African descent. According to the 1810 Census, that year Manette kept five people in captivity and Françoise kept two.[60] At the time, almost half of city households had no enslaved people in them and of those that did, the average number was four. To be sure, there were exceptions: the Ursuline nuns had seventy-two enslaved people at the convent, and some merchants and artisans kept large numbers on-site for business operations. But for the most part slavery in the city existed on a small, domestic scale, at close quarters. In this regard, the sisters were typical.

Some captives stayed with a family for decades, while others were bought and sold as the enslaver saw fit. Recall from the end of Chapter 1 that Françoise's husband, Ursin, purchased an enslaved woman named Marie from his father's estate shortly after they married. At that time, Marie was forty-two years old, twenty years older than Françoise, and had been with the family since Ursin was a boy. Marie was able to help Françoise through the difficulties of childbirth, child rearing, and child death. The last reference I have found has Marie serving as godmother for a free *mulata* child named Juana in 1802.[61] On that occasion the priest identified her in Spanish as "*Maria Durel, Negra esclava de Don Ursino Durel,*" ascribing to her both a forename and a surname. The customary practice was to give enslaved people only one name to reinforce their lower status, since family lineage was one of the indicators of social rank. The priest may have known Marie, who by then was in her fifties and had been with the Durel family for more than thirty years. Longevity and familiarity may have granted her a kind of recognition in the eyes of the priest.

In contrast, Manette's husband, François, purchased African-born Lubin as a boy of eight and sold him as a man of twenty-five in 1803. He sold twenty-five-year-old Minny in 1805, twenty-four-year-old Félicité, a laundress and cook, in 1807, and seventeen-year-old Honoré, skilled as a cook, in 1809.[62] It is clear that François, like his father before him, supplemented his business income with profits from the sale of humans.

A sequence of events in Manette's life reveals yet another reality of urban households where White and Black people lived in proximity. On March 13, 1812, Manette buried her husband, who was fifty-four years old.[63] Less than a month later, on April 8, she buried their fifteen-month-old daughter, named Antonia. The child was interred alongside her father.[64] Then, just four days later, Manette made another visit to church, this time to have a one-month-old *mulato* child baptized.[65] She gave the baby the name François and identified the mother as Ana, "*negra esclava de Mr. Durel.*" That the child was described as *mulato* and the mother as *negra* (Black) suggests that the father was White, although as usual, the priest did not record the father's name.

The child's godparents were free persons of color. Finally, Manette made yet another visit to church, this time to have the priest correct the child's baptismal record to indicate that he was free and not enslaved. In the margin of the record, she signed a statement saying that "my intention and will was and is that the creature . . . in this act was baptized free." This last record is somewhat confusing. It is possible, perhaps probable, that the baby's father was her husband, born just about the time that he died. Possibly Manette entrusted the baby's care to the godparents, who were free, for I have found no record of her freeing the child's mother. Whatever the case, the convergence of these life events—two burials and a christening within a month of her husband's passing—must have left her reeling.

That Black and White women lived in close quarters in the city might have led to cordial relationships, as could have been the case with Françoise and the enslaved Marie; or it may have caused tension if the White woman's husband used his position of power to have sex with young enslaved women, as may have been the situation with Manette and the enslaved Ana. In a culture that gave males ultimate authority, and which condoned sex between White men and enslaved women, urban households could be fraught with anxiety for women of either ethnicity.

With her husband's passing, Manette took on a new identity, that of Widow Durel. At the time she had six living children, four sons and two daughters. The oldest, named Jean Baptiste (3) after his grandfather, was already twenty-seven years old and in business for himself. Over the next decade or so, all the children married, except for the youngest, Michel (whose story appears briefly in the next chapter). The greatest change for Manette was that she became responsible for the family's finances. She took over operation of her husband's dry goods business and put her sons to work.

Manette seems to have embraced her new life. She assumed the role of a Creole matriarch, arranging marriages for her children with other old Creole families and ensuring that her children and grandchildren knew their heritage. These were years in which the word *Creole* took on new meaning. Originally it applied to anyone born in any colony, as distinct from being born in Europe or Africa. With the arrival of increasing numbers of English-speaking Americans, however, the word began to connote local lineage and French heritage. That is, as New Orleans became American and multilingual, the old families emphasized both their local and French origins. French people who arrived after Louisiana joined the United States were called the "new French," to distinguish them from true Creoles. "Creole" also applied to the French-speaking people of African descent born in Louisiana. This differentiated them from the English-speaking Black people who came from other states in the United States.

Manette and Françoise had grown up hearing a story that confirmed their Creole lineage. Their maternal grandmother, Marie Françoise Robinet, was one of the first European children born in New Orleans after its founding. Françoise was probably named for her. As a child, she survived a frontier conflict between French settlers and the indigenous Natchez people. In the early years of the colony, the French established a settlement and a fort near present-day Natchez, Mississippi. Coexistence with the local people was generally peaceful, and some Europeans married Natchez women. In time, however, the French demanded too much land and the locals pushed back. On November 29, 1729, they rose up, killing approximately 230 settlers and burning the fort and the settlers' homes. They did not touch the women and children, including six-year-old Marie Françoise. The French called this incident the "*massacre de Natches.*" It became part of Louisiana lore, and the fact that Marie Françoise had survived it was well known. At her death in 1809, at the advanced age of eighty-six, the priest made note of it in the funeral record.[66] This was just the sort of story that gave Creoles a sense of who they were as a people. Manette and Françoise would have passed the story on to their own children and grandchildren.

In the summer of 1831, Manette took two of her granddaughters, ages sixteen and ten, to Paris.[67] They boarded a ship in New Orleans, sailed to Le Havre, and from there traveled up the Seine River to the city. There, she exposed the girls to their French heritage. The party also included her sons Jean Baptiste (3), age forty-seven, and Justin, thirty. Judging from their luggage on the return home, this was not a short visit. Manette traveled with four trunks, three bags, three boxes, two baskets, and a bed. Between them the girls had four trunks and a bandbox for their bonnets. They probably stayed in a hotel for several weeks and went on daily outings, attending services at the Cathedral of Notre Dame, taking in the view of the city from atop Montmartre, or strolling along the Champs-Élysées in the late afternoon. Manette may have taken the girls to have dresses made in one of the fashion houses. They may even have called upon relatives or acquaintances. Only one generation removed from the

Dejan and Durel families in France, Manette could well have been in contact with cousins. They definitely visited an establishment that sold exotic birds, for they returned home with "3 Canary birds" in cages.

Two of Manette's sons, identified in the ship's register as merchants, used the trip for business as well as pleasure. Justin, who had assumed management of the family's dry goods business from his mother, made arrangements to purchase merchandise while in the city. He returned home with forty-six packages of products to add to his stock in New Orleans. He also brought back a parrot for the enjoyment of his wife and children. (On a subsequent voyage, in 1837, he took his entire family to France, as well as an enslaved woman who later claimed her freedom.) The oldest son, Jean Baptiste (3), may have taken time while in Paris to make contacts and explore possibilities for his son's education. Although the boy was only twelve at the time, by age eighteen he was living in Paris and studying medicine. (His story appears in Chapter 4.)

Trips to France became increasingly frequent for the Creoles of Louisiana. Passenger ships sailed regularly between New Orleans and Le Havre and numerous members of the Durel family made the voyage. Manette made more than one. Tragically, at sixty-five years old, she died at sea enroute to Le Havre on May 23, 1833.[68]

Françoise's experience as a widow and grandmother was different from that of her sister. When Ursin died in 1817, he left her no business to take over. Without his regular income as a sea captain, her future looked precarious. She still had three boys under age eight to raise. Her oldest son, Ursin (2), was in no position to help. He was already married, with an infant son, and had depended upon his father-in-law to buy a house for his own young family. Only her daughter, nineteen-year-old Caroline, was of an age that she might contribute to the household income, perhaps as a tutor of young girls or by taking in sewing, activities appropriate for a lady.

Their house on Toulouse Street was old and in disrepair.[69] Her husband may have left bank stock, a common investment at the time, and there may have been savings. And of course, there was the possibility of selling or hiring out an enslaved person. The 1810 Census reported two enslaved people in the household; the 1820 Census indicates only one.[70] Whatever the case, Françoise managed to have the old house taken down and replaced by a double cottage, one side for the family and the other for rental income.

On top of the financial challenges, Françoise continued to suffer the loss of her children: Hortaire (Arthur) at age thirteen in 1822 and Eugène at age nineteen in 1833.[71] Most devastating was the death of her daughter. Caroline did not marry until she was thirty-four years old, perhaps delaying so that she could stay home to help her mother raise the younger children and make ends meet. During the 1820s, her younger brothers came of age and found employment, freeing her from that obligation. In the spring of 1832 she wed Pierre Messant, a merchant. Then suddenly the next year, on a voyage home from France she died, leaving her husband with an infant daughter named Sophie.[72] This was the same year that Françoise's sister, Manette, died, as well as her son Eugène. Her heart must have broken. Of her nine children, only two remained alive, her sons Ursin (2) and Theodore.

Theodore was a twenty-two-year-old bachelor who worked as an accountant and lived at home with his mother. In 1839, he married and moved with his wife into the rental side of the house. Ursin (2) lived with his family only a few blocks away. In her final years, Françoise lived simply, with her family close by. An inventory of her property taken after her death in 1844 gives a glimpse of her life at the end.[73] She occupied only two rooms in her little house on Toulouse Street. She used one room for cooking and eating. It contained a set of dishes, five spoons and forks, a large stewing spoon, six small coffee spoons, and various plates, bowls, and bottles. The most expensive item was a set of copper andirons for the fireplace. There were two tables and eleven chairs, remnants of a time when she had a large family and many visitors. The other room was her bedroom, in which she had an old armoire for her clothes, a four-poster bed, and a bureau where she kept her jewelry, which consisted of various pins, necklaces, and rings, including one described as having a brilliant stone. There were also several pairs of eyeglasses.

In addition to these simple belongings, the inventory included an enslaved family living in a building behind her house. Arabella, the mother, was fifty-two and infirm. Arabella's daughter, Delphine, age twenty-eight, cooked and cleaned for Françoise even as she cared for her own mother. Arabella's son, Edouard, thirty-one, took care of the house and yard and kept Françoise's fire going. In addition, an enslaved man named Toussaint, about thirty-four years old, was hired out to another family, bringing in a little extra money for Françoise.

Even though she lived simply at the end, Françoise still kept people captive and benefited from their labor. Her generation—the second Durel generation and the first considered Creole—was embedded in a set of assumptions that included the ownership of other humans as a matter of course. After Françoise died, Arabella went to live with Ursin (2), and the others were sold.

=== Clarisse Durel, *née* Andry ===

Clarisse Andry wed Baptiste Durel on March 31, 1785, in yet another example of parents arranging a marriage.[74] Clarisse's father, Louis Andry, had come to Louisiana as an officer of infantry and French royal engineer, charged with surveying tracts of land and designing public buildings. He drew plans to convert a warehouse for church services in 1769, to be used temporarily while repairs were made to St. Louis Church. At the time, Jean Baptiste served on the parish vestry, and the two men probably came to know each other then.[75] Andry was killed in 1778 or 1779 while surveying along the Texas coast, so Jean Baptiste made the marriage arrangements with his widow, Marianne Lapierre.[76]

Baptiste seems to have inherited his father's leadership qualities. Both he and his older brother François served under Galvez, but it was he, the younger son, who rose quickly to the rank of lieutenant and eventually became a captain. Like his father, he became active in civic affairs, served on the cathedral vestry, and was elected to represent Ward One on the city council. He established a residence and successful trading business at the corner of St. Ann and Royal Streets (the building still stands). The value of his estate at the time of his death in 1809 was 34,430 piastres, a substantial sum at the time.[77]

In childbearing, Clarisse fared better than her sisters-in-law. Over the course of a twenty-one-year marriage, she gave birth twelve times and buried only three. Like Manette and Françoise, she spent many years a widow, running the family business, seeing to the education of her children, arranging appropriate marriages, and managing the people she held captive (seven in 1810).

Clarisse's story appears last in this chapter because of an episode in her life that places the Durel family at the center of the most significant event involving slavery to occur in Louisiana before the Civil War. Clarisse's family was wealthy. Her older brother, Manuel Andry, was the largest property owner in St. John the Baptiste Parish.[78] His plantation was on the east bank of the Mississippi River, about forty miles upriver from New Orleans, making him one of the Creole landed elite. He was well connected to the Fortier family. Moreover, he held the rank of colonel in the militia and was a member of the New Orleans territorial legislature.[79] Like the Fortiers, he kept a large number of men and women captive—eighty-six in the 1810 Census—to produce his wealth and uphold an aristocratic lifestyle for his family.[80]

Manuel had two sons, Clarisse's nephews Michel and Gilbert. Michel, the older of the two, was named after Michel Fortier. His first wife died young, leaving him with two children, and he next married Félicité Durel, a daughter of Manette and François.[81] Thus, the Durel and Andry families were connected in multiple ways.

The younger son, Gilbert, married Maria Deslonde, who had grown up on the plantation that bordered his father's. The Deslonde plantation lay just downriver from the Andry property. As a smaller operation, the family held only twenty-three captives. Maria's widowed mother, Margarite, used a mulatto man named Charles Deslonde to manage the work and drive the workers. That Charles had the family name raises the possibility that he was a son of Margarite's husband, Jacques. If this was the case, Gilbert's wife Maria was Charles's half sister. His subsequent actions make clear that Charles was not happy with his situation. He may have chafed at his responsibilities as a driver while his half sister lived in luxury next door. He may have been forced to whip an enslaved worker one too many times. He may have disliked the haughty attitudes of the White enslavers who controlled his life. Whatever the case, in the fall of 1810, Charles began meeting secretly with captives from other plantations to plot an uprising.

Just as White families had social networks along the river, so too did the enslaved. There were opportunities for captives to communicate across plantation boundaries. In the course of a day a captive deemed trustworthy might be sent to a neighbor to deliver a message or borrow a tool. Sometimes a planter hired out his captives to work on another's property. Because enslaved families were often divided and lived on different plantations, an enslaved man might receive permission to visit his wife, or he might visit her at night without permission. The physical layout of plantations, extending back into the swamps, made it possible for the enslaved to meet secretly, especially in darkness.

The men Charles met with were not ignorant. They knew about France's Declaration of the Rights of Man, which asserted that men had a right to "liberty, property, security and resistance to oppression." They were aware that only six years earlier the enslaved people of Haiti (Saint-Domingue) had overthrown their oppressors and created their own republic. Among their number were two men named Kook and Quamana, who only a few years earlier had been Akan warriors in West Africa and knew military tactics that they could teach the others. As they talked, ideas expressed cautiously soon crystalized into a plan. They decided Charles would initiate the attack.

The conspirators organized a network of cells on plantations running from the Andry plantation down to the city. They stockpiled weapons, made flags and drums, and passed along information as to the timing of the uprising. The enslaved people would strike by surprise in the middle of the night and move quickly down the river road, attracting others to their cause. At the time, the territorial army was preoccupied with Spanish forces in West Florida; knowing this, the resistors figured they could move quickly and capture the city with their growing number of armed insurgents.

Whites feared such a possibility. In 1795, they had discovered a planned uprising among captives in Pointe Coupee, farther upriver. Still, they were caught off guard when late on the night of January 8, 1811, Charles led a group of captives into the big house on the Andry plantation with the intent of slaying the men. They succeeded in killing Gilbert and considering that Gilbert's wife was possibly his half sister, this may have been for Charles an act of personal revenge as well as a strike for freedom. In the melee, Manuel, the father, managed to escape with only superficial wounds, but not before he recognized Charles.

The band of insurrectionists, armed with guns, swords, and machetes, then began to march downriver, with Charles in the lead on horseback. As they reached other plantations their ranks began to swell, though not everyone joined. Some captives were afraid, and others calculated that the plan could not possibly succeed. Some even woke their enslavers and urged them to flee. The rebels were hampered by rain and mud, yet they marched on through the day, setting fire to plantation homes and buildings, killing one more planter and wounding others. As word spread ahead of their advance, Whites fled, so the marchers encountered little armed resistance. By nightfall, they numbered in the hundreds and had reached the plantation of Aimée and Jacques Fortier, only about a dozen miles from the city.

When word reached the governor in New Orleans, he raised the alarm and men grabbed their guns. The militia assembled and headed out to confront the rebels. When they reached the Fortier plantation, they found that Charles had ordered a retreat, apparently a tactic used in Africa designed to confuse the enemy. Meanwhile, Manuel had crossed the river to the west bank, raised the alarm, and returned to the east bank with a force of about eighty well-armed men. Marching downriver, they inadvertently surprised the retreating rebels and, in the fight that ensued, the insurgents ran out of ammunition, enabling the Whites to overwhelm them. About twenty died in battle, fifty were taken into custody, and many others, including Charles, escaped into the swamp. Over the next several days, White men hunted them down with dogs and captured most of them.

There were reprisals. When they captured Charles, they broke his thighs, cut off his head, and carried it around on a pole, to the cheers of a gathering crowd. Other captives were brought before a tribunal of five planters, including Michel Fortier's son, Edmond, his grandson, Adelard Fortier, and Jean-Nöel Destrehan, whose son was married to a daughter of Aimée and Jacques. The planters condemned eighteen of the rebels to death, ordering that they be taken to the plantation of their enslavers and shot, and as a harsh warning to others, that their severed heads be placed atop poles along the river levee for all to see.

Clarisse's personal connections to the uprising were many. Her nephew had been killed. Her brother barely escaped harm and then led the counterattack. Her in-laws had fled and later exacted retribution. For White people like her, the story of the uprising lived on in memory, a lesson that said Black people could not be trusted, that one had to be vigilant, that sometimes brutality was necessary to maintain law and order.

Violence was ever-present in the lives of enslaved people, not only in the physical pain they suffered when being whipped, but also in the anxiety over the possibility of a whipping at any moment on any pretense, in the fear of a child or spouse being sold away, and for women, in the frequent occurrence of rape. Black people lived with this reality day and night. In spite of enjoyable times when they were able to be among themselves, violence lurked in the background, like a swamp fog ready to envelop them.

Enslavers in the nineteenth century created myths about the people they held captive: Black people did not feel pain as much a White people; they were like children and needed discipline for their own good; they were like animals that had to be tamed; they were simple people who appreciated and respected their enslavers. These paternalistic myths minimized for enslavers the violence they inflicted on Black bodies and served to assuage any misgivings they may have had.

Even today, many White people show little understanding of and concern for the prevalence of violence in Black lives. After centuries in which Black lives were valued less than White ones, both in the law and on the streets, they object to the simple phrase: "Black lives matter." They counter with "ALL lives matter." Both statements are true, but the fact of the matter is that for much of our history White Americans acted as if Black lives did not matter very much, except for the value placed on their labor and their offspring.

In the uprising of 1811, White people made clear that they would use violence, even brutality, to uphold the system of supremacy that enabled them to exploit Black bodies. Not until the Civil War did Black people rise again in Louisiana, and again Whites responded with violence. During the Jim Crow era, White men lynched Black men with impunity, because Black lives did not matter. And today, the simple truth is that the death rate due to firearms in Louisiana is three times higher for Black people than it is for Whites.[82]

White Durel descendants of every generation have lived in a period of racial violence. At times, some promoted and participated in it. More often, they simply accepted it as normal. That said, there are also stories of close connections and positive interaction between the races. The next chapter tells stories from the third generation, grandchildren of Jean Baptiste and Cécile who had open and lifelong relationships with free people of color.

Chapter 3

The Second Creole Generation

For the second Creole generation of the Durel family in Louisiana, the grandchildren of Jean Baptiste and Cécile, I have chosen stories that show intimate, familial connections between White descendants and free people of color, and in one case with people of American Indian descent. Some of these relationships endured for decades, revealing a surprising openness among White Creoles in acknowledging their mixed-race relatives. Unlike Anglo-Americans such as Thomas Jefferson, who steadfastly refused to acknowledge he was having sex and children with Sally Hemings, the White Creole Durel men in these stories made no attempt to hide their relationships with women of color.

Men and women of African descent, living free of the bonds of slavery, had been a part of the New Orleans population since its earliest years. In 1809, their numbers increased significantly with the influx of more than three thousand free people of color, refugees from Saint-Domingue. The 1810 Census lists approximately 17,000 inhabitants, of whom 37 percent were identified as White, 34 percent as enslaved, and 29 percent as free people of color.[1] Free people of African descent were no small minority tucked away in the shadows of White society. They played a central role in the character of the city.

Their presence in such numbers did concern White enslavers, who feared they would encourage and assist enslaved people in running away. During the first half of the nineteenth century, the legislature passed various laws to limit their number, preventing free people of African descent, especially men, from taking up residence in Louisiana and requiring newly emancipated people to leave.[2] They mandated that free men and women of color be identified with the initials *fmc* or *fwc*, respectively, when writing or giving their names, and attempted to keep the free and the enslaved apart, for example by preventing marriage between them.[3] Nevertheless, strong kinship ties existed among African-descended people, both enslaved and free. There are many examples of a free person of color serving as godparent for an enslaved child or an enslaved person as godparent of a free child of color. The streets and neighborhoods provided plenty of opportunity for free and enslaved to meet and sustain friendships.

Overlaying the legal differentiation between free and enslaved was the customary practice of describing people by skin color: *negro, mulatto, blanc.* Yet this system was not precise: there were people with very dark skin who were free and people with light skin who were enslaved. Moreover, since early settlers of Louisiana came from the southern, Latin countries in Europe where natural skin tones tended to be darker than in northern Europe, there were times when a person of wholly European descent was mistakenly seen as a person of color. It all could be quite confusing, as it was for Gustave de Beaumont, a Frenchman who visited New Orleans in the 1830s. At the theater one evening, he observed a young woman sitting among people of color whom he described as "a dazzling beauty, whose complexion, of perfect whiteness, proclaimed the purest European blood." His companion explained that "everyone knows that she had a mulatto among her forebears." He then observed a woman of dark skin sitting among Whites. His companion informed him that "the blood which flows in her veins is Spanish."[4]

A hierarchy of wealth among free people of color added yet another layer of complexity. Some were prosperous, educated, owned many properties, and wore fine clothes. Others were poor, illiterate, and worked as unskilled laborers. In between, there were artisans, some highly skilled, who owned modest homes and could at least sign their names. A wealthy person of color, especially with light skin and mostly European ancestry, was able to command a degree of respect among White Creoles, in spite of a law stating that they were never to "conceive themselves equal to the white; but on the contrary they ought to yield to them in every occasion, and never speak or answer to them but with respect, under penalty of imprisonment."[5]

Many, if not most, free Creoles of African descent had White relatives—half-siblings, cousins, nieces, nephews, aunts, and uncles. Likewise, many if not most White Creoles had Black relatives. The connection between White people and people of color who had the same White father was generally recognized and could be quite close. The two populations were separate in a legal sense, but in a familial and neighborly way, the dividing line was not so sharp.

Following the Louisiana Purchase, English-speaking Whites from the Eastern Seaboard of the United States arrived in New Orleans in increasing numbers. The business-minded Americans initially located in a section near the river, between Conti and Canal Streets, running from the waterfront up to around Royal Street. As their numbers increased, they moved across Canal Street into the suburb called Faubourg Ste. Marie, which soon became known as the American Sector.[6] This area was never exclusively American—some Creole families lived there—but Canal Street became a symbolic dividing line between the two groups. The American Sector grew into the dominant commercial center, featuring new streets lined with banks, insurance agencies, commercial exchanges, and warehouses. In the newly built houses and boarding houses, one could hear the English language spoken.

In contrast, the French-speaking sections—the original city, which became known as the French Section or Quarter, and the suburbs of Tremé and Marigny—retained their distinctive character and were soon viewed as the old neighborhoods. Here most of the Creoles lived, worked, and played. Although the locus of the city's commerce was in the American Sector, Creole merchants and shopkeepers remained in business along Levee Street, and the old produce market, theaters, and dance halls stayed busy.

A striking difference between the French and American Sectors was the number of free people of color living in each. In 1840, free people of color made up only 8 percent of the total in the American Sector; in the French-speaking areas they numbered more than 30 percent. The easy familiarity among free people of color and Whites that marked life for the Creoles was largely absent from the daily experiences of the Americans, who were far more likely to encounter enslaved people of African descent. This served to reinforce an Anglo-American view of race as binary: White and free or Black and enslaved. Free Black communities had grown in Baltimore and Charleston, but most Americans were uneasy with the idea of a three-part caste system: enslaved, free people of color, and White.

Free people of color living in New Orleans with the Durel surname begin to appear with some regularity in the records during the nineteenth century. Some, no doubt, were formerly enslaved by a White Durel and simply adopted the name, as was the case with Ester Durel in Chapter 1. Others, however, were the children of White Durel men. Still others may have been unrelated, having acquired the name elsewhere. Their names appear in city directories and censuses, a testament to a society in which White people and free people of color mixed openly. Examples include:

- Sophie Durel, a free woman of color who lived in Tremé on Orleans Street between Claiborne and Robinson Streets from the 1830s into the '60s. She had been born in Senegal in the 1790s, captured and taken to Louisiana as a child, and eventually freed in 1835 by "M. Durel," possibly Michel, a son of François and Manette.[7]

- Patrice Durel, a free man of color who was born in Saint-Croix and brought to New Orleans when he was young. By the 1840s he was free, living in Faubourg Marigny, and running a wheelwright business with four employees. His household consisted of ten free people of color and no one enslaved.[8]

- Justine Durel, a free woman of color who lived in the city in 1830 with three children and a young enslaved woman.[9]

- Octave Durel, a free man of color, who was a bricklayer; Madere Durel, a free woman of color; and Carmelite Durel, also a free woman of color, all residing in the city in 1834.[10]

- Jean Durel, a thirty-year-old free man of color who worked as a plasterer and lived in the city in 1850 with his wife and two children.

- Adelaide Durel, a sixty-five-year-old free woman of color who in 1850 lived with a Black West Indian family.[11]

- Jeanne Durel, a free woman of color living on her own, and Anastasie Durel, a free woman of color living with two daughters, both in the city in 1860.[12]

In addition to people of color with the Durel name, the records show White Durel men residing with women of color. For example, in 1830, Valcour, one of the sons of Baptiste and Clarisse, lived on his own with a young enslaved woman in what appears to have been a short-term arrangement. Later, he established a more lasting relationship with a free woman of color from the West Indies named Barbé Thennat. They appear to have been together for more than a decade and, in 1850, they shared their home with Nancy, a free Black woman from Maryland and her two children.[13]

In another example, Michel, the youngest son of Manette and François, had relations with at least two women of color. Unusual for the White Durels of his generation, he was not an accountant or merchant, but instead delivered milk and was the "keeper of stray animals."[14] The city paid him $30 a month in 1841 ($1,087 in 2024) to manage a plot of land in Faubourg Tremé known as the city pound, where he received all sorts of animals found wandering the streets by night watchmen, lamplighters, and policemen. He would then advertise for the owners to come forth and pay a fine to reclaim their beasts (Figure 3).[15]

In 1850, Michel lived with Juliette Lacroix, a free woman described as "black."[16] When he died four years later, he was in a relationship with another women, Marguerite Davis, also a free woman of color. Shortly after his death, she had a child baptized at St. Ann Church in Tremé, giving him the name Firmin Durel.[17]

The relationships above are just a few examples of those found throughout the Durel family tree. In the stories that follow, such relationships and their various permutations are explored in even greater detail.

BROUGHT to the Pound of the First Municipality, corner of St. Claude and Dumain-streets—

A sorrel Horse, with white forehead, and some white spots on his body: no other mark or stamp visible.

A sorrel Mare, with a star on her forehead: no other mark or stamp visible.

If, from the present date to the 18th December, said animals are not reclaimed, they will be sold at that time, by R. Kerrison. Auctioneer.

MICHEL DUREL,
Keeper of the Pound.

d7 3t10d

Fig. 3: Excerpt from *Le Courrier de la Louisiane*, December 7, 1847, page 3.

Fig. 4: *Jean Michel Fortier* by Jean Francois De Vallee.
Courtesy of the Louisiana State Museum.

=== Jean Michel Fortier and Henriette Milon ===

Rose Durel and Michel Fortier had high hopes for their son Jean Michel (Figure 4). Just as they were firstborn of their generation, he was firstborn of his. He carried the names of his two grandfathers, Jean Baptiste Durel and Michel Fortier Sr.[18] In a society defined by lineage and patriarchy, the choice of a name, like the selection of a godparent or marriage partner, was a strategic decision designed to sustain the family's position and wealth. Jean Michel's role was clear; he was to be the head of the family in future years. When he was a teen, his father sent him to France to be educated. French schools for young men provided a liberal education, including classical languages, history, philosophy, logic, mathematics, and the elements of science. He returned to New Orleans in the 1790s an educated and refined man in his twenties. He joined his father in business just as the sugar-based economy was taking off and assumed his position in the family as the eldest of his generation.

Table IV.
Genealogical Reference Chart for Jean Michel Fortier

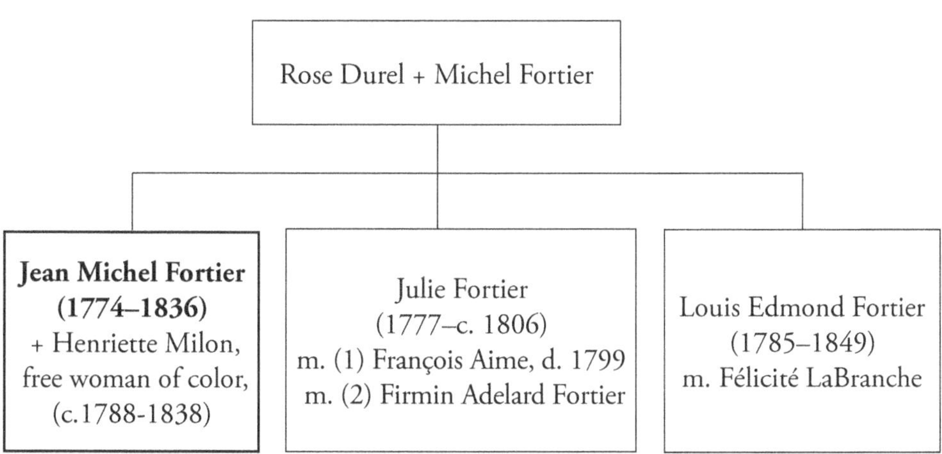

Jean Michel's father probably had already begun thinking about a suitable wife for him when he returned from school. No doubt he attended the fancy balls and social gatherings that characterized privileged society in that era, and he would have been a very attractive prospect for any parent looking for a husband for their daughter. His sister Julie met and married François Aime, son of a planter in St. Charles Parish. His brother Edmond married Félicité LaBranche and moved to St. Charles Parish as well. One would have expected Jean Michel to follow the same path. However, he chose not to. He stayed in the city and remained single. In his early thirties, he began a sexual liaison with a free woman of color named Henriette Milon. This turned out to be no casual encounter. They became lifelong companions, living together on Burgundy Street until his death in 1836 at age sixty-two.[19]

The practice of White bachelors choosing to live with free women of color was long-established in New Orleans, rooted in the demographic fact that, for decades, there were many more White men than White women. In an early example related to the Durel family, Bartholomew Toutant Beauregard, uncle of Elias Toutant Beauregard, who married Félicité Durel, had a lifelong association with a free woman of color named Marguerite, dating from the 1770s.[20] Far from being ostracized by the family, Bartholomew and Marguerite and their mixed-race children were close to the White family. Félicité and Elias even named their first son after him.[21]

The demographic imbalance continued into the early nineteenth century, but Jean Michel did not choose to live with Henriette simply because there were no White women available. Young, educated, and very wealthy, he could have found a White spouse just as his siblings did, had he chosen to do so. Instead, he chose Henriette. Although the two could not marry *legally*, there were no *social* sanctions against their living together and having children. Some may have found the practice objectionable, but it was generally acceptable among the Creoles.

Women in Henriette's position had existed since the beginning of the European enslavement of Africans. Sex between European men and African women was common, and intimate violence spread across the breadth of the enslaved world, from Africa to the Americas. Some women and their female offspring used this to their advantage, attaining power within a racist system designed to oppress them. They used their bodies and sexuality to gain control of their lives and experience a modicum of freedom.[22] For Henriette, this likely meant attending social functions with her mother in order to attract White men. In New Orleans in the 1790s, dances for free women of color were open to both free men of color and White, so that "white men who fancied a dance with a free woman of color had to compete for their favors with men of African ancestry who shared the crowded dance floor." However, in 1805 a new practice was introduced from Saint-Domingue called a "quadroon ball," which excluded men of color, giving White men an unimpeded opportunity to court a woman of color.[23]

Henriette appears as a "mulatto" in some records, but more often she was labeled "quadroon." Strictly speaking, the word *mulatto* meant someone of half African and half European ancestry, whereas *quadroon* indicated one-quarter African and three-quarters European. It is unlikely that the men who created the records took time to inquire about ancestry and rather made a judgment based on appearance.

White outsiders viewed such women, whether mulatto or quadroon, with a mixture of fascination and disdain. One visitor to New Orleans in 1800 described them as prostitutes, "full of vanity and very libertine; money will always buy their caresses. . . . They live in open concubinage with the whites, but to this they are incited more by money than attachment."[24] Another visitor from New York in 1810 portrayed "that unfortunate class of females, the mulattoes, who from their infancy are trained in the arts of love," who contract to be the mistress of a White man and "when the term is expired, or the lover gone, they accept the next best offer that may be made to them."[25] Such descriptions multiplied, with new writers taking their cues from previous accounts, so that New Orleans gained the reputation and allure of an exotic, libertine city of sin. To be sure there were prostitutes, quadroon balls, and White men living with women of color, so that visitors arriving with the anticipation of seeing such women had their hopes fulfilled. But the masculine preoccupation with illicit sex and racial mixing masked a more complex reality for women like Henriette.

In the context of the time, an intimate relationship between a free woman of color and a wealthy White gentleman made perfect sense. Just as White parents sought marriage partners of equal or higher social standing and wealth for their daughters, so too did the mothers of free women of color. Henriette's union with Jean Michel was no different from that of Félicité LaBranche with Jean Michel's brother Edmond, except that the White men who made the laws decided one was legitimate and one was not.

———

Henriette and Jean Michel had ten children baptized in St. Louis Cathedral (Table VI). The oldest child was born in 1805, the last in 1825. In the progression of baptismal records, initially the priest followed custom and did not identify the father. He identified Henriette as *quadroon libre*. However, in 1815, with the baptism of their son Felix, Jean Michel acknowledged that he was the father, and it was probably at this time that he had the priest go back and correct the earlier records. In all cases he signed the record, affirming that he was indeed the father. Henriette continued to be described as *quadroon libre* until 1818, when the designation was dropped. Then in 1820, she was accorded the title *Mademoiselle* (abbreviated *Dlle*). This change suggests a growing acceptance of her as the unmarried consort of a gentleman.

In most of the baptisms, Jean Michel's relatives served as godparents for his children. For example, his brother and sister-in-law, Edmond and Félicité, were the godparents of the third child, Félicité Rosella. Edmond and Félicité's son, also named Edmond after his father, was godfather of Jean Michel's son, Edmond Gustave. Were it not for racial designations, there would be no way of knowing that these children were not part of the White family. Indeed, they were treated as such. The younger Edmond later recalled that he "frequently visited the house [of his uncle] . . . and was in the habit of dining with them."[26]

Table VI.
The Children of Jean Michel Fortier and Henriette Milon,
Free Woman of Color

This information is taken from baptismal records. The early ones are written in Spanish, and I have changed the names to French to reflect what the family would have used. Later records are written in French.

1.	Adelard Murville, baptized March 12, 1806. Born August 7, 1805. Henriette is identified as *quadroon libre.* Initially, the priest wrote that the father was unknown but later corrected it to read Jean Michel Fortier. To affirm the change, Jean Michel signed at the bottom. The listed godparents are Adelard and Aimée Fortier. SLC: B19, 26.
2.	Louise Matilde, baptized March 17, 1808. In this record, the priest identifies Henriette as *mulatta libre.* Again, the father was first listed as unknown and later corrected to Jean Michel Fortier. Her godparents are Michel and Louise Gabriella Fortier. SLC: B21, 70.
3.	Félicité Rosella, baptized March 31, 1810. Born January 11, 1810. In this record Henriette is identified as *quadroon libre* and again the father was at first unknown and later changed. Her godparents are Edmond Fortier and Félicité LaBranche (Jean Michel's brother and sister-in-law). SLC: B23, 70.
4.	Marie Henriette, baptized October 11, 1813. Henriette is identified as *quadroon libre.* Again, the record was corrected, and Jean Michel is acknowledged as the father with his signature. The listed godparents are Phillippe Karo(?) and Louise, the child's older sister. SLC: B26, 159.
5.	Michel Felix, baptized February 2, 1815. Henriette is identified as *quadroon libre.* Michel Fortier the younger (*joven*) is named as the father (no later correction necessary). His godparents are Michel Aime (Jean Michel's nephew) and Victorine Fortier (Jean Michel's cousin, daughter of Aimée and Jacques). Victorine was fifteen years old at the time and represented by Deseada Durel (daughter of François and Manette). SLC: B27, 85.

6.	François Omer (Francisco Omero), baptized February 6, 1816. Born October 17, 1815. Henriette is identified as *quadroon libre* and the given father is Jean Michel. This record mentions the grandparents, Michel Fortier and Rose Durel. The godparents are François Omer Fortier (the child's namesake) and Carlotta Chauvin Delery. In the margin, the child's death is noted: August 28, 1857. SLC: B29, 5.
7.	Gabriel, baptized February 4, 1818. Listed parents are Jean Michel Fortier and Henriette Milon, with no racial designation. The godparents are Gabriel Valcour (possibly Valcour Aime) and Marie Louise Charvenet. SLC: B29, 198.
8.	Lucien Armand, baptized March 20, 1820. "Natural son of *Mr.* Jean Michel Fortier and *Dlle.* Henriette Milon, inhabitants of this parish." The abbreviation *Mr.* stands for *Monsieur*. The abbreviation *Dlle.* stands for *Mademoiselle*. There is no mention of Henriette being a free woman of color and no racial designation. Instead, she is accorded the title of a single lady. The godparents are Michel Lucien LaBranche and Madame Matilda Fortier LaBranche. SLC: B30, 182.
9.	Edmond Gustave, baptized May 12, 1825. Born December 21, 1822. His parents are given as J. M. Fortier and Henriette Milon, *libre* (no racial designation). The godparents are Edmond Fortier and Natalie Fortier. SLC: B35, 48.
10.	Félicité Angela, baptized August 4, 1827. Born October 2, 1825. The parents are listed as *Monsieur* Jean Michel Fortier and *Mademoiselle* Henriette Milon. In the margin, the child is identified as "*enf. d. c. l.*," a free infant of color. Her godparents are Alexandre Septime Fortier and Félicité Fortier. SLC: B37, 124.

They lived on Burgundy Street, which, like others in the Creole section of the city, was residentially integrated. On the street as a whole in 1820, there were 166 households, of which roughly:

- 30 percent were families of free people of color, a man and a woman, usually with children, and about a third of these included enslaved people.

- 30 percent were White families with children, or White adults living on their own. Forty percent of these households included enslaved people.

- 15 percent were single White men living with a woman of color, most often a free woman, but sometimes enslaved; most of these included children.

- 15 percent were free women of color living without a man of either race, often with children. In this category it is possible that the woman had a sexual relationship with a man who did not live with her.

- 10 percent were of various unusual configurations, such as a free woman of color who was the head of the household, living with a White woman, both age twenty-six to forty-five; a free family of color, with three White men living with them, perhaps as boarders; a single White woman and four enslaved females, caring for six free children of color; and a White family with a free girl of color, perhaps employed as a housekeeper.

Burgundy Street was not unusual for streets in the Creole section of the city, except that there were fewer free people of color on streets nearest the river. People of color entered the housing market in significant numbers only in the 1780s and '90s, when land closest to the river was already developed. Bourbon Street was something of a dividing line. Properties between Bourbon Street and the river tended to be more expensive, often used for commerce or government, with fewer houses and more space for grand mansions belonging to the wealthy. Properties on Bourbon and above were smaller, more crowded, less expensive, and primarily residential (Table VII).

Table VII.
Households for Selected Streets Recorded on the 1820 Census

Street	Number of Households	Number Headed by a Free Person of Color	Percentage Headed by a Free Person of Color
Levee (Decatur)	106	1	1%
Chartres	120	6	5%
Royal	139	14	10%
Bourbon	219	76	35%
Dauphine	156	84	54%
Burgundy	166	86	52%

Although White people and free people of color lived within the same households and in the same neighborhoods, racial equality did not exist. Friendships may have formed, but people of color, by law, were always to be subservient to Whites because of their African ancestry. And even though Jean Michel's children had frequent interaction with their White cousins, they could not inherit his wealth. Some White men found ways around the law to ensure that their mixed-race children had at least some resources after their death, as Jean Michel did in 1814 when he donated an enslaved sixteen-year-old girl named Victoria to his "natural" children.[27]

Nevertheless, his children did not benefit when he died; their cousins did. Jean Michel passed away on April 13, 1836. The death notice read: "Jean Michel Fortier a native of this city aged sixty-two years, late a merchant, died in this city at his residence situated Burgundy Street between St. Ann and Dumaine Streets. The said Jean Michel Fortier was not married."[28]

Three weeks later, Jean Michel's cousin, Jean Baptiste Dejan, appeared before the probate judge to swear that "the said Jean Michel Fortier has neither legitimate ascendants nor descendants" and that his nearest relations "are Edmond Fortier his brother, and Adelard Fortier, Valcour Aime and Michel Aime, the nephews of said deceased." These men already owned sugar plantations upriver, and now, because they were White, they added to their wealth.

As a free woman of color, Henriette had no legal standing in the affair. However, she had her own resources, and the very next year she purchased the Burgundy Street house back from the White heirs, as well as a fifty-year-old enslaved man named Lubin, whom they had also inherited. For a price, Jean Michel's heirs allowed Henriette to remain in the house where she had lived for decades, and prevented a man whom she may have known almost that long from spending his remaining years among strangers on a distant plantation. She lived in the house until her death, and then the property passed to her daughters and remained in the family until the end of the century. Their story continues in Chapter 5, wherein the property became the subject of a dispute that landed before the Supreme Court of Louisiana.[29]

Future generations would come to view sexual relationships between a White man and a Black woman as immoral. They characterized the woman as licentious and the man as irresponsible. After the Civil War, most White Creoles condemned, ignored, or even denied that such relationships ever existed. This change in attitude was a facet of the cultural transformation of New Orleans from a Creole to an American city. Yet, at the time, Jean Michel's lifelong relationship with Henriette was not unusual. To underscore the esteem in which he was held by his White relatives, his nephew Septime, son of his brother Edmond, named his first son Jean Michel and engaged the artist Julien Hudson, a free man of color born in New Orleans and trained in Paris, to paint his uncle's portrait posthumously (Figure 5).[30] The portrait stayed with Septime's heirs into the twentieth century.

Fig.5: *Jean Michel Fortier* by Julien Hudson, 1839.
Courtesy of the Louisiana State Museum.

=== Michel, Aimée, and Félicité Durel, *mestizos* ===

In September 1781, a woman identified as Suson, "*mulata esclava de . . . Santilli,*" appeared in church for the baptism of her son Michel. The father was not identified but the godmother was Jean Baptiste Durel (2)'s sister, Victoire (2), and the godfather was his brother-in-law, Michel Fortier. In May 1784, Suson was again in church, this time for the christening of a daughter named Maria Amada (later called simply Aimée, the French version of Amada). Again, no name was given for the father, but the godparents were members of the Durel family, François and Aimée. A third time, in April 1785, Suson was in church for the baptism of a child, this one called Maria Félicité (later called simply Félicité), whose godparents were Ursin and Félicité Durel. Six of the seven Durel siblings of the second generation served as godparents for Suson's children, and each child was named after one of them.[31] Clearly Suson had a connection to the Durel family.

A clue lies in the fact that the only sibling not to serve as a godparent was Baptiste, the second son of Jean Baptiste and Cécile. It turns out that as a young man, prior to his marriage to Clarisse Andry, Baptiste had a sexual relationship with Suson that lasted several years. This is confirmed by alterations made to each of the baptismal records sometime later, not only naming him as the father but also giving each child the Durel surname and identifying Suson's status not as a slave but as a free *mestiza*. A 1773 notarial record states that Pierre François Santilly held six individuals enslaved, five described as *mestizo*. Of the five, one was named Suzana, a version of the name Suson.[32] A plausible interpretation is that Santilly had enslaved Suson's mother, an Indigenous woman belonging to one of the *petite nations*, and that the five constituted a family with him possibly the father. In the document he promised them freedom, but it is not clear when or whether this happened.

The Spanish, by the time they took control of Louisiana, forbade the enslavement of native people, arguing that it would unnecessarily antagonize the local nations. Pragmatically, Governor O'Reilly chose to apply the rule only to future enslavement and allowed enslavers to keep those *mestizos* they already held captive. Nevertheless, enslaved *mestizos* like Suson began to assert their freedom under Spanish rule in the 1790s and had their status changed.[33]

It is notable that Suson's third child was born just weeks before Baptiste married Clarisse Andry and was baptized a few weeks afterward. All of Baptiste's brothers and sisters knew of the children's existence, and eventually he openly acknowledged them. It is likely that Clarisse knew as well, since, as demonstrated below, at least one of her children maintained a lifelong relationship with the *mestizo* Durels.

The lives of Suson's children reveal ambiguous attitudes about people of mixed European and American Indian descent among Creoles in the early nineteenth century. Although a Louisiana Supreme Court case in 1810 defined American Indians as persons of color, they often appear without racial designation in official documents.[34] In a world obsessed with racial identity, Suson's children were at times identified as *mestizo,* especially in the eighteenth century, but as years passed, they usually appeared with no racial identity and may have lived as White.

The children, Michel, Aimée, and Félicité, received no formal education, did not learn to read and write, and did not inherit anything from their father. While their White, "legitimate" half-siblings were mostly merchants, accountants, and landlords, they made their way among the artisans and laborers of the city. Michel became a cabinetmaker, worked in a shop on Chartres Street, and purchased a house on St. Philip Street in 1811. The census taker in 1820 listed him as living with a free woman of color, although he appears with no racial label.[35]

In 1818, Félicité married a free man of color, also a cabinetmaker, named Louis Villemont, identified as the natural son of a White man of the same name.[36] Félicité is described as a natural child, indicating that she was recognized as non-White. Her mother, Suson, was present at the wedding ceremony, by this time going by the name Suson Frederic (sometimes spelled Frederick). Also present was a man named Ursin Frederic, identified as *mestizo* (in another document) and presumably her husband. Yet another attendee was Ursin Durel (2), documented as a White first cousin. The record of this marriage shows a web of associations among people identified as White, *mestizo*, and free people of color, all in the Durel family.

Aimée, the oldest child, evidently did not marry, and her early years are difficult to trace. In 1802, she was identified as *mestiza libra* when she stood as godmother for a man from Congo who was enslaved by Ursin Frederick.[37] In 1810, she lived in a house on Royal Street and was categorized as "other" in the census that year, there being no category for *mestizo* or "Indian."[38] I could not find her in the 1820 Census, but in 1830 she appeared without racial designation, living with her sister, who by then was widowed and labeled as a free person of color.[39]

Michel died on July 27, 1828, and left his property on St. Philip Street to his sisters.[40] They preferred a house that was for sale on Bourbon Street but could not afford to purchase it until they sold their brother's home. Not wanting to miss the opportunity, they turned to their White half sister, Victoire Durel (3), whose husband, Antoine Abat, was a real estate broker. He bought the Bourbon Street property on December 1, 1829, held it for twenty days, and then sold it to the sisters on the same day that the St. Philip Street house sold.[41]

The two sisters lived in the house on Bourbon Street for the rest of their lives, some four to five blocks away from Victoire's house on Royal Street. Félicité died in 1857 at age seventy-two.[42] Aimée lived another nine years and witnessed the turmoil of the Civil War. In her eighty-second year, from her sick bed, she dictated her last will and testament, leaving her few possessions to family and friends. [43] This document, written in French, gives a glimpse of her poverty and provides the strongest evidence for a lifelong relationship between the White and *mestiza* Durels.

She owned a large mahogany armoire, perhaps made by her brother, which she gave to Madame Ursin Frederic, and a smaller one which she gave to Margarite Frederic, whom she called "my niece." There was a little altar in her bedroom, at which she likely prayed daily, that she gave to a friend, Mademoiselle Gouite. She gave her house and property to Louise Célestin, whom she had held enslaved until emancipation during the war, and a small chest of drawers to Joseph Henry Célestin, possibly Louise's husband. (Unfortunately for Louise, she could not afford the real estate taxes on the property, and later it was seized by the Seventh District Court and put up for sale.) [44]

By this time, Victoire (3) had died, but her children remained close to Aimée. She named Paul Emile Abat, Victoire's son, as her estate executor, and notably she left the few pieces of silver that she possessed—three silver knives and a silver serving spoon—along with six coffee cups and two empty flowerpots, to Victoire's daughter Clara (Figure 6). The simple gesture of leaving her only silver to her White niece, who was far wealthier, speaks to a bond that had lasted a lifetime. Although one was poor and one was wealthy, one labeled a natural daughter and one legitimate, one of mixed European and American Indian descent and the other wholly European, Aimée and Victoire had stayed close.

Fig. 6: *Clara DeJan* [sic], née *Abat* by Adolphe Rinck, 1841.
Courtesy of the Louisiana State Museum.

=== Jean Florent Durel and Idalise Manadé ===

Jean Florent Durel was the eldest son of Baptiste and Clarisse, named for his uncle, Louis Florent Basile.[45] Like his cousin Jean Michel Fortier, he had a lifelong relationship with a woman of color, in his case lasting nearly sixty years. The story of Jean Florent and Idalise Manadé reveals shifting attitudes toward free people of color as the nineteenth century progressed.

When his father died in 1809, Jean Florent was twenty-three years old, and he assumed the role of head of his family. He assisted his mother in managing the family's business and rental properties and eventually started a business of his own. J. F. Durel & Co. had offices on Levee Street. He shared an address with B. Beauregard, probably his cousin Bartholomew. Close by was the office of his Fortier cousins, Jean Michel and Edmond.

He remained a bachelor and continued to live at home into his thirties. At age thirty-two he began a sexual liaison with Idalise, who at the time was sixteen years old and had come with her mother from Saint-Domingue in the wave of refugees in 1809. Idalise became pregnant and gave birth to a daughter in 1819, whom they named Marie Idalise. A second child, Marie Odile, died young, and Jean Florent had the child's body interred in a tomb that he purchased in St. Louis Cemetery #2.[46] Notably, the inscription on the tomb gives the child's surname as "Durel," recognizing her as a member of the Durel family. The tomb also contains the remains of Idalise's mother, Marie Rose Manadé. Clearly from the beginning, Jean Florent viewed his relationship with Idalise as a joining of his family to hers, a relationship that would be publicly acknowledged and lasting.

A third child, Jean Victor, was born in October 1825, and baptized on December 29, 1826, with Jean Florent's mother, Clarisse, and brother Adolph as godparents.[47] By 1830, he and Idalise were living together, with two enslaved females, at the corner of Bourbon Street and St. Ann, just a block from his mother's house. The property was in Idalise's name. She may have had money of her own, or Jean Florent may have provided the money for the purchase.

Unlike his cousin, Jean Michel, who could not legally provide for his mixed-race children, Jean Florent was able to take advantage of a law passed in 1845 to give his daughter and son property. In a compromise with the Creoles, the state legislature, which was controlled by Louisianians with

Anglo-American roots, made it possible for White males to donate property to their publicly acknowledged "natural" mixed-race children. In 1846, Jean Florent stood before a notary and formally recognized Marie Idalise and Jean Victor as his natural children and authorized them to use the surname Durel. That same year, he gave Marie Idalise a rental property at the corner of Levee and Madison Streets, valued at $14,000 ($573,275 in 2024). Five years later, he did the same for his son, gifting Jean Victor a rental property on Bourbon Street.[48]

While he took care of his children, Jean Florent also remained close to his siblings and their families, most of whom lived nearby. At one point, one of his nephews lived with him and Idalise, and another time he engaged a nephew to handle some of his business transactions. He had an especially strong attachment to his sister Victoire (3), the same who maintained a lifelong connection with their *mestiza* half sister Aimée. He may have named his son Jean Victor after her, and years later, when he wrote his will, he singled out her children for specific bequests.

Although Black and White Creoles remained connected, mixed openly within their families, and lived close to one another in neighborhoods, things were different in public spaces. An 1816 law, seemingly aimed directly at respectable mixed-race couples like Jean Michel and Henriette and Jean Florent and Idalise, forbade Whites from sitting in the Black section of theaters, and vice versa. When streetcars appeared in the 1820s, there were separate cars for Black passengers, indicated by a star affixed to the sides. Some owners of restaurants and taverns chose to segregate their clientele, or to refuse service to Black people altogether. Fraternal organizations were generally segregated, with men of color having their own associations. Similarly, their children could not attend schools for Whites, so people of color instituted schools of their own.[49]

It took four decades, but in the 1840s the English-speaking Anglo-Americans finally gained the upper hand in the rivalry with the Creoles. By then, they were no longer newcomers, many having been in New Orleans for a generation, with children who had grown up there. Most of the lawyers and doctors practicing in the city were Anglo-American. Increasingly, English was used in official records and newspapers. By 1850, Creoles were a clear minority not only in the city as a whole, but even in their own neighborhoods.[50]

The arrival of Irish and German immigrants, beginning in the 1830s, hastened the change. The Irish did have Roman Catholicism in common with the Creoles, but they spoke English and both they and the Germans came with the intention of becoming American, not French. By 1850, New Orleans was a city of immigrants, just as other major American cities were. In the census taken that year, 49 percent of the residents were foreign-born, and adding the children of immigrants born in Louisiana, these foreigners were a majority.[51] As in other cities, New Orleans experienced a rise in nativism and violence against immigrants.[52]

At the same time, enforcement of segregation and other restrictions that targeted free people of color intensified. Years later, Black citizens would look back on 1852 as a turning point.[53] This was when the state legislature acted to limit their number, passing a law requiring any newly emancipated person of African descent to leave the United States at their former enslaver's expense.[54] Free people of color started to see the limited rights that they had managed to gain for themselves disappear. They sensed a change in attitude, as emboldened Whites felt empowered to challenge and insult them with no fear of reprisal. The simultaneous rise of xenophobia and overt racism caused an upsurge in acts of antagonism and aggression on the streets of New Orleans. This did not always come in the form of physical violence; a haughty stare, a degrading remark, an unreasonable demand, would have put people of color on guard. Hostility was in the air. In this climate, the genial relationships between White Creoles and Creoles of color began to slip away.

In 1850, there were 9,905 free people of color recorded by census takers in New Orleans, down from a peak of 15,072 ten years earlier. While some have questioned the accuracy of these numbers, it is clear from other sources that many free people of color were choosing to leave.[55] French-speaking free Black Creoles did not take the Underground Railroad north, as did so many men and women of African descent in the American South. Rather, they departed by ship for Latin America, especially Mexico and Haiti, and notably for France itself, their ancestral and cultural homeland.[56] At a time when the situation in New Orleans was becoming more repressive, France was moving in the opposite direction. Not only did people of color have full political rights in France itself, but in 1848 the government extended citizenship to all inhabitants of the French West Indies. A Black man could step ashore in Martinique, or walk down a street in Paris, with his head held high. A Black woman did not have to submit to the whims of a White man.

It is no surprise, then, that Jean Florent and Idalise decided to move to Paris in the late 1850s. He was close to seventy years old, and they had been together for more than thirty-five years. He had deep roots in New Orleans. Born in 1786, he had spent his adult years living within blocks of his boyhood home at the corner of Royal and St. Ann Streets. Throughout his life he had stayed close to his brothers and sisters, especially his sister Victoire. It must have been with deep regret and disappointment that he and Idalise felt compelled to leave. In Paris, at least, she could be herself and her natural talents could flourish. No more stepping aside for White women, no more abusive looks and comments, no longer constrained by the prejudices of others. Henceforth, she would be addressed, not simply by her first name Idalise, but as Madame Durel.

Jean Florent arranged for his nephew, Eugène Dejan, son of his sister Eloise, to manage his properties in New Orleans, which continued to provide income in his old age. He and Idalise settled at 21 Rue de Teheran, a twenty-minute walk from the Champs-Élysées. Their daughter had died in 1850, but their son Victor and his wife, Marie Adele Morin, moved to Paris as well, bringing with them a newborn son, named Louis Florent. Thus, on the eve of the Civil War, the family of Jean Florent Durel—husband, wife, son, daughter-in-law, and grandson—became residents of Paris. He never returned to the city of his birth.

Two decades later, at the advanced age ninety-two, Jean Florent Durel wrote his last will and testament. With Idalise at his side, he bequeathed property in Paris to his daughter-in-law, Marie Adele, his son having predeceased him. He also left money for the *Sœurs de l'Espérance* (Sisters of Hope) to support their work with the poor and sick in his adopted city. Significantly, he willed his property in New Orleans to nieces and nephews who had stayed in touch, including Clara Abat Dejan (Figure 6), who had also remained loyal to her *mestiza* aunt.[57] (Table VIII shows Clara's genealogical connections to both her Aunt Aimée and her Uncle Jean Florent.)

Following Jean Florent's death, Idalise continued to live at 21 Rue de Teheran for another seventeen years, until her death in 1894. Like her husband, she died at age ninety-two. She had lived a long and remarkable life.

Table VIII.
Genealogical Reference Chart Showing Relationship of Clara Abat Durel to Her Uncle, Jean Florent Durel, and Her Aunt, Aimée Durel, *Mestiza*

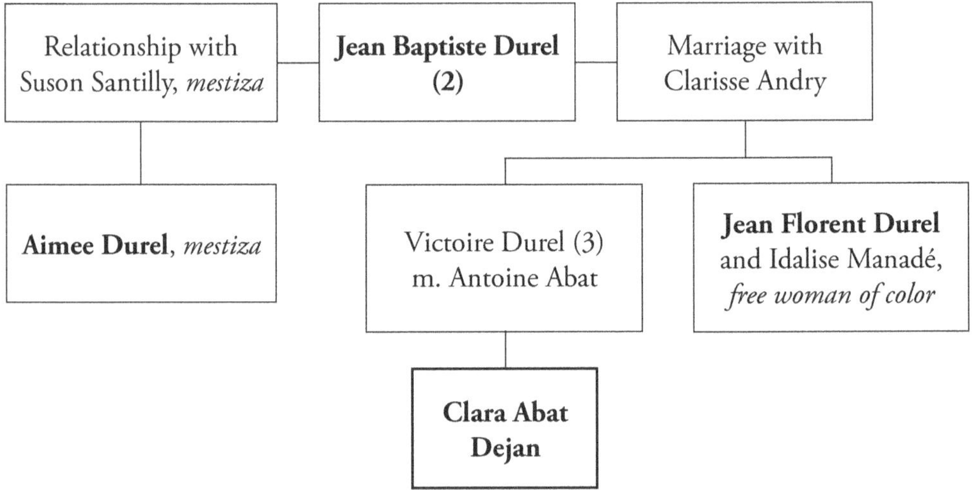

She was born in 1802 in Saint-Domingue. As a child, she escaped the revolution, arriving in New Orleans at age seven with her mother in the wave of refugees that engulfed the small city. As a teenager, she attracted the attention of Jean Florent, most likely at a quadroon ball that her mother had taken her to. She and Jean Florent began an intimate relationship that lasted a lifetime. For nearly forty years, she lived as the respectable consort of a wealthy White man, raising their children and managing his household. Then, when she was near sixty, she moved with him to Paris and resided there for another thirty years. The forces of racism had shaped the contours of her existence for almost an entire century.

=== Jean Baptiste Durel (4), Free Man of Color ===

This brief story attempts to resolve a mystery. A man bearing the name of the founder of the Durel family in Louisiana, Jean Baptiste Durel, died at his home in Faubourg Tremé in 1837. He is the fourth person in this book to have this name. Unlike the previous three, he was a free man of color, and it is not clear from the records who his father was.

The death certificate of Jean Baptiste Durel (4) states that he was the natural son of the late Jean Baptiste Durel and the late Mathilde Martin, a free woman of color.[58] His baptismal record describes him as *quateroon libre*, indicating that his father was White. He was born on February 26, 1813, but not baptized until he was six years old, on May 17, 1819. He had a younger sister, Marie, who was baptized at the same time, when she was eighteen months old.[59] Although the children's mother, Mathilde, was at the christening, the father did not attend. His identity is revealed only in a note the priest received before the ceremony. It seems the children's father wished to acknowledge his paternity but could not or chose not to be present at the ceremony.

An issue arises in the designation of the father as "late" in the death certificate. At the time, Jean Baptiste (1) and (2) were long dead. Only Jean Baptiste (3), the eldest son of Manette and François, was living when the children were baptized. However, he was not "late" at the time of the death of Jean Baptiste (4) eighteen years later, for he did not die until 1857.[60] It is possible that the death certificate that identified him as "late" was simply wrong, that the friends of Jean Baptiste (4), the free man of color, who reported his death believed that his White father was deceased.

At the time of the christening, Jean Baptiste (3) had recently married a White woman, Elizabeth de Glapion, who was pregnant and would give birth to a son that December.[61] It is plausible that before the birth of a legitimate child, Jean Baptiste (3) was in the process of ending his intimate relationship with Mathilde. Perhaps she demanded that her children be baptized and that he acknowledge them. Thereafter, he may have had nothing to do with them and, hence, was presumed dead by those who came to know Jean Baptiste (4) as an adult.

Whatever the case, when he was nineteen, Jean Baptiste (4) married a free woman of color named Barbé Aimée Loiseau, from Cuba. Their marriage was short-lived, for he died only four years later. He was survived by three children, two girls named Marie and Cécile, and a boy named Jean Baptiste, all having the last name Durel. I have been unable to track the lives of the children beyond their mention in the probate record.

If Jean Baptiste (3) was indeed the father of this free man of color, it gives an interesting dimension to the story of Forester Durel in the next chapter.

Forester was Jean Baptiste (3)'s legitimate son, and hence, would have been Jean Baptiste (4)'s half brother. Forester became a leading proponent of the separation of the races and a denial of Black relatives. The next chapter also features yet another free man of color with the founder's name. That two such men were given the most prominent name in the Durel family underscores once again the openness of White Creoles in acknowledging their familial relationships with people of color during the first half of the nineteenth century. That openness would come to an end with the next generation.

Under Jim Crow, there were two overarching strategies employed to maintain White supremacy. The first was to keep Black and White people separated; the second was to ensure that Whites had more advantages. Although the Supreme Court called for "separate but equal" treatment of Black people, in reality it was separate and unequal. This was the world of my childhood, and so I was both surprised and heartened by the proximity of Black and White homeowners in Creole neighborhoods and the openness and acceptance of intimate relationships between White and free people of color. The stories in this chapter revealed to me a new way of thinking about race.

Durel descendants who came of age at the turn of the nineteenth century saw nothing wrong with a White man having children with a free woman of color, as long as it did not jeopardize the man's fortune and the inheritance of his White children. They had no concern about White and free Black people living next door to one another, their children playing together and becoming friends. Perceived differences were due to class, not race. That is, instead of the so-called "separate but equal" doctrine I lived under, they lived in a time of connectedness and inequality. Black and White people could be friends and relatives, but Whites still had advantages.

In the prologue, I wrote about Johann Blumenbach, who published a hierarchy of human types in 1795 that placed White people at the top and Black people at the bottom. Blumenbach thought in terms of skin color, deeming "white" or light complexions more beautiful than "black" or dark complexions. From what I am able to discern from descriptions in the records, the Durel descendants who had long-term relationships with women of color tended to agree. Both Henriette Milon and Idalise Manadé appear to have had very light skin and had more typically European than African features. Only one White descendant, Michel Durel, the keeper of stray animals, lived with a woman described as "black."

The period of time in which men like Jean Michel Fortier and Jean Florent Durel could live openly with free women of color was relatively brief. What Creoles found acceptable at the beginning of the nineteenth century came under attack as the years passed. For me, the glimmer of hope I felt in seeing what was possible faded. I would like to have lived in a time when I could have Black neighbors and friends and even Black relatives, openly acknowledged and loved. I would have been better off for it.

Table IX.
Genealogical Reference Chart for Henry Durel, J. B. "Numa" Durel, and Pierre Forester Durel

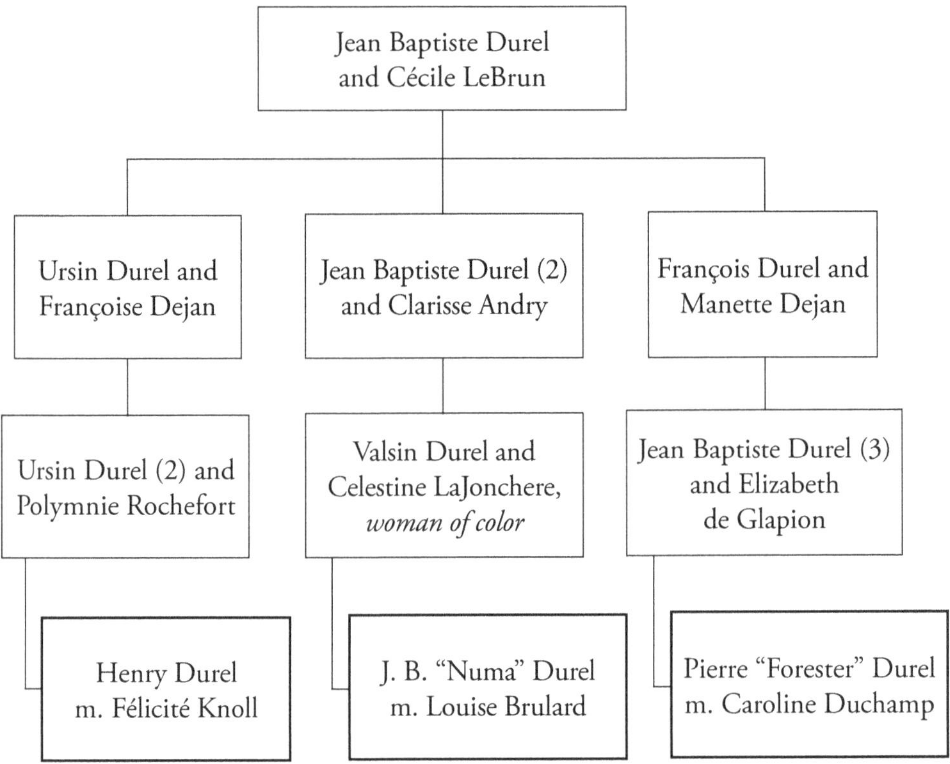

Chapter 4

The Civil War and Reconstruction Generation

When I was in school, all eighth graders in the state studied Louisiana history. In the school textbook from 1959, the section on the Civil War was titled "Louisiana and the War for Southern Independence." The next section was called "The Period of Military Occupation." I recall learning that the war was a conflict between the industrial North and the agrarian South, and that the North's victory put an end to slavery. I also learned that following the war, Black men were given the right to vote and hold political office, but they were not ready for such responsibility and fell under the influence of corrupt northerners, called carpetbaggers, who took control of the state. Eventually, respectable White southerners regained power and reestablished order and good government. It was a simple lesson, but it was wrong, glossing over a complex reality.

The three stories in this chapter reveal the complications and difficulties experienced by ordinary people as they grappled with political and social upheaval. For most generations, change comes gradually. For the fourth generation Durel descendants, those who came of age in the 1840s and '50s, change was rapid and violent.

=== Henry Durel and Félicité Knoll ===

Henry Durel grew up in a household where a particularly heinous form of slavery existed. With the end of the importation of African captives into the United States in 1807, some enslavers sought to meet the demand for new enslaved workers by "breeding" children to be sold when they were old enough to bring a good price. "Breeding" was a term used at the time. One such enslaver, Thomas Jefferson, wrote that a breeding woman who gave birth to a healthy child every two years was more profitable than an enslaved man's labor in producing a successful harvest. Given the frequency of the death of a mother, child, or both during and immediately after childbirth, this was a risky business. Some enslavers were careful not to overtax the woman and to feed her better than usual during the late stages of pregnancy. When the child was strong enough to be placed in the care of an elderly female captive, the mother went back to work. The enslaver expected her to become pregnant again as quickly as possible, with her husband if she was married or with a man selected for the purpose. Enslavers preferred women who were strong and healthy, increasing the odds of commanding a higher price. If a woman proved unsuccessful in giving birth to healthy children, she would be sold.

Evidence in the probate record of Henry's father, Ursin (2), strongly indicates that he was in the business of breeding. In 1845, at the time of his death, Ursin (2) kept fourteen people of African descent in captivity, far exceeding the average of three per slaveholding household in the urban neighborhood where he lived. The fourteen consisted of five women and nine children under the age of fourteen. They were:

- Arabella: a fifty-year-old woman, whom Ursin (2) had recently inherited from his mother.

- Betsy, thirty-five, with three children: Noël, thirteen; Beloxine, eleven; and Henriette, six.

- Celie, no age given, with Marie, eleven, and four more children under age seven: Victor, August, Octave, and Octavie.

- Melice, twenty-two, with no children.

- Genie, twenty-four, and her son Pierre, age five.

With the exception of Arabella, all the women were of childbearing age.

When it came to estimating the financial value of the enslaved, the appraisers combined each woman with her youngest children and singled out the older children for separate sale. Thus, for example, they gave Betsy and six-year-old Henriette a value of $600 (the equivalent of $24,900 in 2024) and estimated separately that eleven-year-old Beloxine was worth $300 ($12,450 in 2024) and thirteen-year-old Noël was worth $400 ($16,590 in 2024). In another year or so, Noël could be sold for $500 ($20,470 in 2024), and with eight more children queued up behind him, Ursin (2) had a steady flow of income. In addition, with the exception of the weeks immediately preceding and following a birth, he could hire the mother out to someone in need of domestic help. The elderly Arabella would have cared for the children while the mothers worked. All in all, Henry's father seems to have had a profitable business, so much so that after he died, Henry's mother continued the enterprise. She appears in the 1850 Census with fifteen enslaved people: an older woman, two men, five women of childbearing age (ages eighteen to thirty-four), and seven children under age fifteen. The addition of two enslaved men raises the question of who fathered the children earlier. It could well have been her husband.

Such was the daily reality of slavery for Henry Durel growing up. When it was time for him to set out on his own, he took a different path.

Henry was born around 1825 and came of age at a time when New Orleans experienced a significant change in the composition of its population. Beginning in the 1830s and continuing through the '40s and '50s, European immigrants, mostly from France, Germany, and Ireland, arrived in large numbers. Many were rural people who continued upriver to settle on farmland, but others chose to remain in the city. The newcomers could not afford to enslave anyone. On the contrary, female immigrants competed with free women of color for domestic work, and immigrant men sought jobs in warehouses and at the port, providing an alternative to enslaved labor. It was a gradual process, but over time the number of people of African descent held in captivity in the city declined as the population grew. Specifically, according to the census, the number of enslaved people declined from roughly 18,000 in 1840 to 14,000 in 1860, while the overall population more than doubled, from about 84,000 to 170,000. Proportionately, the enslaved went from 12 percent of the population to 8 percent.

This change explains Henry's circumstances as he began life on his own. He went to work as a clerk in the office of the city comptroller and met and married Félicité Knoll, whose family had come from Alsace in France when she was a child. Their first baby, named Henry Bernard, was born in 1848 and soon thereafter, the young family rented rooms in the house of a woman from Germany. By 1860, Henry and Félicité had six children and were living on St. Ann Street, not far from

POLICE JAILS—OFFICIAL.

Was brought to the City Police Jail on the 1st of June, 1860, the mulatto boy ALBERT. Says he belongs to Mr. Robinson, who lives in Chatanooga, and formerly belonged to widow Tyler. He is 5 feet 5¼ inches high, has curly hair, and is aged about 21 years.

The owner will call and claim his property according to law.

ED. PLANCHARD,
Keeper of City Police Jail.

Registered June 16, 1860.

HENRY DUREL,
For Comptroller.

je18 15t

Was brought to the City Police Jail on the 8th of June, 1860, the black boy NELSON alias JIM. Says he belongs to Mr. Stanfield Reeves, who lives in St. Francis county, Arkansas. He is 5 feet 3 inches high, has a cut on the left hand index, a double range of teeth on the lower jaw, and is aged about 23 years.

The owner will call and claim his property according to law.

ED. PLANCHARD,
Keeper of City Police Jail.

Registered June 16, 1860.

HENRY DUREL,
For Comptroller.

je18 15t

Was brought to the City Police Jail on the 13th of June, 1860, the black boy THOMAS. Says he belongs to Mr. George Payne, who lives near Bonnet Carré, Louisiana. He is 5 feet 7 inches high, of pleasing countenance, griff complexion and good address, and is aged about 23 years.

The owner will call and claim his property according to law.

ED. PLANCHARD,
Keeper of City Police Jail.

Registered June 16, 1860.

HENRY DUREL,
For Comptroller.

je18 15t

Was brought to the City Police Jail on the 15th of June, 1860, the black boy SHEDRICK. Says he belongs to Mr. Anthony Hardman, who lives on Four-Mile Bayou, Atchafalaya, 18 miles above Berwick's Bay. He is 5 feet 9 inches high, wears a goatee, has a cut on the lower jaw, is aged about 33 years, and has several of the upper jaw teeth missing.

The owner will call and claim his property according to law.

ED. PLANCHARD,
Keeper of City Police Jail.

Registered June 16, 1860.

HENRY DUREL,
For Comptroller.

je18 15t

Was brought to the City Police Jail on the 5th of June, 1860, the black boy LEWIS. Says he belongs to Dr. Loughborow, who lives in the parish of St. John Baptist La. Said boy is about 5 feet 6 inches high, and has one of his upper front teeth missing, and is about 40 years of age.

The owner will call and claim his property according to law.

ED. PLANCHARD,
Keeper of City Police Jail.

Registered June 9, 1860.

HENRY DUREL,
For Comptroller.

je11 15t

Was brought to the City Police Jail on the 5th of June, 1860, the negro boy LIGY. Says he belongs to Gen. Davis, who lives in the parish of St. Bernard. Said boy is 5 feet high, and has one or two small scars on the forehead, and is about 18 or 19 years of age.

The owner will call and claim his property according to law.

ED. PLANCRAHD,
Keeper of City Police Jail.

Registered June 9, 1860.

HENRY DUREL,
For Comptroller

je11 15t

Was brought to the City Police Jail on the [illegible] of May, 1860, the black boy GIPPY. Says he belongs to Mr. Henry Grayton, who lives at Oyster Creek, Texas; he is 5 feet 1 inch high, and has a scar on the forehead, and is full breasted.

The owner will call and claim his property according to law.

ED. PLANCHARD,
Keeper of City Police Jail.

Registered June 1, 1860.

HENRY DUREL,
For Comptroller.

je2 15t

Was brought to the City Police Jail on the [illegible] of May, 1860, the black boy FRIDAY. Says he belongs to Mr. Henry Grayton, who lives at Oyster Creek, Texas; he is 5 feet 6 inches high, and has one of his front teeth caved in.

The owner will call and claim his property according to law.

ED. PLANCHARD,
Keeper of City Police Jail.

Registered June 1, 1860.

HENRY DUREL,
For Comptroller.

e2 15t

Fig. 7: *New Orleans Daily Crescent*, Tuesday, July 3, 1860

where he grew up. On one side of their house lived a man who owned a dry goods store with his wife and a servant. They, like Félicité, were "new French," not Creole, having immigrated in the nineteenth century. Next to them was another couple from France, and next to them a house with four single White men: a waiter, two confectioners from Germany, and a French cook. In the other direction, a local family lived with a German servant and two immigrant boarders. Next lived a single man from France, and then two French families with White servant girls. On this street, which was in the heart of what had been the old Creole section of town, most residents were foreign born.

Significantly, unlike Durel descendants of previous generations, Henry did not enslave anyone. He followed the growing practice of hiring a live-in servant to help Félicité with the housework and raising the children. Her name was Célma Lafitte, a seventeen-year-old Creole girl. Enslaving someone required an outlay of cash, whereas employing a servant was a weekly or monthly expense. Henry's salary was modest, and Félicité, to make ends meet, purchased a sewing machine to make and sell clothes. They did not enslave anyone because they could not afford to do so.

The contrast between Henry's life, with no one held in bondage, and his father's, in keeping fourteen women and children in captivity, is striking. However, it is in no way a sign of growing antipathy for slavery. Henry did not oppose the enslavement of people of African descent. On the contrary, like most ordinary White men of his class and status, he supported the practice and the supremacy of White people over Black people.

One of Henry's duties in the comptroller's office was to place weekly notices in the newspapers alerting the public to the recapture of enslaved people who had escaped. The listing from July 3, 1861 (Figure 7) may give the impression that only young enslaved men escaped, but that was not always the case. In an example from the Durel family, in 1860, Henry's cousin, Clara Durel Forstall, whose husband had made a fortune in international banking, reported that of the fourteen captives she held at her mansion in New Orleans, four had escaped: a twenty-seven-year-old man and three women, two in their early thirties and one aged fifty.[1] That a fifty-year-old woman chose to flee challenges notions that only the young escaped and that older workers remained loyal to the Whites who held them in bondage.

When presented with an opportunity and a reasonable chance of success, enslaved people of any age always chose freedom over the violence inflicted daily on their bodies and in their hearts.

The persistence of escape gave rise to the Fugitive Slave Act of 1850, which required officials in all the states, including the North, to apprehend those who ran away. Anyone aiding a fugitive was subject to six months in prison and a $1,000 fine ($40,420 in 2024). Northerners, many of whom had long ignored the existence of slavery, were now compelled to enforce it. This brought on a groundswell of opposition. In 1852, Harriet Beecher Stowe published *Uncle Tom's Cabin*, a novel that tugged at the hearts of many Northerners. The *Dred Scott* decision, handed down by the US Supreme Court in 1857, further fueled opposition to slavery. It stated that the rights of citizenship as set forth in the Constitution were never meant to apply to any Black person, enslaved or free. As attitudes shifted in the North, Southerners began to talk about the possibility of seceding from the Union.

Meanwhile, Henry took an active interest in politics. In September 1860, he joined a "great torchlight procession" from Lafayette Square to Place d'Armes in support of John Bell of Tennessee, the candidate for the Constitutional Union Party, who was pro-slavery but opposed secession.[2] Bell felt there was room for compromise and that if the rulings of the Supreme Court were fully enforced there would be no need to secede. He also believed that the majority of Northerners supported slavery, but their voices were being drowned out by radicals. As it turned out, Bell placed third in the November election. The Southern Democrat John C. Breckenridge carried the South, and the Republican candidate, Abraham Lincoln, won the more populous North. Soon thereafter, Southern states began to secede. Louisiana did so in January 1861.

Although the most enthusiastic men began organizing themselves into militia companies, eager to defend their city and their state, Henry continued working, transferring from the comptroller to the city treasurer's office as assistant bookkeeper at a higher salary.[3] However, in the spring of 1862, as an attack on New Orleans grew imminent, he was drafted into an artillery company organized hastily by Captain Armand Guyol, who had been an officer in the US Army before secession.[4] A fleet of Union ships had sailed into the Gulf of Mexico, making its way toward the mouth of the Mississippi River. Within days, army private Henry Durel was marching downriver to Forts Jackson and St. Philip.

The Union fleet reached the mouth of the river and began bombarding the forts on April 18. The Confederates returned fire, but they proved to be no match for the Union force. For days, the mostly inexperienced and ill-prepared soldiers sheltered in dank casements with insufficient food, blankets, and drinking water and with the incessant din of mortars falling from the sky. Sickness and fear began to overwhelm them, and on the tenth day the men at Fort Jackson mutinied. Meanwhile, Union ships broke through a chain that had been strung across the river between the forts and soon reached the city. It quickly became apparent that New Orleans could not withstand a heavy bombardment, and so Confederate troops withdrew to the countryside. The city surrendered.

The First Louisiana Artillery Regiment, of which Henry's company was a part, next moved northward and participated in defending Vicksburg, which fell to Union forces in July 1863. In that battle, the regiment surrendered and later was exchanged for Union troops that had been captured by the Confederates. After reorganizing, with a reduced number of companies and men, the First Louisiana Artillery marched through Alabama to take up position for the defense of Mobile, the last major port under Confederate control. Henry's brother Gustave, who had been drafted with him, died in early 1864, possibly on this march. The Battle of Mobile Bay occurred on August 5, 1864, resulting in yet another Union victory. Thereafter the regiment remained in Alabama until the end of the war.

Upon his return, Henry went back to work for the city treasurer.[5] On the surface, his life seems to have returned to normal, unaffected by his wartime experience. He reconnected with friends and participated in church and community activities, as when he played the role of Sir Henry, Knight of the Crescent in a jousting contest at a festival to raise money for a new Catholic church on Bayou Road.[6] He even found time to go on a hunting vacation. The following notice appeared in the *New Orleans Crescent* on Sunday, October 13, 1867:

> Vacation—Mr. Henry Durel, a nice gentleman and warm friend, and probably the oldest clerk in the treasury department of this city, has obtained a fortnight's leave, which he will spend at Mandeville. Mr. Durel, being an expert at handling a fowling piece, promises each clerk at the treasury one dozen *cailles* (quail), in default of which to forfeit a flannel shirt to each.[7]

These few mentions of his social life just after the war reveal a man who was active, engaged, popular, and good-natured. But something was amiss.

While he was at war, Félicité continued to raise their six children on her own, earning money as a seamstress and living either in the rented house on St. Ann Street, where they were living at the outbreak of hostilities, or perhaps she moved in with her mother who had a house on Orleans Street. Curiously, when Henry returned, rather than moving in with his family, he took a room at the City Hotel in the business district and stayed there for three or four years. This may have been a pragmatic choice, enabling him to reside close to work instead of in an overcrowded house across Canal Street in the French Quarter. That said, as later evidence reveals, it could well have been an early sign of marital stress. At this point, however, they were not totally estranged, for they had another child in February 1868, a boy named Beauregard in honor of the Confederate war hero, General P. G. T. Beauregard.[8]

Shortly after the baby's birth, Henry lost his job through no fault of his own. In the nineteenth century, patronage was a chief component of government employment at all levels. Indeed, Henry likely got his initial position in city government through a family connection. Following the war, however, many newcomers entered local politics—men who had no roots in the city—and the fact that Henry came from an old Creole family counted for little. The mayor who took office in 1868 was a Virginian who had moved to New Orleans in 1862. With the new administration came a new treasurer, who cleaned house and brought in his own men to staff the department. Henry was able to find a new position within a year as bookkeeper for August Koenig & Bro., a business on Canal Street that sold toys and fancy goods.

Signs of employment difficulties for Henry and marital stress between him and Félicité became obvious during the 1870s, when he was in his fifties and she in her forties. They began the decade living together on Burgundy Street. In 1871, he was able to get their son, Henry Jr., a position as clerk at Koenig & Bro., where he continued to work as bookkeeper. However, at some point he and Félicité started living separately. By the end of the decade, Henry Jr. was still at Koenig & Bro., but Henry had moved on and was employed simply as an office clerk at some other business. Notably, he resided with his grown daughter, Nezida, and her husband in their house on Peace Street, whereas Félicité lived with their two youngest sons in a boarding house on Dumaine Street. Through the 1880s they remained separated, she earning a living as a dress maker while he worked intermittently as a clerk.[9]

Henry remained involved in politics after the war, a time of intense political volatility and violence. During the war, the area of the state occupied by Union forces, including New Orleans, came under the authority of a federally appointed military governor, with state and local governments continuing to function under Union oversight. Almost immediately, free people of color began to call for full citizenship, including the right to vote, reasoning that as free men before the war, the state had denied them this fundamental right. Now, under Union control, they deserved it. They sent a delegation to Washington to meet with President Lincoln to make their case. Although he was impressed and sympathetic, Lincoln made no commitment. He did, however, send a private letter to the governor, urging him to consider the possibility of enfranchising a limited number of Black men, especially those who were intelligent and who had served honorably in the Union Army.[10] A new state constitution, adopted in 1864, abolished slavery and called for racially integrated public schools, but left open the question of Black suffrage.

Once the war ended, White men like Henry faced the prospect of having to pledge allegiance to the United States in order to vote. Some were resistant, bitter over the defeat of the Confederacy. Others were willing to accept the loss on the battlefield and the end of slavery, but not full citizenship and equal rights for Black people. They were determined to maintain White control of local and state government, and some were prepared to use violence to do so. In Washington, President Andrew Johnson of Tennessee, who became president after Lincoln's assassination, also favored a return to White control. Things came to a head when Congress passed, over Johnson's veto, the Civil Rights Act of 1866, intended to protect the rights of formerly enslaved people of African descent. Fearing that the Supreme Court would find the act unconstitutional, in June 1866, Congress passed and submitted to the states for ratification the Fourteenth Amendment to the federal Constitution, giving Black people equal protection under the law, but leaving it up to the states to determine who could vote.

In New Orleans, some were eager to affirm their rights and explicitly include the right to vote, even before the Fourteenth Amendment was ratified. Black leaders and their White Republican allies—those who had drafted and passed the Louisiana constitution in 1864—called for a meeting on July 30, 1866, to amend the constitution. Word of the meeting spread. Some Republican leaders were warned not to attend. On the day, enthusiastic Black supporters marched in a parade to the meeting place, joined by other Black people along the way, and were jeered by Whites who gathered along the route. Scuffles ensued, men drew weapons, and soon an armed force of policemen and firemen arrived, sent by the mayor to maintain "the peace and good order of the city."[11] In the end, about forty supporters of suffrage were killed, thirty-seven of them Black. One policeman died from his wounds.[12]

There is no evidence that Henry participated in what became widely known as the New Orleans Riot of 1866, although it would not be surprising if he did. In a congressional investigation following the incident, a White man who was a clerk, not unlike Henry, declared that when he heard something was going on, he "went to the chief of police's office, which was already crowded by citizens ready to be sworn in as special officers, but that the chief of police told them that if they had arms they should go immediately to the scene of the riot."[13] Henry was a hunter. He could easily have grabbed his rifle and joined the melee.

The riot of 1866 and its widespread condemnation in the North contributed to the emergence of Radical Reconstruction in the South. In elections that year, Republicans won a veto-proof majority in Congress, passed laws requiring southern states to ratify the Fourteenth Amendment in order to be readmitted to the Union, and sent the US Army to protect Black citizens in the former Confederacy. In Louisiana, the Republican-controlled state government, backed by the military, approved the Fourteenth Amendment, took control of the government of New Orleans, created a new police force that reported directly to the governor, reduced the power of the mayor, and appointed several Black leaders to the city council. Democrats were outraged.

Four years later, at the time of the 1870 presidential election, the following headline appeared in the New Orleans *Times-Picayune*.[14]

NOVEMBER 10, 1870

DONALDSONVILLE IN DANGER

The Town in the Hands of a Negro Mob.

Judge Lawles and Mayor Schaumburg Killed by the Mob.

The Citizens Fleeing for their Lives.

The article claimed that at the closing of the polls in Donaldsonville, a town about seventy miles upriver from New Orleans, a Black unit of the state militia removed ballot boxes to a nearby plantation, and that when White citizens objected, a Black mob formed and killed the mayor and a judge, both White. The *Times-Picayune* presented the situation as Democrats saw it. The *New Orleans Republican* described it differently, stating that armed White men surrounded the courthouse where the ballots were to be counted, so the election supervisor arranged for an "unarmed" unit of militia to take the boxes to a more secure location.[15] As to the killings, the *Republican* stated that it was actually the judge who shot the mayor "in the presence of a crowd, who then became excited," and "in the confusion that ensued, [the judge] was killed."[16] In New Orleans that evening, in response to claims that "Donaldsonville is in flames" and "Our citizens are being murdered," a crowd of White men gathered on Canal Street in New Orleans. This time, there is evidence that Henry was there, his name appearing on a list of "alarmists" published by the *Republican*.[17]

The story played out over the next several days, as more information reached the city, each paper giving a different version of events. On Friday the *Picayune* reported that "a great fire was raging in Donaldsonville"; the *Republican* said all was quiet and campfires had been mistaken for burning buildings.[18] Saturday's account in the *Picayune* admitted only that "a small outbuilding . . . was destroyed by fire" and focused on the reported brutality of the murders, the mayor's body "literally riddled with bullets" and the judge receiving "two gunshot wounds and seven fearful cuts (from cane knives)." The *Republican* countered by mocking the Democrats for believing that "because a kitchen burned in Donaldsonville the entire city of New Orleans was threatened with destruction."[19] The dueling newspaper accounts both reflected and intensified deep divisions in the citizenry.

Henry was a minor player in this episode, but his presence shows his readiness to believe reports of Black mobs setting fire to a town and murdering the town's leaders. He, like many other ordinary White men in the city, was caught up in the racial tension, misinformation, and violence that permeated Louisiana politics during Reconstruction. The divisiveness continued until a victory for Whites came in the "Battle of Liberty Place," a clash described later in this chapter.

For now, let me turn to the story of another Durel descendant, a second cousin of Henry. He was a little younger than Henry and also served during the Civil War. Their stories run in parallel. A major difference, though, is that he was a Black man.

=== Jean Baptiste "Numa" Durel and Louise Brulard ===

Six days before Henry joined the throng on Canal Street after hearing the news about Donaldsonville, a Black man named J. B. "Numa" Durel applied for a marriage license at the office of the Orleans Parish justice of the peace. The clerk who took his information entered his father's name as Valsin Durel and his mother as C. LaJonchère, abbreviating her name to fit the space on the form.[20] Valsin Durel was a White man, a younger brother of Jean Florent Durel, whose lifelong union with Idalise Manadé is described in Chapter 3. Unlike his brother, Valsin's relationship with Numa's mother appears to have been short-lived. There is no evidence that he was involved in Numa's life beyond giving him the family name. While Numa grew up, Valsin remained a bachelor, worked as a bank clerk, and lived with his mother until she died. He then moved in with one of his sisters. For a while, he lived with a White woman, and late in life, as an old bachelor, he married a woman twenty-six years younger and moved to New York City.[21]

The identity of Numa's mother is more difficult to establish. In 1833, a woman of color named Celestine LaJonchère gave birth to a son named Joseph. The name of the child's father was also LaJonchère, with no first name given.[22] Numa was born some five years earlier, around 1828, so if Celestine was his mother, Joseph was his younger brother. In addition, there is a connection between the Durel family and a White LaJonchère family in the 1833 marriage of Valsin's brother, Adolph, to Celestine Forstall, whose mother was Marie Celeste LaJonchère d'Aunoy.[23] It is conceivable that Valsin and Adolph, as young bachelors, attended social gatherings at the LaJonchère home, and on one such occasion Valsin had a sexual encounter with Numa's mother. Given the vulnerability of young enslaved women, he may have forced himself on her. Whatever the case, it is clear that Numa knew the identity of his father, but probably had nothing to do with him growing up.

Numa spent his childhood years in the community of free people of color and eventually learned to make cigars. The art of rolling a quality cigar had come to New Orleans with refugees from Saint-Domingue and Cuba and was a skill at which many free men of color excelled. Around age thirty he met Louise Brulard, a free woman of color whose father was most likely Sebastian Brulard, a White farmer from Plaquemines Parish.[24] By 1860, Numa and Louise had two children and lived in a small house on the outskirts of the city, and Numa worked at a nearby cigar factory.[25] It was a good job, earning him enough to buy the house in which they lived.

When the Civil War came, Numa signed on as a private in the "Native Guards," a military unit comprised of free men of color, so named to underscore that these men were native to Louisiana and their intent was to defend their homeland. They did not yet know which way the war would go, and as they had done in past conflicts, they used military service as a means to enhance their standing in the eyes of White authorities.[26] White leaders actually had no intention of using them in any meaningful way, but it made good press to have Black men fighting on the Confederate side. As Union ships threatened the city, the Native Guards were handed obsolete muskets and stationed along Esplanade Street. When it became evident that the city would fall, the White military withdrew to the countryside, leaving the Native Guards behind. This was just as well, for when Union General Benjamin Butler took control, Black leaders approached him and offered their services. They were now in a position to fight for equality and the end of slavery.

Initially, Butler was reluctant to accept their offer. White prejudice and ignorance, in the North as well as the South, raised concerns. White military officers believed that Black soldiers could be trained and would follow orders; after all, they surmised, those were traits that made them suitable for slavery. But there was doubt that they would fight and stand their ground in the heat of battle. Also, there was concern that Northern troops would refuse to fight alongside them. Certainly, no White soldiers would agree to salute a Black officer. However, despite these concerns, Butler needed to expand his force. Thus, Black men from Louisiana, Numa among them, joined the Union Army and eventually became part of the Corps d'Afrique. On the first of September 1862, Numa stood before a recruiting officer and identified himself as J. B. Numa Durel, age thirty-six, cigar maker. The officer noted that he was five foot, seven inches tall, with hazel eyes, auburn hair, and a light complexion. The attending surgeon found him to be free of bodily defects and mental infirmity. Numa swore allegiance to the United States of America and signed the document with a flourish.[27]

General Butler did not want to keep Black troops in the city and risk increasing racial tension. He sent two regiments to Bayou Lafourche to help clear Confederate forces from that area. They did not get a chance to fight, for the Confederates had withdrawn by the time they arrived. Instead, they went to work rebuilding and guarding the rail line that ran between Lafourche Crossing and the city. The commanding officer for the Lafourche region assigned them another task, that of going into the fields and harvesting the sugar crop.

These regiments saw action at Port Hudson, north of Baton Rouge, in May 1863. In a Union attack against a Confederate stronghold, they demonstrated they were willing to fight and die. Still, many Northern troops refused to salute Black officers. This caused Butler's successor, General Nathaniel Banks, to purge the cadre of Black field officers and replace them with mostly mediocre White ones. The Black officers were natural leaders, and they did not sit idly waiting for the war to end. Instead, they organized themselves for the political arena.

Port Hudson proved to be an exception for Black soldiers, who spent most of the war not in battle but doing menial tasks behind the lines. They dug latrines, constructed earthworks, hauled supplies, and stood guard. Under the mistaken (and prejudiced) belief that Black people were more resistant to disease, commanders stationed them in defensive forts in the steamy, mosquito-infested Louisiana wetlands. Black people, of course, suffered from sickness just as Whites did, and even more so because many White physicians refused assignments to Black units.

This was the situation for Numa, whose unit was not sent to Port Hudson. Instead, he went initially to Ship Island, part of the coastal defenses around New Orleans. Then, in 1863, he received training as a hospital nurse and was assigned to Fort Macomb on Chef Menteur Pass, just twenty miles east of the city. He cared for soldiers suffering and dying from chronic fever and disease, including yellow fever, pneumonia, dysentery, and diarrhea. Numa mustered out of the service on September 26, 1865. He had less than a day's walk home.

Like his White second cousin, Henry, Numa engaged in politics. He was one of the free Black men, all owners of property, who signed the petition to President Lincoln in 1863, requesting support for their claim to full citizenship.[28] After the war, Numa joined the Republican Party and on Saturday afternoon, April 11, 1868, he was present in a crowd at a rally in Washington Square to show his support for the party's candidates in the elections that spring.[29] It was a dangerous time. In spite of the presence of the US Army, which was stationed in New Orleans following the riot of 1866, bands of armed White men still "robbed, terrorized and even killed working-class Black men who had dared to register to vote."[30] Nevertheless, Numa was at the rally specifically to back Oscar Dunn, a forty-two-year-old Black man running for lieutenant governor.

Although Southern historians would later characterize Black leaders from this era as incompetent, Oscar Dunn was a man with remarkable leadership skills and experience. He had grown up in a free Black household before the war and earned his living as a painter and music teacher. In the 1850s, he joined the Freemasons, where he proved to be an effective leader and rose to be grand master of his lodge. When lower Louisiana fell to the Union Army in 1862, he took the initiative to meet with formerly enslaved men who flocked from the plantations to the city and helped them find employment with fair wages and work contracts. In the immediate postwar period, he played a leading role in gaining Black men the right to vote. Initially, only White men who supported the Union had that right. To demonstrate the potential impact Black voters would have on an election, Dunn funded at his own expense a statewide registration of would-be Black voters and asked them to submit voluntary ballots in elections that occurred in the fall of 1865. More than sixteen thousand did so; had their ballots counted, they would have made up 87 percent of the Republican tally. Radical Republicans in Congress took note.

Black working men like Numa were drawn to Dunn because of his grass-roots work with the newly freed people of African descent. He handily won the Republican nomination for lieutenant governor in 1868. His running mate was Henry Warmoth, an aspiring young White man from Missouri who had come to Louisiana with the Union Army during the war and had decided to stay. Warmoth proved to be a divisive figure and narrowly won the nomination for governor over a wealthy, light-skinned Creole man of color.

Although the Republicans ultimately won the election in 1868, the Democrats were not yet done with violence. The combination of an ambitious northerner as governor, a Black man (Dunn) as lieutenant governor, and a platform that called for racial integration alarmed conservative Whites who believed that they were the rightful leaders of the people. For them, this was going far beyond what they believed the war had been about. They were determined to regain control.

For his part, Numa returned to making cigars. It was a skill that stood him well throughout his life. In the mid-nineteenth century, smoking cigars became immensely popular among men. Cigar manufacturing was a growth industry in New Orleans, with 171 men identified as cigar makers in 1860 and 534 in 1880.[31] Numa was able to provide for his family, although the 1880 Census notes that he was unemployed for four months that year. He and Louise continued to have children, eight in all, some of whom were of the right age to take advantage of integrated public education during Reconstruction. Life looked promising for this branch of the Durel family, but it did not last. In many ways, the children faced greater obstacles than did their parents. Their story continues in Chapter 6.

=== Forester Durel and Caroline Duchamp ===

In 1873, eight years after the end of the Civil War, Forester Durel wrote in French to his fellow Creoles:

> The time has come to indicate what the sons of Louisiana want—that one must be either WHITE or BLACK, that each person must decide for himself. There are two races here: one superior, the other inferior. . . . Their separation is absolutely necessary. So let us

separate ourselves as of today into two distinct parties, the White Party and the Black Party.[32]

Forester was reacting to the political situation at that time. A year earlier, the Republican Party split into two factions, and Democrats, seeing an opening, countered with a Fusion ticket, a fragile coalition with moderate Republicans. They presented a platform of racial moderation, acknowledging the right to vote for Black people but urging caution regarding the integration of schools and public transportation. They hoped to attract some Black voters while keeping a large base of White support. In the end, the election was marred by widespread corruption—intimidation of would-be voters, stuffed ballot boxes, secret polling places—and was settled only when a federally appointed judge by the name of Edward Durell (no relation) ruled in favor of the Republicans.

Many were dismayed by the continued bloodshed and political polarization. In the summer of 1873, a group of pragmatic capitalists, fifty White and fifty Black, formed a secret "Committee of One-Hundred" and launched a "Unification Movement." They were more concerned about reviving the local economy than they were about issues of race. They wanted a government that focused on support for sugar and cotton production and reestablishing New Orleans as a great trading port. It was an effort to unite the citizens behind moderate leaders who sought racial harmony, economic prosperity, and an end to political corruption. Many of the leaders were Creole, Black and White, who had conducted business with one another before the war and understood instinctively that it was possible to work together.[33]

This was the situation that Forester reacted to. The disputed election of the previous fall had convinced him that moderation and compromise would not work. He felt that things had already gone too far, and that his fellow Creoles needed to choose either the Democrat (White) Party or the Republican (Black) Party. His phrasing, however, reveals a deeper meaning beyond political choice. He wrote that "there are two races here: one superior, the other inferior. . . . Their separation is absolutely necessary." After more than a century in which White and Black Creoles maintained warm and friendly relationships, he was now calling for complete separation. No longer would there be room for a third category, people of color. Henceforth, anyone of African descent, no matter how much European ancestry they possessed, would be classified as Black.

Fig. 8: *Pierre Forester Durel* by Clara Monvoisin, c. 1840.
Courtesy of the Louisiana State Museum.

Pierre Joseph Marie Durel, who later adopted the name Forester, had deep roots in Creole culture. He was born around 1819, the only "legitimate" child of Jean Baptiste Durel (3) and Elizabeth de Glapion. His grandmother was Manette Durel, *née* Dejan, whose own grandmother had survived the "Natchez Massacre" (Chapter 2). Like others of his generation, he grew up in a residentially integrated neighborhood. His parents' house was on Dauphine Street, where roughly half the households were White and half free people of color.[34] Nearby, he had White relatives living with free women of color. His father's cousin, Jean Michel Fortier, lived with Henriette Milon around the corner and up a block on Burgundy Street. Another cousin, Jean Florent Durel, lived with Idalise Manadé two blocks in the opposite direction at the corner of Bourbon and St. Ann. His uncle Michel, his father's youngest brother, resided with a woman of color in Faubourg Tremé, as did a free man of color named Jean Baptiste Durel, who may well have been his father's mixed-race son and hence, Forester's half brother (Chapter 3). Forester's life growing up was typical of Creoles of his time, a world in which familial interracial relationships were common and openly acknowledged.

When he was young, Forester went to Paris to study medicine. A miniature of him painted in Paris reveals a poised and precisely groomed man in his early twenties (Figure 8). At the time, French medicine attracted aspiring students and practicing physicians from across the United States. The American medical profession was not yet fully formed, and the French had the best training that could be had. Scholars have described the time from 1830 to 1860 as the French period of American medicine.[35] As a French-speaking Creole, Forester may have taken pride in this.

It was not all study for Forester. While in Paris, he met Caroline Duchamp from New Orleans, who was on an extended stay in Paris with her widowed mother and younger siblings. Her father had died in 1832, leaving her

Fig. 9: *Clarisse and Caroline Duchamp* by Pierre Raymond Jacques Monvoisin, 1840. Courtesy of the Louisiana State Museum.

mother with several investment properties, business assets, and five minor children to raise. In 1838, after selling some properties, her mother took the children to Paris in order to give them an "education which their best interests require."[36] While there, Caroline and her sister, Clarisse, had their portraits painted by the Parisian artist, Raymond Monvoisin (Figure 9).

Caroline, on the right, was sixteen years old at the time. Clarisse was fifteen. It is a striking pose of two young ladies in white dresses, seated against a dark brown background, their hands intertwined. Their hair is dark, their eyebrows full, and their white skin glows with a rosy tinge. The artist captured their budding beauty, especially that of Caroline. This is the way she looked when Forester first met her, and soon they were courting.

Caroline sailed back to New Orleans with her family in January 1841.[37] The courtship continued through correspondence, and by early 1843 she was back in Paris. That April, she and Forester wed in the church of St. Thomas Aquinas on Rue de Montalembert, in the university district on the Left Bank of the Seine River.[38] They remained in Paris for two more years while Forester completed his studies. Caroline gave birth to their first child in 1844, and the young family returned to New Orleans in March 1845.[39] They moved into his parents' house, and Forester opened a doctor's office in the same building on Bourbon Street where his father ran his mercantile business.[40]

Forester was soon in a position to enlarge the house on Dauphine Street to accommodate his growing family. In 1849, his parents gave him the house, in recognition of the improvements he had made at his own expense.[41] The money may have come from his wife's inheritance, which she would have received when she married. By 1850, the household consisted of Forester and Caroline, his parents, four children, and old Lanu, an enslaved man from Africa, who by then was in his nineties.[42]

Things began to change for Forester in the 1850s. Politically, this was a decade marked by both the rise of anti-immigrant sentiment and the curtailment of the rights of free people of color. Perhaps more relevant for Forester were the epidemics of yellow fever that plagued the city every summer, especially in 1853 when more than seven thousand people died. At that time, in addition to his private practice, he was an administrator at Charity Hospital and on the front line of battling the disease.[43] In 1854, he seized an opportunity to sell his house in the city and relocate his family to the Lapice plantation on the west bank of the river in St. James Parish, where he set up practice to care for the planter's family and his enslaved workers. In the 1860 Census,

Forester's family is listed in a house standing between the dwellings of the plantation manager and overseer.[44]

This living arrangement came to an abrupt end when the Civil War broke out in 1861. Caroline took their children back to New Orleans and moved in with her mother, who still lived in the house on Toulouse Street where Caroline had grown up.[45] Forester went to war, commissioned as a surgeon in the Confederate Army. He spent the next four years caring for the sick and wounded on the battlefield.[46]

Following the war, Forester returned to New Orleans much disillusioned. He joined his family in the Duchamp house on Toulouse Street and opened a medical practice.[47] But his heart was not in it. With dismay, he watched the political turmoil playing out as Black and White leaders vied for power. Initially, he observed from the sideline, but in September 1869, he decided to join the fray. His weapon of choice was neither the gun nor the ballot box. Instead, he picked up a pen and began to publish a weekly paper called *Le Carillon*, meaning "The Alarm Bell." In its pages, he used satire and caustic wit to alert his fellow French-speaking Creoles to what he saw as the danger of the current state of affairs. He targeted Black politicians and, in so doing, revealed a deeply held racism at odds with the views of his Creole ancestors. [48]

Forester was an intelligent and educated man. It is clear from his writing that he was familiar with the work of race theorists, most notably Josiah Nott, a medical doctor from Alabama. It is possible that the two men knew each other personally, since each had served as a surgeon in the Confederate Army. Fifteen years older, Nott was already well known before the war. He had received a medical degree from the University of Pennsylvania, followed by the expected further study in Paris, and then settled in Mobile, where he became a leading citizen and founded the Medical College of Alabama in 1859. However, he was best known for his views on race.

As mentioned in the prologue, Johann Friedrich Blumenbach had constructed a racial hierarchy that placed White people at the top and Black people at the bottom in 1795. Others did the same, always placing people like themselves at the top. They began to elaborate on the characteristics of White people, deeming them superior in a surprising number of ways. White men were more intelligent, civilized, courageous, heroic, manly, honorable, just, and merciful. White women were more beautiful, pure, virtuous, dutiful, and kind. In every favorable way, White Europeans and people of wholly European descent were superior. For some, it was not enough to lump all Whites together. The eighteenth-century German scholar Christoph Meiners placed Germans above all other Europeans and Protestant Germans in the north above Roman Catholic Germans in the south (Austria). The Englishman Thomas Carlyle took his cue from Meiners and extolled the Anglo-Saxons who had settled England from the north of Germany. Carlyle's American colleague, Ralph Waldo Emerson, followed suit and placed Anglo-Saxon "stock" above all other Americans, most notably the Irish, who were Celtic in origin and Catholics to boot. The Catholic, French-speaking Creoles fared little better. "White Anglo-Saxon Protestant" became the American ideal.[49]

Fundamental to this racial thinking was the notion that outward appearance equated to inner qualities. For example, phrenology, the practice of measuring the shape and dimensions of the human skull, was deemed a scientific way to discern a person's character. Not surprisingly, these race theorists claimed that European skulls were most like those of the ancient Greeks, whereas African skulls showed similarities to apes and monkeys. While most American scholars were skeptical of such interpretations, those intent on justifying slavery and White superiority embraced them. Josiah Nott was such a scholar.[50]

In 1844, Nott published "Two Lectures on the Natural History of the Caucasian and Negro Races," in which he purported to prove that the races were in fact different species, created separately by God, and that the Black species was inherently inferior to the White one. Called polygenesis, this theory had been debated for at least sixty years. When Nott presented it in a lecture in New Orleans in 1848, Roman Catholic Creoles in the audience would not have been enthusiastic. They took their religion seriously and believed what the priests taught: all humans descended from Adam and Eve and all had souls. It was for this reason that they had ensured that the Black people they enslaved were baptized. They saw polygenesis as a challenge to their faith.

Nevertheless, there were plenty of apologists in Louisiana who found Nott's ideas useful to bolstering their argument that the two groups were unequal and should be kept separate. Nott wrote against racial mixing on grounds that it would lead to the degradation of the superior White species. He noted the word *mulatto* had the same root as the word *mule*, the infertile offspring of a male donkey and female horse. He alleged that this would be the inevitable result of sexual unions between Black people and White, choosing to ignore the reality of healthy and fertile mixed-race people all around him. This kind of selective argument became the underpinning for laws against miscegenation, a term that first came into usage in the 1860s. It was the basis for the "one drop rule," the notion that even a single drop of African blood would corrupt the character of offspring.

Nott was not alone in promulgating the theory of polygenesis. Harvard professor Louis Agassiz and Agassiz's protégé, Nathaniel Southgate Shaler from Kentucky, gave the theory respectability. At Harvard they taught a generation of future American leaders who, in the late nineteenth and early twentieth centuries, would use assertions of White superiority to justify not only continued suppression of Black people, but also restrictions on immigration from southern and eastern Europe. Long after polygenesis was rejected by American scholars, its lingering influence could be seen in public policy. Indeed, it has yet to fully disappear.

A more immediate impact of Nott's ideas came through Forester's pen. Forester was a clever man, able to use rhyme and wit to get a laugh and make a point. In the following example, he chose the Havana cigar, widely considered to be superior to all others, as a symbol of racial purity. His readers were sure to get it. The French title for the poem is "*Mélange des Races*."

> Whites—they're a real race
> Blacks—they're a real race
> Horses—they're a real race
> Cattle—they're a real race
> Havana cigars—they're a real race;
> But mulattoes—they're no more a race
> Than mules are a race,
> Or mixed cigars are really a race.[51]

For race theorists, keeping the races separated was more than a biological concern—it was also a moral one. For them, just as the shape of one's skull signified intelligence, white skin attested to one's spiritual character. Unblemished pure Whiteness meant an unblemished soul. For women, fair white skin, especially tinged with a little pink on the cheeks, showed a graceful woman. Even better, skin that was slightly transparent, revealing veins of "blue blood," was evidence of noble character. It fell to honorable White men to protect these virtuous White women from violation by Black men.[52] It is worth noting that in her teenage portrait, Forester's wife, Caroline, has the appearance of an unblemished, wholesome girl (Figure 9). That she and her sister are portrayed in modest, white dresses adds to the sensation of innocence. This idealized, romanticized view of young women fed what became an obsession among racists, the irrational belief that Black men preyed on White women.

It is no coincidence that in 1867, when White supremacist Alcibiades DeBlanc created an organization to intimidate Black people, he chose the name "Knights of the White Camellia." He and his followers envisioned themselves like knights of old, pledging fealty, in their case not to a nobleman or monarch, but to the White race. Theirs was a moral crusade to uphold racial purity. They vowed to protect the race "from amalgamation and miscegenation and other degradations."[53] Their romantic views had real-world consequences, for like the better-known Knights of the Ku Klux Klan, they rode at night to intimidate, assault, and even murder Black men.

In the pages of *Le Carillon*, Forester's favorite target was Caesar Antoine, a Black Creole who served as lieutenant governor from May 1873 to April 1877. He routinely described Antoine as a creature of another species. In one piece alone he called him an "orangutan," a "monkey," a "noxious beast," a "biped," and a "being of this species." At one point he referenced "the narrow skull of a baboon."[54] Antoine was a successful barber, an occupation that brought him into frequent contact with both Black and White businessmen before the war.[55] He joined the Republican Party to fight for universal suffrage, was a delegate to the 1868 constitutional convention, served in the state senate from 1868 to 1872, and then as lieutenant governor.

Forester's writing in *Le Carillon* helped to popularize stereotypes of Black people as ape-like in appearance, incapable of doing more than the most menial work, and driven by sexual desire. His use of satire and humor made these characterizations seem funny and harmless; he could claim that he was only kidding, just having a bit of fun. Racists still use these images. I recall seeing a picture of a grinning White college student holding a photograph in which President Barak Obama's face was superimposed on the body of a monkey. He may have thought of that as just a joke, but his action was rooted in stereotypes and prejudices that have caused real harm to people of African descent for more than two centuries.

In 1874, the racial violence that had plagued New Orleans politics since the end of the Civil War erupted into full-fledged warfare on the streets of the city. What had been intimidation and murder of Black men by small bands of White men gave way to organized military action on a far larger scale. Conservative White leaders had given up on attempts to regain power through the ballot box and instead recruited working men to create a trained military force called the Crescent City White League, with the intent of overthrowing the Republican government.[56] They professed this in moral terms: the *redemption* of Louisiana for the White race.

That summer, White supremacists spread false rumors of an imminent attack on the city by a so-called Black League, claiming that Black men intended to kill "as many white men as possible . . . and *keep all the women*."[57] Whites who believed the stereotype of Black men as sexual predators were alarmed and flocked to join. The league's leaders, for the most part, had battle experience from their time in the Confederate Army. Most of the recruits were men too young to have served in the war and this was their chance at glory. (Among them was a Durel descendant, eighteen-year-old Alcée Fortier, whose story appears in the next chapter.)[58]

The battle came on September 14. The White League set up barricades along Poydras Street and gathered its forces in the vicinity of Tivoli Circle.[59] The Republican-controlled state militia and metropolitan police set up a line of defense at the foot of Canal Street. Federal troops stationed downriver at Chalmette were not available to help since most had been sent away to avoid yellow fever. At midafternoon, league forces advanced along the levee and down Tchoupitoulas Street, where the battle commenced. Within twenty minutes, it became a rout, as league forces quickly overwhelmed the police. Although federal troops returned and retook the city four days later, the league had made its point. It had killed no Black civilians and presented itself to the nation as a legitimate organization with a justified concern. By then, the national mood was shifting away from the initial postwar enthusiasm for Reconstruction. The league's leaders, instead of being prosecuted as rebels, were deemed saviors of the White race. Their victory was dubbed the "Battle of Liberty Place."[60]

The following presidential election of 1876 resulted in disputed returns from Louisiana, South Carolina, and Florida. In a compromise, Democrats agreed to hand the presidency to the Republican candidate, Rutherford B. Hayes, in exchange for the removal of federal troops from the South and increased federal spending for transportation and other improvements in the three disputed states. This marked the end of Reconstruction. Violent resistance had won the day. Almost immediately, White supremacists took control of government in Louisiana.

Forester died in early summer 1875.[61] He did not live to see his state "redeemed" for the White race. But he had made an impact. Over the next two decades, the 1880s and '90s, White Creoles heeded his call for the absolute separation of the races. They separated themselves from their Black Creole friends and relatives. By the end of the century, White Durel descendants—the fifth generation—denied that close relationships with Black people had ever existed.

In preparing for this chapter, I chose to write about Henry Durel because his name kept appearing in newspapers in the late 1850s and early 1860s, advertising the capture of enslaved people who had escaped from their enslavers. I had a hunch that this ordinary clerk with such an unusual task would lead me to insights about New Orleans on the eve of the Civil War. Little did I suspect that I would discover, in the life of his father, a dimension of slavery that I find especially abhorrent. Up to this point, I had simply accepted the fact that members of my family had enslaved Black people, whipped them, and worse, and that some had, in all likelihood, raped vulnerable Black women. I attributed their actions to the racist and sexist systems of the times in which they lived. I went along with the comforting notion that even good people do harm when immersed in a culture that condoned such behavior. But what the story of Henry's father, Ursin (2), revealed to me is a deeper truth, that in an evil system, some people can be exceptionally evil.

Ursin (2) was my third great-grandfather. As I came to realize that I descend directly from a man who held four women in captivity for two decades or more, for the sole purpose of getting them pregnant and selling their children, I found myself getting angry. I came to see him as a callous man, living off the harm he inflicted on these women and their children. City directories suggest that although he started out as a cabinetmaker, he eventually had no gainful employment and lived off proceeds from his property. His income seems to have been meager, to the point where he failed to keep his own house in good repair. He comes across as a man who took the easy way, enjoying the benefits of being White without meeting his basic responsibilities as a husband and father. I may be wrong, but I can think of no other way to read the evidence.

When I turned to the story of Forester Durel, my anger returned. I was incensed by his use of racist stereotypes, under the guise of satire, for I grew up at a time when those stereotypes were common, and I know the harm they did. To this point, of all the family members I had studied and written about, he was the first to not only go along with racism, but to actively promote it. Indeed, his dictum that the races needed to be separated foretold the racist, segregated world in which I lived. I have come to resent the White men who created segregation and the adults of my youth who through their own words and behavior led me to believe that although I was to be kind and compassionate, it was not my responsibility to challenge the system. I had to go along with it, as my ancestors had always done.

This chapter marked a turning point for me. In Chapter 3, I had discovered White Durel descendants who had lasting, warm relationships with free people of color, for whom racial differences were less important than family ties. They showed me that another path forward was possible, that segregation was not inevitable. But when Reconstruction ended, White supremacists like Forester had the upper hand. Forester's elderly cousin, Jean Florent Durel, who still lived in exile in Paris with his wife, Idalise, had become irrelevant.

Table X.
Genealogical Reference Chart for Delphine Fortier and Alcée Fortier

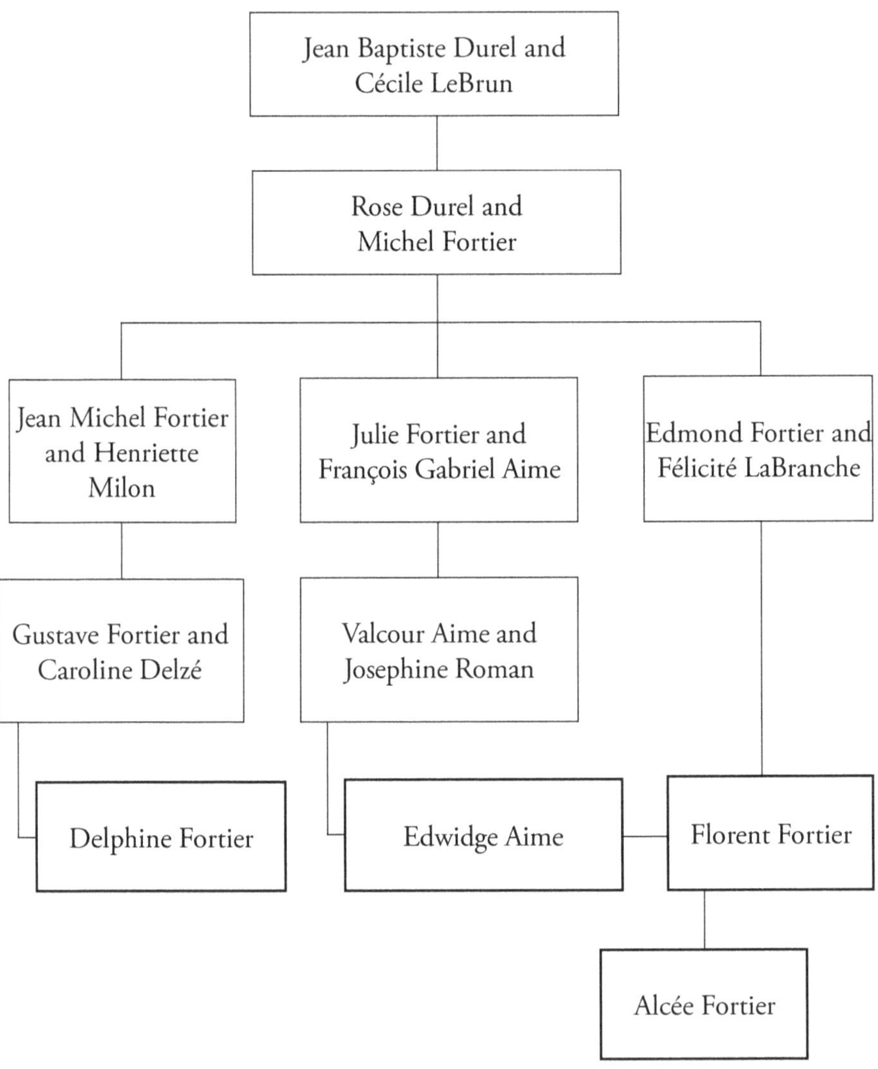

Chapter 5

The Divided Generation

In the final decades of the nineteenth century, states across the South, including Louisiana, were once again under White control and began creating a new racial order, which eventually would become known as Jim Crow. Henceforth, Louisiana would be segregated, by law and by custom, with a strong "color line" dividing people into two races: Black and White. In the new order, there would no longer be a middle ground for people of mixed European-African ancestry. One drop of African blood placed an individual on the Black side of the color line.

The change did not occur overnight. The price of returning to the Union after the Civil War was a pledge of allegiance to the United States and its constitution, including three new amendments: the Thirteenth, which abolished slavery; the Fourteenth, which gave all people born in the United States citizenship and equal protection under the laws; and the Fifteenth, which guaranteed all male citizens the right to vote. Southern Whites reluctantly accepted the Thirteenth as the price of defeat on the battlefield. For the other two, legislatures sought ways to separate Black people and White without incurring constitutional challenges. Through the 1880s and '90s, White leaders chipped away at Reconstruction-era gains for African Americans and resegregated public spaces and institutions, including schools, theaters, streetcars, and hotels.

Louisiana became obsessed with racial identity and blood purity, putting White Creoles in an awkward position. Northerners viewed Creoles as an exotic people who spoke a foreign language and practiced unusual customs, and for whom racial identity could be suspect. In the new order, White Creoles felt compelled to assert their Whiteness and emphasize their commitment to White supremacy. Meanwhile, Black Creoles found themselves lumped together with all people of African descent. Some objected, having long considered themselves superior because of their French heritage and light skin. Others, however, embraced the opportunity to become leaders of the Black community and were in the forefront of pushing back against what one described as "a government determined to develop and establish a system by which a portion of the people would have to submit to the rest."[1]

This chapter highlights the lives of two Durel descendants who lived through this period of divergence. Alcée Fortier, a professor at Tulane, became a leading voice in ensuring that Creoles of wholly European descent were defined as White. Delphine Fortier, an impoverished Black seamstress, late in life found herself in a court battle for her inheritance. They were second cousins, each descended from Rose Durel and Michel Fortier (Chapter 2). Their respective stories, told together, bring into sharp relief differences in lives and fortunes due solely to racial identity.

Their stories begin where the story of Jean Michel Fortier and Henriette Milon ended in Chapter 3. When Jean Michel died, his natural children received no inheritance because their mother, Henriette, was a free woman of color. Instead, his considerable wealth was divided among his "legitimate" heirs: his brother, Edmond, and three nephews, Michel and Valcour Aime and Adelard Fortier. Professor Alcée Fortier descended on his father's side from Edmond and on his mother's side from Valcour. He benefited from the transfer of generational wealth. Delphine Fortier, the seamstress, was a granddaughter of Jean Michel and Henriette. The property she went to court to claim (when she was a grandmother herself) was the house on Burgundy Street that her own grandmother had bought back from Jean Michel's heirs in 1836.

=== Alcée Fortier, *White* ===

Alcée Fortier was born in 1856 on the Valcour Aime plantation and liked to call himself a child of the Civil War. One of his earliest memories was huddling in the lee of the levee with his sisters and the enslaved women who cared for them as Union gunboats on the river fired over their heads. The shots never hit the big house, but there were plenty of cannonballs scattered about the fields to excite a boy of six or seven. His childhood was also marked by loss: his older brother, Louis, a private in the Confederate Army, succumbed to illness marching home at the end of the war, and both his grandfather, Valcour, and his mother, Edwidge, died two years later.[2] They had lived just long enough to see their world turned upside down. For decades, they had lived in comfort and extravagance; the war brought financial ruin.

Fig. 10: *Alcée Fortier* (1856–1914). Louisiana State Archives. Public Domain.

At least, that is the way Alcée described it as an adult. He was fond of saying that he and others of his generation had pulled themselves up by their own accord after the war:

> Ruined by war, accustomed to luxury. . . . Some took to the plow handle, some the pen of the clerk, some studied law, medicine or engineering, while others sat in the professor's chair. They are not rich, but have kept intact the honor and name of their fathers and they are earning their bread by the sweat of their brows.[3]

His family was not so destitute that he could not attend a private high school in New Orleans after the war, where he observed firsthand the volatile politics of Reconstruction. His sympathies lay with the Democrats and in particular with the wealthy planters who considered themselves to be the natural and rightful leaders of Louisiana. At the age of eighteen, he joined the White League and fought to "redeem" Louisiana for the White race.[4]

Alcée proved adept at languages and in the mid-1880s, in his late twenties, he became professor of French language and literature at Tulane University. The timing was fortuitous. By then, Reconstruction had ended and White supremacists had begun the process of imposing the sharp color line that separated people who were "pure" White (those of solely European descent) from anyone who had even a trace of African ancestry. White Creoles feared that other Americans perceived them as foreign, not truly American, and even worse, as not being pure White. They needed to distance themselves from their Black relatives. Alcée's appointment to Tulane set the stage for him to become a leading voice in their defense.

It is likely that Alcée was in the audience that gathered at Tulane on Saturday, April 25, 1885, to hear the elderly Creole historian Charles Gayarré speak.[5] Warming to his topic, Gayarré pronounced that it was "high time to demonstrate that the Creoles of Louisiana . . . have not, because of the name they bear, a particle of African blood in their veins." He told his audience that, based on the best dictionaries produced in Europe, the word *criollo* in Spanish, and *creole* in French, had originally been used only for the children of European settlers. In fact, he said, "to be a *criollo* was to possess a sort of title of honor—a title which could only be the birthright of the superior white race." He said that over time the word was naturally extended to delineate things produced in the colony—creole horses, creole cattle, creole corn, and so forth—and so it was applied to the offspring of "imported Africans." His argument was etymological, not historical. That is, Creoles could not have African ancestry because anyone with African ancestry could not, by definition, be a Creole. It was a clever strategy that enabled him and his listeners to ignore the fact that, for generations, their forebears had acknowledged openly their mixed-race relatives as fellow Creoles.

Gayarré's adversary was George Washington Cable. A White New Orleans native, but not Creole, Cable had begun publishing short stories about Creole life in *Scribner's Monthly*, a magazine produced in New York City with a national readership. The popularity of his stories led to the publication of *Old Creole Days* (1879), followed quickly by *The Grandissimes: A Story of Creole Life* (1880), and *Madame Delphine* (1881). Cable became a rapidly rising star in the American literary world, and his stories introduced the Creoles to a wide American public.[6]

In his stories, Cable accentuated the Creoles' use of the French language and gave his less educated characters a kind of Creole dialect, translated into English.[7] He described the quaint streets and architecture of the old French Quarter and the tropical-like climate of New Orleans, all of which his northern readers found exotic and picturesque. He also emphasized the openness with which White Creoles acknowledged their Black relations. One story tells of two half brothers, sons of the same White father, a prominent and respectable Creole merchant. The older brother was born to a free woman of color, the younger to the man's White wife. Not only does the father acknowledge both sons, but he also sends them to school in Paris. The brothers become close and in one intimate conversation the older one says, "You are the lawful son . . . I had no right to be born," to which the younger responded, "By the laws of men, it may be so; but by the law of God's justice, you are the lawful son, and it is I who should not have been born."[8]

Gayarré found this story preposterous and dangerous, for it indicted the entire White Creole people. As long as the existence of mixed-race people could be excused as the unfortunate result of a few disreputable White men, then the Creoles, who were by definition pure White, could claim to have God on their side. If, however, man's law contradicted God's law, then the entire social order would be turned upside down. The bastard son would be made legitimate, and by implication the legitimate son would become a bastard. This must have made Gayarré's audience squirm, aware as many surely were of the behavior of their own fathers and grandfathers in this regard. Cable was attacking the very moral and financial underpinnings of their White identity. This, Gayarré said, was Cable's real purpose. From the podium he used his considerable oratorial skills to belittle the author, calling him at various times a "romancing libeler," a "modern slanderer," and a "literary dime speculator," and describing his work as an "audacious mutilation of what is truth."

Gayarré presented, and White Creoles adopted, a mythical history of their ancestors. According to this myth, they were a people of noble origin and character, a superior people that had always separated themselves from those of African descent and had always condemned anyone who transgressed the color line. They pretended that men who had lifelong unions with women of color, men like Jean Michel Fortier and Jean Florent Durel (Chapter 3), never existed or at least never counted for much. They wiped all mention of such men from their historical accounts. This imposed historical amnesia lasted well into the twentieth century. For example, when

Estelle Fortier Cochran published a detailed genealogy of the Fortier family in the 1960s, she listed Jean Michel simply as "unmarried" without any further description or reference to his mixed-race children, whereas she gave Alcée's grandfathers, Edmond and Valcour, extensive biographical coverage.[9]

———

As a professor of the French language, Alcée conducted field research, which consisted of trips into the Louisiana countryside, visiting rural communities, meeting local inhabitants, recording local customs, and transcribing the way they spoke. He became expert in the use of French among White Creoles, Black Creoles, and Acadians, the other major French-speaking population to settle Louisiana. He noted how striking it was that unlike immigrant groups, whose language disappeared in favor of English after a few generations, the French-speaking people of Louisiana continued to speak their mother tongue for five or six generations after they became American. Louisiana was bilingual during the nineteenth century and into the twentieth. Even in my own youth in the 1940s and '50s I had elderly aunts and uncles who still spoke French at home.[10]

Using his field notes, Alcée wrote and had published two books, *Louisiana Studies,* in 1894, and *Louisiana Folk-Tales* the following year.[11] In the latter, he presented tales he had collected, as he had heard them in French, with an English translation and notes for the benefit of other folklorists who could use them for comparative research. In these published writings, Alcée embraced the White Creole myth. He regularly refers to Whites as people of good quality and Black people as ignorant and benefiting from White tutelage. As for people of mixed African-European ancestry, since their existence could not be denied, he simply did not mention them, or when he did, he did not identify them as such. For example, in *Louisiana Studies* he reviewed literature written in French by local authors, and in the section on poetry included works by several free men of color, including Camille Thierry and "Victor Séjour, whose work 'Le Retour de Napoléon' was favorably received in France." However, he did not identify them as Black, leaving the reader to assume they were White.[12]

Most often Alcée depicted Black people as childlike. He took his own superiority, and that of the White race, for granted and, as these examples show, wrote in a condescending, paternalistic way.

> [The enslaved] were, as a rule, well treated by their masters and, in spite of their slavery, they were contented and happy. Not having any of the responsibilities of life, they were less serious than the present freedman, and more inclined to take advantage of all opportunities to amuse themselves.
>
> —*Louisiana Studies*, 125.

> While reading these [folk tales], one must bear in mind that most of them were related to children by childlike people; this accounts for their *naïveté*. . . .
>
> It is interesting to note what changes have been made in some well-known tales by a race rude and ignorant, but not devoid of imagination and poetical feeling. . . .
>
> It is curious to see how the ignorant African slave transformed his master's language into a speech concise and simple, and at the same time soft and musical. . . .
>
> —*Louisiana Folk-Tales,* Introduction to the 1895 Edition.

From his lofty perch, Alcée failed to comprehend the true nature of the people he thought he knew so well. He found it "a strange fact that the old negroes do not like to relate those tales with which they enchanted their little masters before the war."[13] It never occurred to him that they shared these stories under duress. He did not comprehend that Black people owned these stories, that they had received them through a long oral tradition that came with their people from West Africa. Barred from learning to read and write, this was a way that they preserved their history and culture and recorded their experiences in America. Some stories they never told Whites, and those that they did share often had double or hidden meanings. It is no accident that so many of the tales Alcée recorded were about a smaller, trickster animal outwitting a larger, more powerful one.

Through his publications, Alcée established himself as a respected scholar and a recognized expert on Creole culture and Louisiana history. Following in the footsteps of the elderly Gayarré, he continued the defense of White Creoles against their critics. In an address to teachers at the ninth annual meeting of the Louisiana Educational Association in 1892, he stated:

> I know that all Louisianians are brothers, whether they be of Anglo-Saxon or of French descent and the Creoles wish to be nothing more than Louisianians, than Americans. . . . Because they wish to keep at the family hearth the French language, the beautiful speech of their fathers, they are not, I repeat it here, any less patriotic than other Louisianians.[14]

Alcée went on to describe his Creole forebears as pioneers, not unlike the Pilgrim fathers of New England and the Knickerbockers of New Amsterdam. They had "cleared the land by cutting down the primeval forests" and "curbed, by strong dykes, the devastating power of the greatest of rivers," and "fought and repulsed the Indians." Although some "descended from the best nobility in France," many more traced their lineage "to that excellent middle class, *la bourgeoisie.*" He made no mention of slavery. In short, he depicted White Creoles as typical, hard-working, freedom-loving Americans.

The state superintendent of public education thought so highly of Alcée's talk that he decided to have it printed and distributed to teachers around Louisiana, with the intent that it would "induce some to strive to perpetuate the memory of the State's founders in the public schools as a means of instilling patriotic ideals into the minds of the children."

In 1895, Alcée became president of the Louisiana Historical Society and in that position wrote a four-volume *History of Louisiana* to coincide with the centennial of the Louisiana Purchase in 1903. Again, his writing betrays an assumption of White superiority and Black ignorance. The following passage, which refers to the riot of 1866, in which Whites killed thirty-seven Black men, is typical of his preconceptions:

> It is impossible to excuse, in any way, the killing the negroes on July 30, in New Orleans; but we can understand the feelings of the men of 1866 with regards to the conventionists, whose purpose was to enslave the majority of the honorable white population, and to give political power to ignorant negroes.[15]

As an apologist for White supremacy, Alcée helped to establish the narrative of the Lost Cause, which stated that slavery was a benign institution that benefited Black people and that the Civil War was about a noble people defending their homeland and agrarian way of life against Northern aggression. Notably, the *New York Times* gave Alcée's history a glowing review:

> Patient, critical examination and intelligent study may cause it to take its place among the great sectional histories of this country. . . . Prof. Fortier has given a splendid narrative of episodes, graphic, well balanced, and of dramatic conclusions . . . [marking] an event in the book year, if not an epoch-making work in the writing of history.[16]

In the first decade of the twentieth century, the principle of White supremacy in the South became accepted in the North. Alcée was celebrated as an authority on Louisiana history and his version of past events and persons became standard. This was the history that entered into my school textbooks, ensuring that I and other White children learned about the past in a way that justified the segregated world in which we lived.

White Creoles succeeded in separating themselves from their Black relations by choosing racial purity over common heritage. Early in the nineteenth century, both Black and White Creoles took pride in the fact that they were born and raised in Louisiana, shared the Roman Catholic faith, and spoke the French language. By the end of the century, what they once shared became less important than skin color. Although Alcée, and many others, promoted the continued use of French in everyday discourse, the use of English spread. With each new generation, fewer and fewer people of Creole descent spoke the language that had once bonded their forebears and set them apart from non-Creoles.

Likewise, the Catholic faith began to separate White Creoles from Black. The local parish church had once been a place where Black and White Creoles freely mixed. For example, in St. Augustine Church, which opened in Tremé in 1841, wealthy free persons of color occupied the most prominent pews alongside wealthy Whites. The only discrimination was that enslaved people were required to sit in smaller pews in the side aisles. As late as 1874, a newcomer was surprised to see "lips of every shade, by hundreds press with devout kisses the same crucifixes, and fingers of as great variety in color, are dipped in the 'holy water.'"[17] However, small acts of prejudice began to appear, as when an 1875 visitor observed a priest in St. Louis Cathedral refusing to give communion to a Black soldier. White Creole Catholics were not immune to the racism sweeping the city. Some White laity began to complain that priests spent too much time ministering to Black people. Some wanted the children separated by race, with White children receiving religious instruction, first communion, and confirmation first, followed by Black children. By the late 1880s, even the Holy Family sisters, a religious order founded by free Creole women of color, were assigned a pew at the rear of the cathedral, at the behest of White nuns who continued to sit up front.[18]

The process of separating Black from White altered the meaning of the word *Creole*. In the new racial order, to be Creole meant something very different on either side of the color line. Following Gayarré's etymological argument, Whites succeeded in making their definition the official one. The following quote is taken from the 1927 city directory, in a section in the front designed to give visitors and newcomers an introduction to the city's history:

> CREOLES. Creoles are the white descendants of Spanish and French colonists. There are no negro Creoles, but there are Creole negroes who belonged to Creole families, just as there were Creole horses, or eggs or corn.
>
> The Creoles love home life, reverence women for whom they used to fight duels, and have many of the finest qualities. Creole slaves spoke a dialect related to French about as the negro dialect is to English. The "Vieux Carré" was the Creole part of the city.[19]

New Orleans had begun to promote itself as a tourist attraction in the 1880s. Promoters started referring to the oldest part of the city as the *Vieux Carré*, a French phrase meaning the "Old Square," thereby giving the place an old-world European charm. The word *Creole* became a marketing tool for historic landmarks, houses, plantations, restaurants, and food. There were creole pralines, gumbo, jambalaya, coffee, cocktails, and even toothpaste.[20]

By the twentieth century, Whites were more likely to think of their ancestors as having *been* Creole, rather than themselves as *being* Creole. As they intermarried with other White demographic groups, their Creole ancestry became one among many. Creole identity became a historical detail, not a living phenomenon. Some, of course, continued to tout their Creole lineage, often involving themselves in genealogy and historic preservation, just as New Englanders delved into their Anglo-Saxon origins.

For Black Creoles, the story was very different. Black historian Alice Moore Dunbar-Nelson, writing in the second issue of the *Journal of Negro History* (1916), put it this way:

> The Caucasian will shudder with horror at the idea of including a person of color in the definition, and the person of color will retort with his definition that a Creole is a native of Louisiana, in whose blood runs mixed strains of everything . . . with the African strain slightly apparent. The true Creole is like the famous gumbo of the state, a little bit of everything, making a whole, delightfully flavored, quite distinctive, and wholly unique.[21]

Black Creoles looked to their history for inspiration. Rodolphe Desdunes, whose parents had come to New Orleans as free people of color following the Haitian Revolution, published *Nos Hommes et Notre Histoire* (*Our People and Our History*), in which he profiled poets, musicians, politicians, soldiers, businessmen, and philanthropists.[22] He and others like him saw themselves as heirs to a great tradition of accomplishment and leadership in the Black community. It was they who organized the fight against the segregation that was being imposed on their people by White supremacists in the 1890s. Desdunes was a founding member of the *Comité des Citoyens* (Citizen's Committee), which sent Homer Plessy to take a seat in a Whites-only railroad car. Because of his light complexation, Plessy went unnoticed even when he gave his ticket to the conductor. However, as soon as the conductor punched the ticket, he identified himself as a Black man and refused to move until he was arrested. Found guilty in a Louisiana court, he appealed to the US Supreme Court, which, in the landmark case *Plessy v. Ferguson*, ruled that racial segregation was constitutional under the pretense of providing "separate but equal" facilities and services.[23]

In his history of Louisiana, Alcée did not mention the Supreme Court's decision. But he did write about a new state constitution adopted in 1898, stating that the articles referring to suffrage were the most important. The new constitution included a section that added a requirement that citizens meet certain educational or property requirements in order to vote but exempted anyone whose father or grandfather had had the right to vote prior to Reconstruction. Alcée explained that "the purpose of this section, known as the 'Grandfather clause' was to allow many honorable and intelligent but illiterate White men to retain the right of suffrage, and the purpose of the educational or property qualifications was to disfranchise the ignorant negroes who had been a menace to the civilization of the State since the adoption of the Fifteenth Amendment to the Constitution of the United States."[24]

Thus, on all fronts, White supremacists were succeeding in separating the races, imposing a new order that brought advantages to White people and disadvantages to Black. Alcée had done his part.

=== Delphine Fortier, *Black* ===

While Alcée Fortier promoted and justified the new racial order, his second cousin, Delphine Fortier, went to court to claim the property on Burgundy Street where her grandparents had lived. There was no prohibition against a Black child inheriting property from a Black parent; only the transfer of wealth from a White parent to a Black child was forbidden. Thus, when her White grandfather, Jean Michel Fortier (Chapter 3) died, his White relatives, two of whom were Alcée's grandfathers, inherited his estate. However, when Delphine's grandmother Henriette Milon, a free woman of color, died in 1838, each of her children received the equivalent of $4,365 (approximately $181,000 in 2024) in credit notes, property shares, and cash. Rosella, the eldest child, inherited the house. She continued to live there with her younger sisters, Henrietta and Angela, and with Delphine's father, Gustave, who was the youngest son.[25]

Gustave was born in 1822 and was sixteen when his mother died. Although he lived at home, he was already in a relationship with Caroline Delzé, a free woman of color who was a few years older than he. Less than a year later, in February 1839, Caroline gave birth to Delphine. He and Caroline did not marry, but their relationship lasted. The 1850 Census has him still residing with his sisters on Burgundy Street while Caroline and

Fig. 11: *Edmond Gustave Fortier* (1822–1862).
Historical Archives of the Supreme Court of Louisiana. Public Domain.

Delphine are listed in a household at another location. Delphine had the surname Fortier, whereas her mother continued to use Delzé.[26]

Gustave used his inheritance to invest in property and set himself up as a shoemaker. By 1860, Gustave, Caroline, and Delphine were living together as a family, all using the last name Fortier. They resided at 223 Dumaine Street, and Gustave had a shoe store at the corner of Dauphine and Bienville.[27] A photograph of him taken around this time (Figure 11) depicts a man of some means, gazing directly at the camera, a gold watch chain draped across his vest. He bears a strong resemblance to his father, Jean Michel Fortier (Figure 5).

In July 1862, Gustave fell seriously ill. Sensing his end was near, he asked for the priest to come to administer the last sacrament. When he came, the priest asked Gustave if he and Caroline had been married in the church, and when Gustave replied they had not, the priest offered to marry them. On his deathbed, with his sisters present, Gustave and Caroline became, legally, husband and wife. The priest also asked if he wished to acknowledge Delphine as his daughter, and he said yes. He died a few days later.[28]

Then came a surprise. Two months after his death, his sisters (Delphine's aunts) filed a petition with the Second District court asking that they be recognized as their brother's legal heirs, arguing that he had never officially declared Delphine to be his daughter in a notarial act or in a record of births or baptisms, as required by law. Delphine, now in her early twenties, countered with her own petition, claiming to be:

> The duly-acknowledged natural child and only surviving legal heir of the late Edmond Gustave Fortier, *f. m. c.* and that her mother, Caroline Delzé, was publicly known as living in a state of concubinage with her father, and residing as such in his house, at the time when petitioner, his child, was conceived, and that petitioner was acknowledged as his child, and called so by her said father in conversation, both in public and in private, and that he caused her to be educated as such.[29]

Yet there was no legally executed record to this effect, and the judge found in favor of Delphine's aunts.

The aunts may have disapproved of their brother's relationship with Caroline Delzé. They were of an old Louisiana Creole family, their ancestry was mostly European, and their skin complexion very light. Caroline's mother, Camile Delzé, was identified in the 1850 Census as having been born in the West Indies. She may have come to New Orleans as an adolescent girl in the wave of refugees that arrived in 1809 after being expelled from Cuba. Delphine's aunts grew up in the 1810s and '20s, when women like Camile were viewed as outsiders and stereotyped as licentious.[30] The aunts may have harbored such feelings and projected the stereotype onto Caroline. Also, it appears that at the time of their brother's death, they were in the process of transitioning to living as White. Although they were described as mulatto in the 1860 Census, in both 1870 and 1880 they were listed as White.[31] Their consciousness of color may have added to their disapproval of Caroline and Delphine, whose complexions may have been darker than theirs. Whatever their motivation, Delphine's aunts succeeded in taking Gustave's property as their own.

No doubt embittered by the experience, Delphine and her mother moved on. The Civil War raged, and New Orleans fell into the hands of the Union Army. Accustomed to a degree of security and comfort when Gustave was alive, they now faced a rapidly changing, socially chaotic, and often violent city. Around 1864, Delphine began a relationship with a man named John Jourdain, with whom she had five children. He evidently died in the late 1870s, following the birth of the last child and before the 1880 Census, in which Delphine identified herself as a widow. At that time, she used his surname, worked as a seamstress, and resided with her children in half of a double house on Laharpe Street that her mother rented.[32]

Meanwhile, Delphine's aunts continued to live in the house on Burgundy. The only one to marry was Angela, the youngest, but she and her husband had no children. By the 1890s, the others had died, and Angela lived alone, an elderly widow in her late sixties. Following her death in 1896, Orleans Parish took possession of her property under the assumption that she had no living heirs.

Delphine had been estranged from Angela for decades and was probably unaware of her passing. She must have been surprised when a White lawyer named Gustave Soniat contacted her. Soniat had researched the property records and tracked down Delphine, who was by then a grandmother and living with one of her married daughters. Soniat convinced her to sue the parish and in May 1898, he filed a petition on her behalf in the civil district court in New Orleans claiming her aunt's estate, which included, in addition to the house on Burgundy, three other properties in the old French section and seven more in Tremé.[33]

With the lawyer's help, Delphine was better prepared to contest her inheritance than she had been immediately following her father's death. The trial played out over the summer and fall of 1898. The court arranged to have Angela's personal belongings inventoried, the eleven properties appraised, a privy vault for one property in Tremé emptied, mislaid stock certificates duplicated, and property taxes paid. The trial date was postponed twice and finally set for November. Soniat called several witnesses, who were in their seventies and eighties, to testify. One eighty-four-year-old woman stated:

> I visited the house one or two days after the birth of Delphine, when Caroline Delzay [*sic*] was in bed, confined for Delphine. Gustave Fortier presented me to Delphine as his daughter, a day or two after the birth of Delphine. He always treated Delphine as his daughter, and played with her and nursed her as an affectionate father, and told her that Delphine was his only child.

Another woman, a hairdresser who "belonged to Madam Rosella" testified that she had been present at the deathbed marriage of Delphine's parents. Another said that Gustave often visited his sisters with his daughter and that they referred to her as their niece. On November 18, 1898, the judge, after "considering the law and the evidence," rendered a judgment in favor of Delphine.

Almost immediately, a woman named Estelle Fortier, in the hope of getting a share of the money, challenged the decision. She claimed to be Angela's first cousin by virtue of the fact that her father, Norbert Fortier, had been Jean Michel Fortier's brother. This suit was settled in January 1899, when Soniat produced copies of records that showed that Jean Michel had no such brother.

Then, in what must have seemed to Delphine like yet another attempt to deprive her of her rights, the Louisiana attorney general filed an appeal with the state's supreme court, claiming that "Delphine Fortier was only the illegitimate and unacknowledged child of Edmond Gustave Fortier" and that the district court had made an error in judgment. The attorney general argued that the state should have received the estate for the "benefit of its school fund" (which, incidentally, benefited White children far more than it did Black). This time, the case rested not on proof of Delphine's legitimacy but on whether a natural niece could inherit from a natural aunt. After extensive examination of the evidence, relevant laws, and previous cases, the supreme court justices allowed the lower court's ruling to stand.[34]

The appraised value of the estate came to more than $24,000 ($911,700 in 2024). Three properties were sold in November 1898 to cover court costs of $7,000 ($266,000 in 2024). This left Delphine in possession of real estate, stock certificates, cash, and her aunt's personal effects at a total value of approximately $17,000 (close to $646,000 in 2024 dollars). She had waited a lifetime for this. After decades of laboring as a seamstress, raising her children on her own, and living in rented houses, she finally received her due.

Or did she? In one last, surprising twist to her story, it turns out that Delphine was not Gustave's biological daughter after all. Only recently discovered, there is a record of her birth under the name Delphine Joublanc. The record states that on April 29, 1846, seven years after her birth:

> Gustave Fortier, a proprietor, native of New Orleans, aged twenty-three years & residing on Burgundy Street between St. Ann & Main Streets . . . declared that on the tenth of February eighteen hundred and forty-nine [*sic*] (10th February 1839) at eleven o'clock p.m. was born in a house situated at the corner of Bienville & Marais . . . a female child named Delphine Joublanc, a natural issue of Adolphe Joublanc, a builder native of this city aged about 30 years, with Caroline Delzé a f.w.c. native of New Orleans, aged about thirty years.[35]

Delphine's natural father was Adolphe Joublanc, with whom Caroline may have had only a brief encounter. The fact that it was Gustave and not Joublanc who registered the birth seven years later supports the claim that Gustave took responsibility for Delphine and treated her as his own. Apparently, Delphine was completely unaware of her true origin and grew up believing that Gustave was her father. Indeed, the only people to know the truth may have been Gustave and Caroline. Gustave took the secret to his grave and Caroline kept it in her heart. Had the truth been known to the courts, regardless of Gustave's wishes, Delphine would have inherited nothing.

Evidence is scant as to how Delphine spent her final years, but she and her children certainly did not live extravagantly. She remained in Tremé, where she had lived much of her life, and resided in various rented houses. At one point, she lived with a daughter, at other times she seems to have been on her own. She had four surviving children, all of whom worked for a living: one daughter was a seamstress, another was a presser at a pants factory, one son was a cigarmaker, the other a laborer. None appears to have ever owned a house.[36]

What became of her wealth is a mystery. Since her father's death, Delphine had worked for a living. As a widow, she had earned enough to raise four children, but never enough to purchase her own home. To receive, in one fell swoop, titles to multiple properties and shares of stock may well have bewildered her. In the hands of unscrupulous attorneys or prey to devious con artists, she could easily have been swindled. She was also elderly and may have preferred to sell everything and simply live off the cash. She survived for eighteen years after being awarded her aunt's estate, passing in October 1917 at the advanced age of seventy-eight.[37] One can conceive of her spending the money down year by year, paying rent, buying food, putting something into the collection basket at church, and occasionally helping out one of her children or grandchildren with a little cash. The circumstantial evidence suggests that by the time she died, there was no great sum to distribute among her heirs.

The differences in life and fortune between Alcée Fortier and his cousin Delphine are palpable. To paraphrase George Washington Cable, by man's law each received what they deserved, but by the law of God's justice, Delphine should have enjoyed the same benefits as Alcée: a higher education, a comfortable existence, and recognition as a person of value. Instead, because of her African ancestry, she labored as a seamstress, earned a meager income, and was stereotyped as "ignorant," which was Alcée's favored term when referring to Black people.

These two stories raise the question of reparations, of making amends for the wrongs Black people suffered because of slavery. A common argument against reparations is that no one alive today is responsible for slavery. While that is certainly true, it seems to me that a different question needs to be asked. The issue is not who caused slavery, but who benefited from it. Also, as Delphine's story shows, it was not only slavery that harmed Black people. Even those who were ostensibly free faced discriminatory laws and practices that prevented them from enjoying the full benefits of citizenship.

Two forms of deprivation stand out when contrasting their stories: educational opportunity and intergenerational wealth. With the exception of a brief period during Reconstruction when public schools were integrated, Whites in Louisiana in the nineteenth century had far more opportunities to go to school and receive even a basic education, let alone any sort of advanced learning. As shown in the next chapter, this discrimination continued into the twentieth century, as White supremacists in power deliberately and consistently provided better schools and more funding for White students. Regarding generational wealth, by deeming a union between White and Black parents both immoral and illegal, the state prevented the children of such a union from inheriting wealth from their White parent, and hence, unable to pass that wealth along to their own children. From generation to generation, Whites had an advantage in terms of accumulated wealth and education. The impact of that discrimination lingers in the lives of many Black people today.

Table XI.

Genealogical Reference Chart for the Families of Edward Durel, *Black*, and Walter Durel, *White*. Arrows indicate stories contrasted in the text.

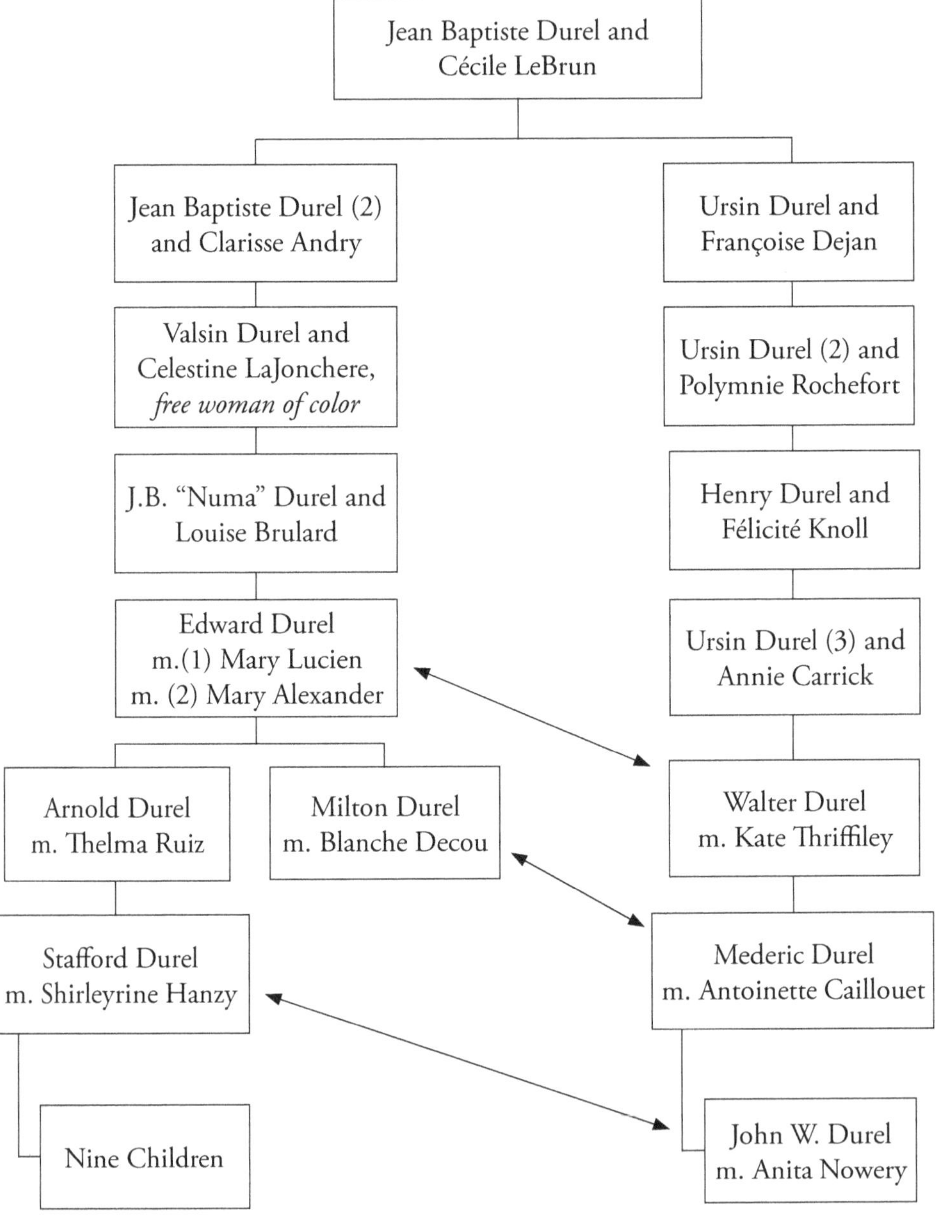

Chapter 6

The Jim Crow Generations: Two Durel Families, One Black and One White

In 1917, a Black Creole man named Edward Durel resided at number 2250 North Johnson Street with his wife, Mary Lucien, three sons, and a daughter. He was forty-three years old, worked as a cooper, and was one of the sons of the Union soldier Numa Durel, discussed in Chapter 4. Just a block farther up the street, at number 2361, lived the family of a White man named Walter Durel. He was thirty-one years old, employed as a bookkeeper, and was a grandson of the Confederate soldier Henry Durel, whose story also appears in Chapter 4. The serendipity of these two Durel-descendant families living on the same street at the same time in the early decades of the Jim Crow era presents an opportunity to examine closely the impact of segregation on either side of the color line.

Edward and Walter lived within sight of each other and in genealogical terms were third cousins, once removed. Yet, in all probability they did not know one another and may not have been aware that they shared the same surname. The section of North Johnson Street where they lived was still unpaved in 1917, part of an expanding city where streets often remained unpaved for years. The area was called St. Roch, named after a cemetery and shrine built there following the 1867 yellow fever epidemic. It was a racially integrated, working-class neighborhood, home to various trades that served or depended upon the port.

In spite of their residential proximity, these two Durel families lived very different lives. In this chapter, I have chosen to link their stories, referencing one another in the text in order to highlight the differences. Also, the stories are personal for me. Walter was my grandfather, and his family included my grandmother, Kate, and my dad, Mederic, who at the time recounted here was nine years old. I never knew my grandfather, who died six years before I was born, nor my father, who passed away when I was only two. I grew up with stories about them, about how my grandfather built the apartment house where my grandmother lived and about when he got sick. A few years before he died, he went into a hospital where my mom was a nurse, and that was how my parents met. I heard about my dad serving in the navy during World War II, and how when he came home, he opened a life insurance office, became president of the father's club at school, and joined the local chapter of the Veterans of Foreign Wars, where he helped to establish an annual citizenship award. Just a few stories, not much to go on as I started my quest to understand their lives. By then, there was no one still alive for me to ask. Their stories, like all that I have written to this point, have depended upon written records.

Note that in the comparisons that follow, the generations are staggered. Edward was the youngest male in his family and was a fifth-generation descendant of Jean Baptiste Durel. Walter, on the other hand, was the oldest male in his family and a sixth-generation descendant (See Table X). Nevertheless, their lives overlapped for forty-four years, the years in which the racist Jim Crow system became firmly established. Similarly, their sons were of different descendant generations but shared a lifetime of events and forces that shaped their respective experiences.

=== Edward, *Black*, and Walter, *White* ===

Edward was a short man with brown complexion and black hair. He was born on October 16, 1874, at a time of cautious hope for Black people in New Orleans.[1] When born, he was the youngest of six boys and a girl, the children of Numa Durel and Louise Brulard. One more child, another daughter, came later. His father was gainfully employed as a cigarmaker, and his mother stayed home to care for the children and the house they owned on North Claiborne Street. Edward grew up speaking French and attending Catholic Mass, probably at Annunciation Church, which served their section of the city. On Sundays, they were accustomed to sitting in pews surrounded by other parishioners, both Black and White. Edward's older siblings had the opportunity to attend a racially integrated school, possibly the Catholic elementary school next door to their church, or perhaps the Marigny School, a public school on nearby Marigny Street.

Indeed, New Orleans public schools had a stellar reputation before the Civil War, at least for White students. New Englanders who migrated to the city brought with them a strong tradition of public education, and by the

1840s the American section of the city had a tax-supported (albeit Whites-only) system of public schools based on the Massachusetts model created by the noted education reformer Horace Mann.[2] White Creoles, for their part, were slow to adopt public schools. Traditionally, they provided education for their children through Catholic academies and small, independently operated private schools. The very wealthy hired private tutors or sent their sons to school in France. Only when Creoles became a minority in the city did they adapt to the American approach.

Free people of color, whether Creole or not, were left out of public education altogether, in spite of the fact that their taxes supported the schools. Instead, they engaged individual adults who taught basic literacy in their homes, and the very few who could afford it sent their sons to France. Notably, in 1837, Marie Couvent, a wealthy free woman of color, bequeathed to the Catholic Church a sum of money for the creation of a school for impoverished children of color. It opened in 1841 with an independent board of governors, faculty, and staff—all Black.[3]

During Reconstruction, a new state constitution called for the racial integration of public schools statewide, although it took two years and a court order for New Orleans to comply. Nevertheless, from 1870 to 1877, New Orleans had integrated public schools. Enrollment dropped initially as some White parents, but not all, removed their children, and Black parents, for the first time, had the ability to register theirs. Within three years, enrollment surpassed prewar levels as many Whites reenrolled their children because of the high cost of private schools and the superior quality of education in the public system.[4]

Black people had good reason to be cautious about such progress. As described in Chapter 4, White supremacists used violence repeatedly to resist racial integration and equality. In yet another example, in 1874, "white high school boys, cheered on by the newspapers, raced through the integrated schools of the city, intimidating teachers and physically evicting Black children."[5] They smashed windows and only when they killed a Black man and child did their adult backers call for an end to the rampage.

White supremacists regained control of state and local government in 1877 and set about dismantling integration. In 1874, the year of Edward's birth, the state had seventy-one integrated public schools. Fifteen years later, that number had shrunk to fifty-six schools, of which forty-five were for White children and eleven for Black students. Over the same period, the number of private and parochial schools doubled from seventy-four to 148.[6]

Not only were the schools resegregated, but the state also cut funding by 40 percent. The New Orleans school board closed some schools, deferred maintenance on others, laid off a number of teachers, and reduced the salaries of the rest. The school superintendent, who had spent his career promoting public education, resigned. Many good teachers chose to leave and take jobs in private schools. The public school system was a mess. That it survived at all was due in large part to mostly female teachers who continued to work for lower wages.[7]

When it was time for Edward to begin school, his parents had to choose between the severely underfunded Marigny School, which was designated for Black children, or the Annunciation parochial school, where discrimination against Black families was beginning to emerge. In either case, Edward likely left school after—perhaps even before—eighth grade, the limit of formal schooling for most Black youth. Only very wealthy Black families could afford more.

Whereas Edward spent his formative years coping with the impact of legislated racial discrimination, Walter's childhood experiences were markedly different. Born in 1886 and christened John Walter Durel, he went by Walter (I was named in his memory). He was the third child and eldest son of John Ursin Durel (3) and Annie Carrick, whose parents had come to New Orleans from Ireland. Irish immigrants had first arrived in numbers in New Orleans in the 1840s and '50s, at the time of the Great Famine. By the 1880s, they had begun to gain a foothold in the economic, political, and cultural life of the city. That they were White no doubt made a difference at a time when the government was fixated on race. Although his father was Creole, Walter was raised among his mother's people, the working-class Irish Americans who made a home for themselves in the suburbs of Marigny and Bywater, just downriver from the old French Quarter. Walter's parents moved in with his mother's parents when they first married, and as they raised their children, they remained in the area.

Walter attended McDonogh School No. 3, a segregated, boys-only public school in the neighborhood. Before the Civil War, a planter named John McDonogh bequeathed to the city funds to be used for the education of both White and free Black youth. Hiding the stipulation about Black children, the school board initially used proceeds from the bequest to build four new schools for Whites. During Reconstruction, however, a newly formed, multiracial school board used the fund to build six integrated schools and began the practice of naming them after McDonogh. Then, with resegregation, four of the newer schools were redesignated for White children only. The school board tried to make it five, but Black citizens, who at the time could still vote, pushed back. From then on, none of the eighteen new McDonogh schools built between 1877 and 1889 taught Black students.[8]

In school, Walter had opportunities to develop qualities that would serve him well in life. In sixth grade, he became president of the Hobson Club, a student organization that focused on good citizenship, the kind of activity often found in big city schools with large immigrant populations. Walter's younger brothers were members and his maternal uncle was chairman of a parent's group that supported them.[9] When he was in the eighth grade, Walter was selected as one of two students to represent his school at the annual Founder's Day ceremony, a citywide event organized to honor John McDonogh.[10] Dozens of White children, including Walter, representing nineteen schools lined up to lay flowers at the McDonogh memorial in Lafayette Square. Representatives from two "colored" elementary schools, Marigny and Tomy Lafon (which would be set on fire by a White mob the very next month), also attended.[11]

For Walter, school was a time for building self-confidence and honing leadership skills. He found the same nurturing environment at church. His family belonged to the parish of Saints Peter and Paul, a center of White ethnic life in their part of the city. It had long been standard practice in the Catholic Church to define parish boundaries geographically, and anyone living within the bounds would belong to that parish. This assumed a degree of homogeneity within the bounds, which was generally true before the Civil War. The practice began to change with the arrival of large numbers of immigrants, and some parishes came to be identified by the dominant ethnic group in the immediate area. There were predominantly Irish parishes, as well as German, Italian, and French. By the 1890s, this practice faded as church leaders began to emphasize race over ethnic identity. Saints Peter and Paul's congregation was mostly Irish but welcomed Germans, Italians, and others, so long as they were White. There may have been a few lingering Black families, for segregation had not yet fully taken over.[12]

Walter's family was active in parish affairs. His father served on various committees, including the Benevolent Association, which raised relief funds for poor parish families.[13] One of Walter's older sisters sang in the church choir, and Walter joined the Usher's Society.[14] This was perhaps his first direct encounter with questions about racial identity. The traditional role of an usher was to escort people to their seats. However, by the turn of the twentieth century, the duties included ensuring that Black people who entered sat in designated rows in the rear of the church. This could be a challenge, for the usher had to decide on the spot a person's race. There is an account from another church of an usher who conducted a light-skinned, Black Creole man to a seat midway up the aisle and left his wife standing in the rear. To the usher, the man appeared to be White, "unlike his wife whose facial features were more clearly negroid [*sic*]."[15] Walter might well have found himself in this position, just as Edward at some point in his youth almost certainly witnessed the humiliation of his parents as they were told they could no longer sit with White parishioners and had to move to the back.

White Catholics had first started to complain about the Black people in their parishes in the 1880s. Creole parishes that had long been integrated began to relegate Black parishioners to pews in the rear and prevented them from participating in parish activities. Eventually, over the objection of Black Catholics, the bishop started to create separate Black and White parishes. The story of the opening of St. Dominic's parish in 1909 reveals the methods the bishop used. The uptown parish of Mater Dolorosa had both Black and White congregants. The parish council decided to raise money to build a new church building, larger and more conveniently located, and asked all parishioners to contribute. Then, on the Sunday before the opening of the new facility, Black members were told that they would remain behind to form a new parish in the old church, renamed St. Dominic's. The Black members, who had no say in the matter, complained that "they contributed for the new church and if they knew of the change, they would have kept their money for their church."[16] The bishop arranged for the Josephites, a religious order dedicated to serving the spiritual needs of Black Catholics, to send priests from Baltimore to staff the parish. This enabled him to avoid the controversy that would have arisen by assigning local White priests. To add to the insult, he refused to let Father John Plantevigne, a Black Josephite priest who was Louisiana-born, participate in the opening ceremony.

The segregation of the Catholic archdiocese into Black and White parishes continued as both Walter and Edward became adults and started families. In 1917, when they lived on North Johnson Street, Walter's family joined Our Lady Star of the Sea Church, which they could see from their front porch. True to his leadership style, Walter volunteered and chaired the arrangements committee for the annual parish picnic that year.[17] Edward's family, who had moved to the street a few years earlier, may have initially attended Our Lady's and sat in the rear, but in 1916 a new church opened for Black people on St. Bernard Avenue, about a twenty-minute walk away. It had been twenty years since the first Black parish opened, and although some Black congregants continued to protest and remained in a White church, many had come to accept and even prefer their own churches. Rather than suffer the humiliation of sitting in the back and waiting until Whites had received communion, they favored a church where they were welcomed and could participate fully in parish life.[18]

Racially segregated parishes meant that on Sundays, Black and White children living on the same street belonged to different communities. Edward's son, Milton, went in one direction, Walter's son, Mederic, who was Milton's age, went in another. Church, like school, was one of the institutions that taught them from an early age that they were different.[19]

———

Edward's name first appears in a city directory in 1894, when he was nineteen years old. He is listed as a laborer and living at home with his mother, Louise. His father had died a few years earlier, and Louise still lived in the family's house on Claiborne Street, supplementing her husband's military pension by keeping a few cows and selling milk to her neighbors.[20] Edward's brothers lived nearby and were employed as coopers, a trade open to young Black men coming of age in the 1880s and '90s. Edward soon followed suit and landed a job at the Louisiana Manufacturing and Cooperage Company.

Coopers made barrels and other containers used in shipping produce, both wet and dry. Unfortunately, by that time, the industry was in decline and the work could be unsteady. New Orleans never regained the prominence in trade that it had before the Civil War. Wartime disruptions and competition from railroads meant that much of what once flowed up and down the Mississippi River now traveled overland, east and west. At the same time, metal drums began to replace wooden barrels for shipping. The impact was gradual but steady. In 1879, there were sixty-two cooperages operating in the city; by 1920 there were only twenty-seven.[21] This meant periods of unemployment for the workers. On one such occasion, one of Edward's brothers was laid off for three months and found work as a day laborer, and another moved back in with his mother and helped her sell milk. Still, for Edward, coopering provided more income than unskilled labor and enabled him to start a family of his own.

He married Mary Lucien, a Black Creole woman who, like so many women of her race and class, worked as a seamstress. The young couple did not earn enough to have a place of their own, so they lived initially with her widowed mother and later with his mother. In 1910, Louise Durel's household consisted of herself, age seventy-three; a son, age fifty-six, and a daughter, age forty-four, both unmarried; and Edward, thirty-five, Mary, thirty-three, and their four children, ranging in age from two to twelve.[22] By 1917, Edward and Mary were earning sufficient income to rent their own place, the house at 2250 North Johnson Street. Then, at some point while living there, Mary became sick and died. In 1921, Edward married again, to a woman also named Mary, Mary Alexander.[23] She would finish raising his children and become an anchor for them into the 1950s. They called her "Babelle."

Whereas Edward's work and family life was rooted in the St. Roch neighborhood, Walter's first job took him to the downtown Central Business District, where he landed a position working as a clerk in a cotton brokerage.[24] Work brought him a degree of independence and freedom. He was seventeen and soon moved out of his parents' house and into an apartment of his own. Three years later he met Kate, who lived in the neighborhood. This fortuitous meeting brought him into the orbit of politically powerful Irishmen.

Across urban America, the Irish gained political influence by building coalitions with other European populations, often with Catholicism as a common thread. These political machines, as they were called, ensured that the working class had a share of a city's wealth through government jobs and contracts.[25] Kate's father, Frank Thriffiley, was active in the local machine called the Ring, which was led by an Irish American named John Fitzpatrick. Frank ran a corner grocery, a place where neighbors went not only to buy produce, but also to pass time, gossip, and complain. Frank listened to their concerns, allowed his customers to buy on credit, did them favors from time to time, and earned their votes. In the New Orleans municipal elections of 1892, the Ring defeated the incumbent government that was backed by the city's business interests and middle class, and Frank joined the city council as a representative from the Eighth Ward. He served only two years of a four-year term, resigning along with nine other councilmen when a grand jury indicted them for bribery and irregularities in city contracts.[26]

Frank was never brought to trial and, far from losing favor with his constituents, he remained a popular force behind the scenes in ward politics, promoting his son, Thomas, and another young Irishman, Billy McCue, as a new generation of leaders. Tragically, Thomas was shot in an altercation following a political rally in 1899 and died two days later. Billy, a man with a "winning personality," went on to become the acknowledged ward leader and married Frank's daughter, Kate's older sister, Loretta.[27]

This all happened years before Walter met Kate, although as a thirteen-year-old kid he may have been at the rally where Thomas was shot, for it took place only half a block from where his parents lived. Shortly after he started seeing Kate, he took a job in Mobile, Alabama, as cashier for a wholesale fruit company. He was then twenty years old; Kate was eighteen. He moved in September, she soon followed, and they were married by a priest in the Catholic cathedral in downtown Mobile on October 23, 1906.[28] They returned to New Orleans six months later, perhaps because the job did not work out, but just as likely because Kate missed her family. The sting of her brother's death was still with her, her sister Bernadette was courting, and her other sister, Loretta, was pregnant with her first child.[29] Kate herself became pregnant that December.

Back in New Orleans, Walter got to know his brother-in-law, Billy, who was twelve years his senior. No doubt he was drawn to Billy's success, for when he invited friends to his house in 1908 to form an amateur baseball team, he named it the McCue Baseball Club. Indeed, Walter might have had a career in politics had Billy not suffered a cerebral hemorrhage and died suddenly, at the age of thirty-nine, in 1913.[30] Walter did get involved, briefly, as a supporter of the Progressive Party candidate for governor in 1916. His man lost, and Walter's fleeting participation in politics came to an end.[31]

Walter's future, it turned out, lay in lumber. After returning to New Orleans, he found a position as bookkeeper for the Hugo Forchheimer Company, an exporter of lumber and timber, one of more than one hundred lumber companies in the city. This was a fortunate move, for lumber exporting was a booming industry. After the Civil War, large lumber companies, having mostly depleted the forests of the Great Lakes region, began purchasing vast tracts of timberland across the south. The Forchheimer

Fig. 12: *John Walter Durel* (1886–1939). Courtesy of the author.

Company, headquartered in Frankfurt, Germany, chose New Orleans as its main American location, with branch offices in New York City; Beaumont, Texas; Gulfport, Mississippi; and Pensacola, Florida.[32] For Walter, this meant a much larger network of contacts and greater opportunities to advance.

Over the next thirteen years, as he entered his thirties, he went from the position of bookkeeper for Forchheimer to being a stockholder and member of the board of Southland Lumber Corporation, and to junior partner of Hillcoat-Durel Lumber Company. Robert Hillcoat was new to the city, having come from Mexico, where he was an executive of a major oil company. Wanting to get into lumber exporting, he tapped Walter for his expertise and contacts. Hillcoat put up most of the capital and held the title of president; Walter was vice president and secretary.[33] A photograph of Walter, taken on one of several voyages to meet with potential customers in the Caribbean, shows him as a stout man with an easy smile (Figure 12). He was in his prime.

During this stretch of time, and reflecting his growing income, he moved his family every few years but always within the neighborhood and close to parents and siblings. It was between 1915 and 1920 that they lived on North Johnson Street. That Edward's family lived down the street was pure coincidence, the intersection of two life trajectories. Edward had lived within a few blocks of North Johnson since he was born and would continue to do so until he died. Walter, on the other hand, was on his way up and out. The house on North Johnson was just a way station. No longer just a bright young man from a downriver Irish neighborhood, Walter had begun to establish himself as a successful uptown business executive.

As an aside, Edward had a nephew, a son of one of his brothers, who also left the neighborhood. Faced with a future of low wages and periodic unemployment, Joseph Durel, in his midtwenties, joined the Great Migration of Black men and women who fled the South to escape the daily degradation and violence of Jim Crow and to seek better employment opportunities elsewhere. While most went north, Joseph headed west to California, where he found work on a farm owned by the Pacific Farms Land Company, outside of the town of Tulare, in the San Joaquin Valley. He left his family behind, although he did send money home when he could to support his widowed mother. In California, he met and married a woman from Alabama named Hattie. They were two among many who made the same journey for a fresh start.

Their neighbors in 1920 came from thirteen different states, as well as a family from Mexico. All the men worked as farm laborers except for one who worked on the railroad, one who was a school janitor, and another, a clergyman. With the exception of the Mexican family, all were Black.[34]

By 1930, Joseph and Hattie had left the farm and moved to Los Angeles, where he got a job handling baggage for a company that transferred people and their belongings between railroad stations or bus terminals and hotels. They had two children and owned the house they lived in, which was valued at $5,000 ($93,000 in 2024). He was only able to purchase the house because he received an inheritance from his grandmother, Louise, back in New Orleans, after she died in 1927. Louise's eldest son, who was near seventy himself, simply assumed ownership of the house on Claiborne Street at her death. When Joseph got word of this, he took his uncle to court. The house was sold at auction in May 1928, and Joseph received his share, which he then used as a down payment on his house.

In Los Angeles, all of Joseph's neighbors were Black and had come from the South. All the men were employed, a sign of the prosperity of the Roaring Twenties. They mostly worked as laborers for the city or in the construction industry; the women worked as well, many as maids in private homes. There were exceptions, reflecting diverse opportunities in a growing twentieth-century city: one man was a car mechanic, one woman was a waitress in a hotel restaurant, another was an attendant at a city comfort station (public toilet).[35] Joseph's house was just off Central Avenue, which had already emerged as the center of a burgeoning Black community. Although there were more opportunities than in New Orleans for gainful employment, Whites in Los Angeles were no less prejudiced, and Black people were still subjected to insults and abuse. Hence, they clustered among themselves in what came to be known as "South-Central LA."

In New Orleans, the burgeoning economy of the 1920s favored both Edward and Walter. Edward had steady work and was able to buy property situated at the corner of Mandeville and North Tonti Streets, only three blocks from where they rented on North Johnson.[36] It was a smart move. The lots in the area were generally narrow and deep, just large enough to hold a single, one-story, wooden-framed house, typical of New Orleans. Edward's corner lot had two houses on it, a larger one facing Mandeville Street and a smaller one behind it facing North Tonti. Additionally, each house was divided into two units. This provided Edward not only a place for his family to live, but also rental income. In 1929, the property was valued at $3,000 ($55,300 in 2024). Edward, Mary (Babelle), and two unmarried sons lived in half of the larger house; their daughter, Lena, and her husband rented the other half. A married son, Arnold, rented the closest half of the house facing Tonti and lived there with his wife, Thelma, and two children, Arnold Jr. and Stafford. The other half was rented out. In short, Edward was able to create a small family compound. Living was cramped and the shared yard space was limited, but they had the security of home ownership, a rarity among working-class Black people at the time.

For Walter, the prosperity of the 1920s was a godsend. The lumber trade flourished. Ever ambitious, in 1926, while serving as vice president of one lumber company and secretary-treasurer of another, he started a third, John W. Durel & Son, wholesale lumber exporters with an office downtown in the Canal Bank building. He intended that Mederic, once his son graduated from Loyola College in New Orleans, would join him in business. Around the same time, he invested some of his excess capital in newly claimed land, the result of the city's decades-long process of digging canals, installing pumps, and draining the cypress swamps that bordered the original city. Walter purchased property on a new stretch of Conti Street, about four miles from downtown, upon which he built a two-story, three-unit apartment house. His family moved into the largest unit, and the other two they rented out.[37]

In the process of draining the wetlands, New Orleans became residentially segregated. While Black people continued to live in proximity to Whites in the older sections of the city, newly developed areas were for White people only. Of 370 households enumerated in the section of the 1930 Census that includes Walter's apartment house, not one was occupied by a Black family. Only seven individuals were so identified, and they were live-in servants for White families.[38]

The stock market crash in October 1929 changed everything for both families. For Walter, the lumber export market collapsed, and within a year, not one of the companies he had a financial stake in was still in business. Faced with catastrophe, he quickly shifted his focus to the domestic construction industry. He likely still had an inventory of lumber and had gained experience with the construction of his own apartment house.[39] In order to increase his income, he had workers reduce the size of the apartment his family occupied in order to create a third rental unit. Then, in the middle of the Depression, he contracted multiple sclerosis and could no longer work. He died on February 20, 1939, only fifty-two years old.[40]

In the St. Roch neighborhood, the 1930s began with Edward already out of work, although it is not clear if this was due to the faltering economy or sickness. He died on October 12, 1930, four days before his fifty-sixth birthday.[41] His wife and children continued to live in the family compound and faced an uncertain future.

=== Milton, *Black*, and Mederic, *White* ===

Walter's only son and Edward's youngest son faced the coming Great Depression from distinctly different vantage points. Milton and Mederic were the same age, each born in 1908, Milton on April 26, and Mederic on August 9. Although Milton was Black and Mederic was White, from age nine to twelve they lived on the same street, a block apart. Mederic was my dad, and I sometimes like to imagine him as a nine-year-old, tossing a ball to himself in the street, catching Milton's eye, and the two of them playing catch together. Young children are often immune to racial categorization, and such a scene could conceivably have happened. On the other hand, by age nine, each of them had already been exposed to segregation at church and at school and might well have avoided one another. In any event, Mederic soon left the neighborhood, and their paths diverged.

Milton was the youngest of Edward and Mary's children. Like his siblings, he completed the eighth grade, continued to live at home, and went to work. The general prosperity of the 1920s made it easy for him to find a job, although his limited education meant that he would be employed in low-skilled work. One of Milton's brothers helped out at a stationery store, the other worked at a bakery. His sister was a machine operator in a garment factory and her husband (she married in 1922) was a porter, whose job was to carry heavy items and keep the workplace orderly and clean. Milton started out at age fifteen helping at the Royal Typewriter Company. Then, for the next two years he worked in a mattress factory. Next, he got a job as a porter for a year, and by the time he was twenty-one, he was a tin cutter.[42]

Meanwhile, Mederic went to high school. His father was doing well in business, and his parents could afford to send him to a boarding school in Mobile, Alabama, run by the Jesuit priests. His education went beyond school, for in 1923, when he was fifteen, he accompanied his father on a business trip to San Juan, Puerto Rico, and New York City.[43] After graduating from high school in 1925, he entered Loyola College in New Orleans, another Jesuit institution. He completed two years and once again traveled. In 1927, he signed on as a cabin boy on a cargo ship, and that summer visited the Dominican Republic and Columbia in South America, then crossed the Atlantic for stops in Italy and Turkey, and then on to Latvia, then Cuba, and back to New Orleans. (This voyage is one of the stories I heard growing up, about my father and his sense of adventure, that had a significant impact on me.)

When he returned from his adventure, he went to work for his father, starting out as a clerk to gain practical experience. He also worked briefly as a bookkeeper for another exporting company. Then came the stock market crash in October 1929, and life changed.

The Great Depression hit Milton's family hard and fast. The nation's unemployment rate, which sat at about 3 percent before the crash, grew to nearly 25 percent by 1933 and never fell below 14 percent for the remainder of the decade.[44] For Black workers, the situation was even worse. By January 1931, more than a third of working Black men and women in New Orleans were unemployed (compared to 18 percent for White workers).[45] Milton lost his job as a tin cutter within six months of the crash and remained unemployed for two years. In 1932, he was able to get work as a porter, a less-skilled position with lower pay. Although his sister, Lena, was able to keep her job as a seamstress, his brothers, Arnold and Ferdinand, lost their jobs and experienced alternating stretches of unemployment and low-skilled work. The family hunkered down. To make ends meet, Babelle, their stepmother, started taking in laundry. No doubt she planted a vegetable garden and may have raised chickens.[46]

The toll of the Depression was not only financial. Amid the emotional strains of little money, close quarters, and idle time, family ties suffered. Arnold and his wife divorced, and she moved out with their two sons. Lena and her husband separated, and he left. At some point, Milton's elderly aunt Rose, his father's sister who had never married, could no longer live on her own and Babelle took her in. On a positive note, in 1939, when he was thirty-one years old, Milton married Blanche Decou and gave up his room in the larger house to move with his wife into the half of the smaller house that Arnold's family had vacated.

It was fortunate that the family owned this property and that they were able to keep it intact. It provided a degree of stability in otherwise uncertain times. In 1940, at the end of the Depression, Babelle still resided in her half of the larger house with her unmarried stepson, Ferdinand, and her elderly sister-in-law, Rose. Ferdinand was working intermittently as a laborer on road construction and reported earnings of $312 the previous year (the equivalent of $6,900 in 2024). Babelle rented out the other half of the house to a White couple for $15 a month. In the little house on Tonti Street, she rented half to a Filipino man and his family for $12 a month. Milton and Blanche lived in the other half and paid Babelle $10 a month. Milton had recently started working on a road construction crew, although neither he nor Blanche had earned any money the previous year.[47]

Across town, Mederic's family entered the decade of the Depression with greater financial resources. For the first two or three years, Walter was still able to work, and the family relocated temporarily to Houma, Louisiana, west of the city, where Walter hired workers and built two houses. Then, when Walter became debilitated with multiple sclerosis, they returned to New Orleans and Mederic became the family's breadwinner. Like his father, he was outgoing and well-liked, and so he went into sales. It took a year or two, but by 1935 he had established himself as an agent for the New York Life Insurance Company. His commissions, combined with income from the rental apartments, supported the family.[48]

It was at this time that he met my mom. Antoinette Caillouet was from a large, prominent, Catholic family in Thibodaux, about sixty miles to the southwest of New Orleans. She had moved to the Crescent City to attend nursing school and had decided to stay, taking a job at Hotel Dieu, a Catholic hospital. Eventually, when my grandfather's illness progressed to the point that he needed to enter the hospital, by chance my mom was assigned to his care. Courtship followed, and my dad and mom married on October 8, 1938, four months before my grandfather died.

As the Great Depression drew to a close, in the final year of the decade Mederic earned $1,500 ($33,780) to support his young wife and an infant son, born that September. They lived with his mother, Kate, who received about $85 a month in rents. Thus, the family lived on about $2,500 a year (equivalent to $56,000 in 2024). At the same time, the annual income for the Black Durel family in St. Roch was about $460 ($10,360 in 2024) plus whatever money Babelle made taking in laundry.[49]

As boys they lived a block apart and as adults they led very different lives, yet in the fall of 1940, Mederic and Milton had something in common. In anticipation of being drawn into the conflict then raging in Europe, on September 16, the federal government passed a law stating that "any person, regardless of race or color, between the ages of eighteen and forty-five, shall be afforded an opportunity to volunteer for induction" into the armed forces.[50] Both men, at age thirty-two, signed up and waited to be called up.[51]

The military services were racially segregated at the outset of the war, reflecting a belief that any mixing of the races would lead to friction and possibly violence within units and thereby impair fighting efficiency. The Army assigned Black recruits only to support roles, such as cleaning barracks; the Navy enlisted Black men only in limited numbers as messmen, to prepare and serve meals for White officers. However, Black leaders made it clear from the beginning that they wanted more ways in which their people could demonstrate their commitment to the nation. Just ten days after the Japanese attack on Pearl Harbor, the president of the NAACP wrote to President Franklin D. Roosevelt, complaining that the navy's policy did not give Black men enough opportunities. In response to political pressure, the military services slowly expanded the number of support roles open to Black servicemen. Still, it was not until war casualties started to mount and Whites began to complain that Black soldiers were not doing their share that the Army and Navy created Black combat units.[52]

Milton and two others in his family joined the services. His older brother, Arnold, was first, entering the Army in July 1942. At the time, the services preferred single men who were unencumbered by family obligations. Although Arnold had two sons, he stated in his enlistment record that he was separated from his wife and had no dependents, which was technically the case, as the boys were being raised by their mother and her new husband. Following boot camp, Arnold was assigned to an engineering unit, most likely as a laborer for a construction crew. It was taxing work, and after about eighteen months he was diagnosed with joint disease. In January 1945, he was admitted to the hospital at Camp Barkeley, near Abilene, Texas, and in March was discharged for medical reasons. After the war, he found employment at a men's clothing company, married Mathilda Skillman in 1948, and once again rented one of the units in the house on North Tonti that his family owned.[53]

Arnold's son, Arnold Jr, turned eighteen in May 1943 and that fall he entered the Navy. By then, the services had expanded opportunities for Black sailors, and after boot camp young Arnold went to a naval training school and graduated as a pharmacist mate, third class (PHM3C). In March 1944, he sailed on the USS *General George O. Squire* (AP-130), a troop transport ship operating out of San Francisco. When the ship reached Hawaii, he reported for duty at the Aiea Heights Naval Hospital, which served as a way station for wounded sailors and soldiers on their way home from the Pacific front. He worked in the hospital pharmacy, dispensing medicines under the direction of a chief pharmacist mate.[54] He was one of about eight Black sailors assigned to the pharmacy, out of a total of almost six hundred.[55] His was one of the first Navy units to be integrated.

Milton enlisted in the Navy Reserve on February 21, 1944, and attended boot camp at Camp Robert Smalls, a segregated camp for Black recruits at the Great Lakes Naval Training Station in Illinois. Unlike his brother and nephew, he never saw active duty beyond basic training. Although he had volunteered to serve two years, he was discharged at the end of training, based on the "recommendation of the Aptitude Board because of unsuitability for Naval Service."[56] He received an "ordinary discharge certificate issued with character GOOD." On the date of his separation, April 13, 1944, he received an Honorable Service Lapel Button.

He had served honorably, but evidently for some reason the Navy deemed him unsuitable for further military service. His record does not indicate what that might have been. When he returned home, he went to work painting houses, although early on he had a brief job as a merchant seaman. For a time, his wife, Blanche, was a store manager for a dry-cleaning company. They pieced together a life for themselves, continuing to live in half of the house on Tonti Street. Babelle still lived in the corner house, as did Ferdinand, who never married.[57] Milton lived a long life, dying in 1993 when he was eighty-four years old.

Milton's life encapsulates the struggles of many ordinary working-class Black men through the twentieth century. With limited education and low-paying employment, he simply got by. His horizons were limited, and even his aspiration to serve his country was cut short. In the end, he had to accept the life handed to him because of his race. This is not to belittle his life; it is simply to point out that men like Milton lived with little hope of improving their lot.

Mederic was eager to join the armed forces and do his bit to win the war. Delayed because of his age and the fact that he had two young children, he did not enter the Navy until 1944, about the same time that Milton was at Great Lakes. After basic training in San Diego, he went to storekeeper's school at the Naval Training Center in Farragut, Idaho. Storekeepers managed supplies on a ship, and eventually he served on the USS *Lake Champlain* (CV39). In a small way, the Navy introduced him to the possibility of life without Jim Crow segregation. He finished first in his class at storekeeper's school and in a letter home to my mother he wrote:

> Let me tell you about the graduation. It was at 8 o'clock this morning and we were quite a crowd as there were graduating classes from the Gunners Mate School, Electrician Mate School, Radio School and Cooks & Bakers, besides us. All the cooks and bakers are colored and as luck would have it, the honor man from each school had to sit in the very first row and I drew the seat right next to the Black boy—well I guess I will file it away under the heading of experience.[58]

From childhood, he had lived in a world designed to keep him separated from people defined as Black, and that if by chance he encountered one of these others, it would be clear to him that he was the superior of the two. Now, for the first time in his life, he found himself in a situation where a Black man was his equal. Clearly, he found the situation novel. He did not dwell on it or complain about it, which was not always the case when he thought the Navy had made a mistake. But it was notable, and he chalked it up to experience.

On another occasion, he used a common stereotype of Black people when he responded to something my mother wrote: "Do you mean to say that I am slow and lazy—well it may have been but the 'black' has changed."[59] He was a man of his time, never understanding that stereotyping Black people as lacking in ability and ambition served to justify the prejudices they faced in schooling and work. As long as he did not know any Black people on an equal footing, it was easy for him to accept the myth of White superiority. It likely never occurred to him to think about how a Black person felt living in a world where they were reminded constantly of their inferior status. (It certainly never occurred to me when I was growing up.)

The success of integration in the military during the war, as limited as it was, revealed what was possible and emboldened Black leaders to push for more change. In 1948, President Harry Truman issued an executive order ending racial segregation in all of the armed forces.

Even in Louisiana, things were starting to change. Archbishop Joseph F. Rummel had been head of the Catholic archdiocese in New Orleans since 1935. As a young priest, Rummel had once served in a racially integrated parish in Harlem, New York, and had long believed that segregation was morally wrong. Finally, in 1949 he felt he was able to act without causing too much backlash from White laity. That year, he canceled an outdoor religious event because city officials required that it be segregated. The next year, he ordered the pastors of parish churches throughout the archdiocese to remove "White" and "Colored" signs from pews and doorways. Three years later, he put an end to the requirement that Black Catholics wait until all Whites had received communion before doing so themselves. He also directed church pastors to allow Black members to participate fully in parish organizations.[60]

Mederic did not live to see these changes. He returned home at the end of the war and died two years later. While in basic training he had gotten sunburned and later developed a mole that the navy corpsman treated as benign and cauterized. It was actually a melanoma, which metastasized and caused a brain tumor. I was just two years old when he died in October 1947, at the age of thirty-nine.

As I reflect on the stories of my grandfather and father, I am struck by an advantage they had that was denied Edward and his children. Beyond better education, greater opportunities in life, and higher-paying work, there was an expansiveness to their lives. Their horizons were broad, they traveled the world, they were ambitious, they moved forward. I inherited from them a sense of adventure, confidence in my own abilities and conviction that whatever I chose to do would work out. I grew up feeling affirmed, surrounded by family and friends, never experiencing prejudice.

Edward's family, in contrast, was constrained by low wages and uncertain employment. Edward lived his entire life within a ten-minute walk of where he grew up. Milton never ventured far once he returned from the Navy. They suffered from a poverty of possibilities. The deck was stacked against them, and they knew it.

Possibilities and constraints. There is a vast difference between being told, as a child, that if you apply yourself, you can become anything you want in life and being warned, again as a child, about all the things you are not allowed to do. White advantage played out not only in measurable levels of education and wealth, but also more subtly in the hopes and dreams of children.

Chapter 7

The Civil Rights Generation

In the final story of my narrative, I contrast my life with that of Stafford Durel, who was Milton Durel's nephew, the youngest son of Milton's brother Arnold Sr. Although Stafford was born seventeen years before me, our lives overlapped for almost sixty years. In researching the details of his life, I discovered the names of his nine children, seven of whom are still alive today. From my first encounter with a Black person with the name of Durel—Ester, in Chapter 1—I had hoped to be able to identify and speak with Black descendants. I reached out to Stafford's children and have been able to speak with three: Theresa, Stafford Jr., and Catherine. Their memories of their father, as well as their own life experiences, have helped to shape what follows, although the interpretation is mine.

=== Stafford, *Black*, and John, *White* ===

I was born on September 20, 1945, just as World War II came to an end. With the exception of a few discreet instances, my childhood memories are from the 1950s, a decade characterized by economic prosperity and optimism. The United States emerged from the war as a world power, politically and economically. Jobs were plentiful, and after years of economic depression and wartime rationing, Americans were eager to buy new products, in new styles, made of new materials. I remember the day from my childhood, it must have been around 1953, when I and one of my brothers returned home from school, entered the living room, and sensed something was different. The furniture had been rearranged. My mom, grandmother Kate, and other brothers sat there, quietly smiling. As we looked around it came into focus: the television! It was a gift from my grandmother, and the first program we watched, as I recall, was the *Kate Smith Show*, which ended with her singing "God Bless America." In retrospect, it was a quintessential experience for a White kid growing up in the American middle class in the 1950s.

I did not grow up in New Orleans. After the war, my father and mother decided to settle in her hometown, Thibodaux, and after he died, we stayed. My only contact with the Durel family was through my grandmother. She was a big part of our lives, and we saw her often. However, when we visited New Orleans, we saw mostly her sisters and their children, our Irish American relatives. We gradually lost touch with my grandfather's side of the family and grew up not knowing any other people with the last name Durel. I was totally unaware of my Creole heritage.

On my mother's side, I descend from Acadians, or Cajuns, as they are now commonly called. Between 1755 and 1764, Great Britain forcibly expelled thousands of settlers from the French colony of Acadia (Nova Scotia), where they and their ancestors had lived for well over a century. Many found their way to Louisiana. My Caillouet forbears arrived in 1785, a generation after the Durels. They were farmers, eventually owning a sugar plantation near Thibodaux, and had enslaved several dozen Black people to work the land. By my mother's time, they lived in town, her father worked as an attorney, and her grandfather, as a judge. That said, Cajun heritage was a very small part of my identity. While some of the older people in my life spoke French, I learned only English. Although some may have enjoyed traditional music, I listened to rock 'n' roll. Years later, Cajun culture would become popular in America, but in the 1950s it was not something widely celebrated. In truth, I thought of myself simply as an American.

Sixty miles away, in New Orleans, the postwar prosperity that brought a television into my living room provided Stafford Durel with steady employment. He was in his early twenties and getting started with life as an adult. His parents were Arnold Durel Sr. and Thelma Ruiz, who had divorced when he was around seven years old. He and his older brother, Arnold Jr., were raised by their mother and her second husband, a taxi driver and musician named Rodney Richardson. I wrote about the military service of Arnold Sr. and Jr. in the previous chapter. Stafford was too young to serve. He spent the war years in high school and got his first job in 1946, when he was seventeen, as a helper at a venetian blinds company on North Broad Street. Like his forebears, he worked with his hands: his great-grandfather had been a cigar maker; his grandfather, a cooper; and his father, a porter and shipping clerk. It is notable that with each generation the required level of skill declined, not

Fig. 13: *Stafford Durel* (1928–2004). Courtesy of Theresa Durel Reed.

only reflecting limited educational opportunities but also more pronounced racism that pitted a growing White working class against Black workers. Stafford became adept at painting, repairing, assembling, and installing window blinds, shades, and curtains. The pay was low, but the work was reliable, and he stayed with the company until he retired more than forty years later.

Stafford was Creole on his father's side, although that identification probably meant little to him. Like all others of African descent under the Jim Crow regime, regardless of how much European ancestry he had, he was identified officially—and likely thought of himself primarily—as "Negro" or "colored." His children who are old enough to remember his father,

Arnold Sr., say that he had very light skin, and that when they attended his funeral there were many White people there, leading them to believe that he lived as a White person after the war. Stafford's mother, their grandmother Thelma, may have been Creole as well, but what the children recall mostly is that she was part American Indian, a notable fact that had likely been handed down in her family for many generations.[1] For Stafford's children, being Creole is more a curiosity than a significant element of their lives.

Around 1950, Stafford married Shirleyrine Hanzy and started a family. Their first child, Linda, came in 1952, and eventually there were nine children altogether, five girls and four boys. To accommodate his growing family, Stafford rented a large shotgun house on the corner of Conti and North Rocheblave Streets, just a five-minute walk from his work. Shotgun houses were typical of New Orleans in the early nineteenth century, and many have survived. They are simple, narrow structures, one room wide with rooms running in a sequence from front to rear and no connecting hallways. The doorways to each room run along one side of the structure and to get from one room to another one has to pass through the intervening rooms. In popular folklore, shotgun houses were so named because one could fire a shotgun through the front door and the blast would exit the rear without hitting anything. In Stafford's house, the first room was the living room with a couch and television, then came, in sequence, the parent's bedroom, the boys' bedroom, the girls' bedroom, and the kitchen, with a small bathroom just off the kitchen. In addition, they made room for Thelma and her mother, Nellie Ruiz, whom the children called "Bee-bee." They stayed in a small room attached to the rear of the house.

Stafford's pay was insufficient to feed, clothe, and shelter this large family. Occasionally, Shirleyrine brought in extra money by babysitting for White families, but most of her time was taken up cooking and looking after her own children and her aging in-laws. So, Stafford took a second job. Every morning he got up in the dark, at three o'clock, dressed quietly, and either walked or got a ride to a garage on St. Peter Street, which served as a distribution point for the *Times-Picayune*, the city's major newspaper. There, he put several hundred newspapers into a grocery cart and headed out on his route, delivering papers to families still asleep or just rousing for the day. He was back home by six to eat breakfast and then walk to work. After an eleven-hour day, he returned home, sat down to dinner with the family, spent a couple of hours relaxing in his recliner in the living room, having a beer, smoking a cigar, and watching television. To bed around eight, he was up again the next morning at three. The Sunday paper took longer because it included multiple components, like the comics and sales flyers, that had to be assembled and stuffed into bags. In order to speed things up, Stafford enlisted his children to help once they were old enough to do the work. They would take turns getting up early and going with him to assemble the papers. Eventually, some got paper routes of their own. For a time, even Shirleyrine got a route to help pay bills.

The neighborhood in which the family lived was an enclave for Black working-class families, three blocks off Canal Street, the main thoroughfare between the river and the lakefront. The pattern of residential segregation in New Orleans that emerged in the mid-twentieth century was different from other cities, where Black people ended up living exclusively in a few very large areas in what became known as the inner city. Instead, New Orleans developed a checkerboard pattern, with small Black neighborhoods never far from White ones. This facilitated the long-standing practice of Whites hiring Black women as domestic help. A stranger driving along Canal Street would never see the houses where Stafford and his neighbors lived. White families occupied residences in the first two blocks off Canal and then, rather abruptly, the population changed to Black. Also, the nature of the streets changed, the first two blocks being solely residential, the next two having light industrial businesses interspersed among the rental houses. On Stafford's block there was a large warehouse, an autobody shop, and a paint storage facility.[2]

Their enclave, largely invisible to Whites, served as an important center of community. It was a place where Black children played with one another after school and adults gathered on holidays for backyard barbeques, a respite from the White employers who controlled much of their lives.

With one exception, I seldom saw Black people when I was growing up in Thibodaux. I was aware that they lived in certain neighborhoods, but they rarely walked along the streets that I came to know when I went to school and church and visited my relatives. Occasionally, my mother hired a Black man to cut the grass or do some other chore. They would always come to the back door and ask for Miss Nette. But on the whole, in childhood I was surrounded by White people.

Beyond the strictures of segregation, Black people in Thibodaux had good reason to keep to themselves. They were afraid of what might happen if any White person accused them of transgressing the color line. There was a notorious event, of which I knew nothing as a child, that occurred in 1887 and is known today as the Thibodaux Massacre.[3] Following the Civil War, formerly enslaved Black men continued to work on the local sugar plantations and were paid in script that could only be redeemed at the plantation store. That year, during grinding season, the workers went on strike, demanding to be paid in cash. On the night of November 23, White vigilantes, backed by the state militia, rode on horseback through town and into the surrounding countryside murdering dozens of Black men. After that, Black people kept to themselves as much as possible, knowing the extent to which Whites would go to maintain their dominance. This episode was never mentioned by the adults in my life, although I suspect it was told in Black families as a warning to children.

The one exception to the Whiteness of my childhood was Eva Thomas, who came to our house every weekday to cook our meals, wash and iron our clothes, and clean our rooms. My earliest memories of her are few and elusive, mostly images: her standing at the stove cooking dinner, hanging the wash in the backyard, standing at the ironing board in the back hall, and sitting at the kitchen table eating after we had finished. I have a specific memory of once looking at her hands as she ironed clothes and noticing her dark skin against white cloth. I must have been very young, and this was perhaps the first time I noticed skin color. She was present in my life until I left home for college, always there in the background doing her work.

Scholars who have studied the lives of Black women who worked as domestic servants and of the families that employed them have pointed out the paradoxical nature of the relationship: they were intimate but unequal, familial but distant.[4] Whites often said the maid was just like a member of the family, yet the maid had her own family. Black women helped to raise White children, often leaving their own children in the care of a relative or friend. One scholar, reflecting on her own childhood, states: "On some level we white children sensed that something was wrong, but we could not see that we were at the center of it."[5] This statement captures for me my conflicted feelings about Eva.

My mother was a compassionate person and taught my brothers and me to be respectful of Eva and other Black men and women. We learned to be polite and call them "Negro," and never to use what is now called the "n-word." Eva was always present, yet I felt the distance between us. She was a good person who cared for me, and yet I took her for granted. She helped to raise me, and I knew nothing about her own family. When I left for college, I rarely thought of her, except on visits home. And when my mom finally told her she was no longer needed, she disappeared from my life. This was not the case with my brother Tom, who made a point to visit her after she left. It pains me to admit that it never occurred to me to do the same.

In the mid-1950s, as I was becoming aware of a larger world beyond my family and hometown, the TV nightly news started covering the Civil Rights Movement. On the screen I saw White people abusing Black men and women for daring to sit down at a lunch counter or refusing to give up a seat and stand at the rear of a bus. Taking cues from my mother, I admired Dr. Martin Luther King Jr. and felt sympathy for Black people, although I was not moved to action myself. I viewed the protests from afar, as if they had nothing to do with me.

An incident from this time shows how oblivious I was to the benefits I had as a White person. I was hanging out at a soda fountain with high school friends one Saturday night when two boys started egging each other on about who had the faster car. Talking tough, they decided to head out to a sugarcane field north of town and have a drag race. My friends and I followed in another car. We parked alongside the road as the two antagonists positioned their cars side by side and revved the engines. Just then, a police car, with lights flashing, entered the road about a quarter mile away. My first inclination was to dive into the cane and hide, but my friends called for me to get into the car. We started driving fast, hoping to outrun the police. I think we were in the slowest of all the cars, because we were the ones who got caught.

At jail, we gave our names and our parents' names and were locked in a holding cell. I recall being more embarrassed than scared. It was not long before my mother showed up with one of my uncles and I was released after a stern "talking to." For years afterward, I told this story as a humorous anecdote about growing up in the 1950s, as in the movie *American Graffiti.* It was only with the emergence of Black Lives Matter that I looked back and understood it for what it was, an example of the advantages I had as a middle-class White person. I shudder to think what might have happened had I been Black.

When I started high school in 1959, schools in Louisiana were still segregated, in spite of the Supreme Court ruling five years earlier that pronounced segregated schools unconstitutional. It took eight years of legal challenges, legislative maneuverings, and outright disregard for court-ordered deadlines before Louisiana complied. When it came to education, White supremacists in the state had a long history of resisting change. For example, in New Orleans in 1922, the school board faced numerous health code violations at an old elementary school building for Black students. The board was slow to act but finally announced plans to tear the school down and replace it with a new building. White residents showed up at the next board meeting to argue that the new building should be for White children and that Black children should be assigned to other existing and already overcrowded Black schools. The school board president at the time was a Durel descendant, James Fortier, who like his father, Alcée Fortier (Chapter 5), was a staunch segregationist. Fortier sided with the protestors, stating that he was "unwilling to do anything that would affect the white man's supremacy." He added that he was "ready to deny the Negro political equalities and if necessary, to resort to force to do so."[6]

That a recognized White leader threatened publicly the use of force against Black children underscores the determination of White supremacists to maintain power. It was true in 1922, and it was still true in 1954. It was not until Monday, November 14, 1960, that four little Black girls, accompanied by federal marshals, braved jeering and threatening crowds of White adults to attend first grade at two previously all-White schools.[7]

Catholic schools began integrating two years after the public schools. Although Archbishop Rummel had already integrated parish churches, schools presented a greater challenge. Conservative White Catholics organized to block desegregation. The leader of one group, called Save Our Nation, argued that the Bible required segregation of the races. The archbishop, seeking to avoid divisions that would tear parishes apart, delayed, saying that parochial schools would make the move "if and when public schools are actually integrated." By early 1962, he was convinced that public school integration would succeed and announced that Catholic schools would integrate that fall. One opposition leader called the integration order a "Black curse" and urged parents to "take your children out of every parochial school." To quell resistance, the archbishop issued a decree of excommunication against three of the most vocal opponents, barring them from participation in the sacraments and church activities. That fall, integration proceeded without much ado.[8]

Collectively, Stafford and Shirleyrine's children spanned the years of integration and subsequent resegregation of the public system: the oldest child, Linda, started school in 1958; the youngest, Milton (named for his father's uncle), finished in 1984. Initially, the children attended Catholic school, but as reform-minded educators with the aid of federal funds launched innovative programs in public schools, they switched. In high school, Stafford Jr., the oldest son, who by his own admission was not a good student, went to a Job Corps program where he learned carpentry and basic construction. Theresa, the youngest daughter, born in 1963, recalls leaving Catholic school to attend a special program at Phyllis Wheatley Elementary School in Tremé. She went on to graduate from a two-year business college, the first in her family to earn a degree beyond high school. All the children benefited from new educational opportunities, and some broke through the limitations faced by their forbears who eked out a living from low-skilled, low-paid employment. Theresa started work as a medical technician, then switched to the US Postal Service when she was twenty-seven, and soon became manager at one of the branch post offices in the city. Catherine, the middle child, took a job at McDonalds, learned the system, worked her way up, and recently retired as a manager of one of their restaurants.

At first, the New Orleans school board moved cautiously with desegregation in the hope of avoiding a massive withdrawal of White students from the public system, and for a while it worked. By the 1969–70 school year, Black enrollment in public schools had increased 50 percent and White enrollment had declined only 13 percent. However, during the next decade, White enrollment in New Orleans public schools plummeted from thirty-five thousand to thirteen thousand as White families fled to the suburbs or chose to send their children to private and parochial schools. The result was a public system that was 84 percent Black in 1980.[9] At the same time, overall school enrollment decreased by almost a quarter, which meant less money to operate, based on the state's per-pupil funding formula. The school system that had integrated in the early 1960s was essentially resegregated by the late 1970s.

Although I grew up without a father, I heard stories about him, many of which affected me as a youth. In a sense, I grew up with his reputation. In his two brief years in Thibodaux, he served as president of the Father's Club at the Catholic boys' school and organized a fund drive to build a football stadium. He was instrumental in establishing an annual community service award presented by the Veterans of Foreign Wars, which was named in his honor after he died, so that every April my mother went to the ceremony honoring that year's recipient of the "Durel Award." He also joined the Knights of Columbus, a Catholic men's organization, and helped to gain admittance for another newcomer who had been rejected by the older members because of his Italian heritage. In return, Benny Marcello, whom we knew as "Doctor Benny," provided us with free dental care. I took away from these stories not only a sense of pride, but also a nascent understanding of one's responsibility for one's community and especially for the underdog.

Another story had a more immediate impact. The account of my dad's voyage across the Atlantic on a cargo ship when he was nineteen instilled in me a yearning to travel. I recall the very moment I left the state of Louisiana for the first time. I was twelve, traveling in the back seat of my uncle's car on our way to visit my oldest brother, who had gone away to college in Alabama. We left home early, and it was still dark when we reached the Pearl River and crossed into Mississippi. I looked up and saw three green flashing lights marking the middle of the bridge span. An insignificant event for most, but for me it was a moment that remains imprinted in my memory to this day. A few years later I accompanied my mother and another uncle, who was a priest, on a pilgrimage to the Shrine of Our Lady of Guadeloupe in Mexico City. And in the summer between my junior and senior years of high school, I drove another uncle, also a priest, on an extended vacation from San Diego to Seattle. The advantage of growing up in a middle-class family introduced me to a world far beyond my childhood home.

I graduated from high school in 1963, two years before the Catholic Church got around to integrating it. Another advantage I had was the opportunity to go away to college, made feasible because I qualified for tuition assistance under the GI Bill as a dependent of a deceased veteran. My mother's only stipulation was that I attend a Catholic institution. In September 1963, just shy of my eighteenth birthday, I boarded a train for Indiana and entered the University of Notre Dame. I did not comprehend it at the time, but this was my first step in leaving the segregated South behind.

In one of those quirks of life, in 1966, between my junior and senior years of college, I landed a summer job at the Pan-American Life Insurance Company on Canal Street in New Orleans. My work was only three blocks away from Stafford's house on Conti Street. I used to explore the neighborhood on lunch hours and could well have passed his house. But not unlike our respective grandfathers, who lived only a block apart a half-century earlier, our lives were on different trajectories. Truth be told, I would have been incredulous to discover that a Black family with my last name lived there.

After college, I joined the Navy to see the world. I made two deployments to Southeast Asia followed by two years living in London, England. After the Navy, I settled in New England, and subsequently moved with my family to Baltimore. My life since leaving home has been increasingly rich with diversity. At one point, our little street in Baltimore with nine houses had two Black families, one a single, working mother raising three children, and the other a middle-class family with the father in school part-time to earn a PhD in education. There were two families of mixed race, one a Black man and a Chinese American woman, both artists, and the other a Black woman and a White man who had been born in England. There was also a community-based residence for men suffering from schizophrenia, both White and Black, an elderly Jewish widow who had raised her family on the street, and two other White families, like ours. It was a street unlike any I had ever experienced in childhood.

As I left home, Stafford went on working. The older children grew up, left home, and began having children of their own. It was this generation, the grandchildren of Stafford and Shirleyrine, that bore the brunt of a new racist system that emerged in the late 1970s and into the '80s. As had been the case at the end of Reconstruction, White supremacists found ways to undermine Black progress. The new system, rather than focusing on all Black people, targeted the poor. The primary means of persecution was imprisonment, justified by a need to maintain "law and order."[10]

Crime and illegal drugs became national concerns in the 1970s. The causes were many and complex, but rather than analyze and address the causes, White political leaders simply placed the blame on something they called "Black culture." Never mind that the unemployment rate for Black men in cities rose from 8.1 percent to 20.7 percent between 1972 and 1982 as White businessowners moved manufacturing jobs to suburbs or overseas, politicians used the media to portray city-dwelling Black men and women as lazy and drug-addicted, preferring to panhandle and live on welfare rather than do an honest day's work.[11] Never mind that a new and less expensive form of cocaine called "crack" was no more potent than "coke," the more expensive form favored by White users, politicians mandated sentences ten time longer for its possession, leading to lengthier jail time for Black inmates. Never mind that subsequent studies showed that White youth sold and used illegal drugs as much as Black youth, the White media propagated stories and menacing images of young Black men accosting Whites to get money for drugs or hanging out near schools to lure innocent White children into drug use.[12] The depiction of Black men as predators was a tactic that White supremacists had used a hundred years earlier to rouse White resistance to Reconstruction. It worked then, and it worked again.

It was as if the work ethic of underprivileged people like Stafford, Shirleyrine, and their children did not exist. White politicians managed to convince a majority of voters that impoverished Black people were responsible for society's ills, rather than the other way around. Using phrases like "war on drugs," "tough on crime," and "three strikes and you're out," they enacted laws that mandated heavy sentences for drug-related crimes, increased funding substantially for law enforcement and prison construction, and reduced funds for drug abuse treatment and prevention. They also pointed to successful Black citizens who had made it into the middle class as evidence that race was not the issue, claiming their real concern was crime. Yet, during the 1980s and '90s, although the number of White people incarcerated for drug offenses increased eightfold, the comparable number for Black people was twenty-six. That is, for every Black person in prison in the early '80s, twenty years later there were twenty-six. Black people made up only 12.3 percent of the total population of the country in 2000, but they comprised 46.2 percent of federal and state prisoners. Almost one out of every ten Black males between the ages of twenty-five and twenty-nine was imprisoned. Among the states, Louisiana had the highest incarceration rate, with 801 inmates per 100,000 residents.[13]

The intentional targeting of poor Black men by law enforcement and in the media was a game changer for families like Stafford's. During the Civil Rights Movement, they had dared to hope for a better life, but hope soon gave way to fear. The author Ta-Nehisi Coates, looking back on growing up in Baltimore at that time, writes:

> The only people I knew were black, and all of them were powerfully, adamantly, dangerously afraid. . . . It was always right in front of me. The fear was there in the extravagant boys in my neighborhood, in their large rings and medallions . . . in their practiced bop, their slouching denim, their big T-shirts. . . . I saw it in the girls, in their loud laughter, in their gilded bamboo earrings . . . in their brutal language and hard gaze. . . . And I saw it in my own father.[14]

All parents fear losing a child, and for parents of children defined as Black, the fear was especially acute. Coates goes on: "Everyone . . . lost a child, somehow, to the streets, to jail, to drugs, to guns."

On February 15, 1995, Stafford and Shirleyrine's oldest child, Linda, lost a daughter to a gun.[15] Tisha was a student at a once all-White high school still bearing the name of Francis T. Nicholls, a Confederate general, with a school mascot called the Rebels. By the nineties, Whites had abandoned the public schools, and Tisha's school was in disrepair, with some parts of the building unused and left in complete darkness. Years later, a principal recalled that people considered the school totally out of control.[16] Deserted by adult leaders who should have cared, and in spite of the efforts of their teachers and parents, children went to school in fear and acted tough, as if they were the ones in control. But they were not. A toxic mixture of drugs, guns, corruption, unemployment, and racism controlled their lives, and many suffered.

Tisha's death occurred in the midst of an eruption of violence on the streets of New Orleans. The year 1994 witnessed 424 murders, to this day the most ever recorded in the city.[17] Some were caused by police corruption, as when a thirty-two-year-old Black woman from the Ninth Ward was found dead from a single bullet to her head one day after she filed a brutality complaint against an officer for pistol-whipping a teenager. But the majority of the homicides were due to an epidemic of crack cocaine. Rival gangs competed for control of the lucrative business. Young Tisha became involved with a drug dealer, got pregnant, and had their child. Two months later, while riding in a car with him, she was shot and taken to Charity Hospital, where she died. The young man who killed her was convicted of manslaughter and spent twenty-five years in prison. Tisha's child, a boy, was raised by his grandmother.

The Durels gathered at the family vault in St. Roch Cemetery to bury Tisha's body. They had last been there two years earlier for the burial of Stafford's uncle Milton, who had been in a nursing home and died a month shy of his eighty-fifth birthday. This time, the mood was somber as the family grieved the loss of someone so young. It was the kind of grief that Black mothers had often felt over the centuries as their children were taken from them. It was the grief of Marie Jeanne, when my fifth-great-grandfather sold her daughter because the child had reached a profitable age; the grief of the mothers of Cuspin and Felix in Saint-Domingue, when my fourth-great-grandfather took them away and sold them in New Orleans, doubling his money; and the grief of Betsy, Celie, and the other women held captive for breeding by my third-great-grandfather, when he tore their children from their arms and took them to the slave market.

Following the deaths of Shirleyrine (2002) and Stafford (2004), two more of their grandchildren died from gun violence. Stafford Jr.'s son, Edward, was killed mistakenly in a drive-by shooting during the turmoil following Hurricane Katrina in 2005. In 2017, Theresa's son, Terrence, was visiting his eight-year-old son, who lived with his estranged wife, when he was fatally shot in an altercation with the wife's boyfriend. Of Stafford's nine children, three have grieved the loss of a child to a gun. In contrasting my story with his, nothing stands out more. Death by violence is a common occurrence among poor, urban, working-class Black families today, at a rate that would be unacceptable if it occurred among Whites. It is the tragic, living legacy of racist systems that have shaped the experiences of Black families in America for more than three centuries.

The infliction of pain and the experience of loss, from one generation to the next, tears at my heart. Black mothers, especially, have suffered. My thoughts go to a poem by Pádraic Pearse, who fought against injustice in another place and time.[18] In the poem, a mother prays to God, grieving the loss of two sons to violence.

> *I do not grudge them: Lord, I do not grudge*
> *My two strong sons that I have seen go out*
> *To break their strength and die . . .*
> . . .
> *Lord, thou art hard on mothers:*
> *We suffer their coming and their going;*
> *And tho' I grudge them not, I weary, weary*
> *Of the long sorrow . . .*

A long sorrow. A sorrow Black mothers have endured for centuries.

I met Stafford's daughter, Theresa, just three years after her son Terrence was killed. As I have gotten to know her, I have come to admire her strength and fortitude. As one of the last beneficiaries of integrated public education before White parents and their leaders abandoned the public school system, she rose above the limitations that plagued her forbears and was the first in her family to earn a degree beyond high school. Instead of making a living with her hands, she moved into management and has been responsible for a post office branch for nearly thirty years. Her success has been due to her own determination as well as to laws passed during the Civil Rights era that gave Black people greater opportunities for education and employment. Yet, she too has had to struggle and face adversity, especially with the killing of Terrence. She is a strong woman, but the violent loss of her son is always with her.

Fig 14: *The author at the Durel family tomb with Theresa Durel Reed, Catherine Durel Brown, Patricia Durel Bernard, and Stafford Durel Jr.,* St. Roch Cemetery, 2021. Courtesy of Theresa Durel Reed.

Epilogue

The Durel family tomb in St. Roch Cemetery stands against the southern wall and consists of two vaults, the middle and lower ones in a vertical arrangement of three. A marble tablet fronts each vault with names of those buried within. As is the custom in New Orleans, deceased family members are interred in each wall vault, and as another member dies, the longest buried remains are removed from the coffin and pushed to the rear, a new coffin is slid into place, and another name is added to the tablet.

Cemetery records show that thirteen members of Edward Durel's family have been buried in the vaults over the years, although currently there are only six names inscribed. The oldest inscription, on the middle tablet, dates from 1890 and is written in French. It is for Edward's brother, Leon Durel, age twenty-one, who died from tuberculosis at a time when that disease was rampant in the city. An earlier tablet on the lower vault was heavily damaged and replaced by a new one, which is now inscribed with the names of Stafford and Shirleyrine. The missing names include Edward, his wife, Mary, two more of his brothers, one of his sons, and notably, a baby named Stanley, who was Stafford's twin brother.

On an overcast Sunday afternoon, October 24, 2021, I visited the tomb with four of Stafford and Shirleyrine's children—Theresa, Catherine, Patricia and Stafford Jr. (Figure 14). I had made contact with Theresa, the youngest daughter, a year earlier and had had several phone conversations with her. The COVID-19 pandemic prevented me from making a trip to New Orleans until the fall of 2021, and I was eager to make a personal connection, for we were yet strangers. She and her siblings were pleased with the idea that their father's story would appear in a published book and had readily shared their memories of him over the phone; I hoped to create a stronger relationship.

Just before our scheduled rendezvous, I found I had enough time to visit another tomb, that of my fourth-great-grandfather, Ursin (1), in St. Louis Cemetery No. 1 on Basin Street. I opened the prologue to this book with the story of Ursin's purchase of two Black men, Felix and Cuspin. At the time, I did not know what to make of his actions and thus began a nearly ten-year quest to understand race in the history of my family and in my own childhood. Although not preconceived, these visits to the graves of both Ursin and Stafford on that Sunday now feel like bookends to my journey.

At St. Roch, Stafford's children and I stood in silence for a moment and then talked about the names they recognized: Tisha, their sister Linda's daughter, who had been murdered; their father's uncle Milton, who had not played a large part in their lives but for whom their youngest brother was named; and Jean Scott, Uncle Milton's friend with whom he had lived for years after the death of his wife, Blanche. For my part, I explained the French inscription, noting how far back their Creole roots went, and told them about the missing names, especially Edward (their father's grandfather), whose house we would visit next. Before leaving the cemetery, we posed for a picture, and then Catherine, whose husband is a minister, asked that we say a prayer. After that, she blessed me on the forehead with oil from a vial she carried with her.

North Johnson Street is just two blocks north of St. Roch Cemetery. This is where Edward and my grandfather, Walter, lived within sight of each other. When we got there, I positioned us so that we could see both houses and pointed out how my dad and their uncle Milton had been the same age. I said that one might expect that two nine-year-old boys in 1915 would find each other and play together. Jim Crow was just taking hold in working-class neighborhoods, where Black and White families continued to live in proximity to one another. That said, it is just as likely that, even if they did start playing together, their mothers would have called them in and warned them not to, for fear of what neighbors would say or do. The two boys certainly could never have become friends, a simple fact that resonated with me as I thought about my own childhood. It was important for me to share this in order to give them a better sense of why I was so interested in writing about their family and comparing it to mine.

From North Johnson, we continued a few more blocks to the corner of Mandeville and North Tonti Streets, where Edward had created the family compound that served them well through the Great Depression. It was in the left half of the little house facing North Tonti that, on July 19, 1928, their father and his twin were born. I shared with them the evidence I had discovered about his childhood and his grandparents, parents, aunts, and uncles.

This was our last stop on the tour. I would have liked to have gone on by car to the corner of Conti and North Rocheblave Streets, where they had grown up, but there was no time. As we parted ways, I thought about our time together and realized that it was the kind of gathering with Black relatives that I would have been denied growing up, but that would have been possible two hundred years ago when Creole cousins of both races openly acknowledged one another. I felt a sensation of coming full-circle and returning to a time when my Creole family was not ruled completely by racial differences.

I have newfound cousins and a new understanding of our shared Creole history. This is my answer to the question of what to do with the fact that my fourth-great-grandfather enslaved two Black men and quickly sold them for a profit. I cannot change the past, eliminate the sorrow, dismiss the injustice, or disregard the continued effects of racism. I can, however, take heart from those brief moments when our forebears sat at the same dinner table, studied in the same classroom, prayed in the same church, and maybe, just maybe, played together in the street. While the stories of my family show that the forces of White supremacy that have separated us and done grave harm never disappear completely, and that we must be vigilant and ready to push back, the rare moments of friendship and communion reveal what is possible and offer hope.

As I come to the end of this work, my mind turns to the future. I think of my granddaughters and of Theresa's grandchildren, whose photographs are arrayed on the ledge behind her office desk. My dream (inspired by Dr. King) is that they and their children live lives rich in diversity, where strangers are welcomed with curiosity and generosity, where no one is left out, and where no one is judged simply because of their ancestry or the color of their skin.

Acknowledgments

I wish to recognize and thank the unsung heroes of genealogical and historical research: the many archivists who collect, organize, conserve, and make available the documents and images that are the foundation of a book like this. Without their professional guidance and steady commitment, no historical undertaking would be possible.

I thank also my family and many friends for their support and encouragement, in particular Julia Bland, Benjie Castrillo, Jessica Dorman, Justin Durel, Miki Pfeffer, Lawrence Powell, and Theresa Durel Reed.

Above all, I could not have undertaken this ten-year quest without my wife, Anita Nowery Durel, who has been both my rock and my inspiration.

Abbreviations

CD plus year: City Directory for the year indicated (e.g., CD: 1822)

HNOC: Historic New Orleans Collection, New Orleans, LA

LSM: Louisiana State Museum, New Orleans, LA

NARA: US National Archives and Records Administration

NONA: New Orleans Notarial Archives, Orleans Parish Clerk of Court

NOPL: New Orleans Public Library, City Archives and Special Collections

SLC: Saint Louis Cathedral Sacramental Records, Archives of the Archdiocese of New Orleans

Appendix

Durel Family Genealogies

Note: For birth, death, and marriage dates, I have cited primary sources in those cases where I have been able to see the actual source in an archive or an image of the source online. In other instances, I have depended on the work of others, primarily Robert de Berardinis, "Pre-Revolutionary French Marriage Evidences: A Durel-LeBrun Example," *National Genealogical Society Quarterly* 88, no. 2 (June 2000); and Estelle M. Fortier Cochran, *The Fortier Family, and Allied Families* (n.p., 1963).

I. The Founding Generation

Jean Baptiste Durel and Cécile LeBrun

Jean Baptiste Durel was born June 10, 1727, in Bordeaux, France. His father was Jean-Antoine Durel, a master *tapissier* (carpet/upholstery maker). His mother was Marguérite Barreau, who died when he was a child, and he was raised by his stepmother, Catherine Barron. As a young man, Jean Baptiste worked with his father and became a master *tapissier* as well.

Cécile LeBrun was a native of Blaye, across and downriver from the port of Bordeaux. The date of her birth is unknown. She was the daughter of Charles LeBrun, a master joiner, and Magdeleine Coulombrier.

Jean Baptiste and Cécile wed on September 14, 1752, in the church of Saint-Projet in Bordeaux. They departed Bordeaux in the year following their marriage and were in New Orleans by July 7, 1754, when their first child was born.

Cécile died on January 20, 1785, in New Orleans. Continuation of the Book of Funerals for Whites from the first of October 1784 to the conclusion of the book, 2, SLC.

Jean Baptiste died on June 4, 1790, in New Orleans. Continuation of the Book of Funerals for Whites from the first of October 1784 to the conclusion of the book, 23, SLC.

II. Children of Jean Baptiste Durel and Cécile LeBrun

1. Marie Cécile Rose Durel, called Rose

Born July 7, 1754 in New Orleans. Second Register of Baptisms 1753–1759, 25, SLC.

Married Michel Fortier before November 1774, when their first son was born.

Buried August 28, 1788, in New Orleans. Continuation of the Book of Funerals for Whites from the first of October 1784 to the conclusion of the book, 15, SLC.

2. Mathurin Durel

Born March 3, 1756, in New Orleans. Second Register of Baptisms 1753–1759, 53 back, SLC.

Died after February 10, 1761, when he served as godfather for his brother Jean Baptiste, and before June 4, 1790, when his name is not listed among the heirs to Jean Baptiste Durel.

3. Jean François Durel, called François

Baptized February 4, 1758, in New Orleans. Second Baptismal Register, 1753–1759, 89, SLC.

Married Marie Dejan, called Manette, December 9, 1783, in New Orleans. Book of Marriages 1777–1784, 161, SLC.

Died March 13, 1812, in New Orleans. Book of Funerals, 1803–1815, 196, SLC.

4. Marie Félicité, called Félicité

Born April 19, 1759, in New Orleans. Berardinis, "Pre-Revolutionary," 106, 69n.

Married Elias Toutant Beauregard, c. 1782. Elias dropped the use of "Toutant" in many documents and is called Elias Beauregard in the text.

Died July 27, 1809, in New Orleans. Book of Funerals, 1803–1815, 62, SLC.

5. Jean Baptiste, sometimes called Baptiste, referred to as **Jean Baptiste (2)** in the text to distinguish him from his father

Born January 26, 1761, in New Orleans. Berardinis, "Pre-Revolutionary," 106, 67n.

Married Marie Claire Andry, called Clarisse, March 31, 1785, in New Orleans. Book of Marriages from April 1784 onwards, 36, SLC.

Died November 6, 1809. Tombstone, St. Louis Cemetery #2, New Orleans.

6. Victoire (1)

Born January 29, 1763, died young, probably before June 1766 when another child was given this name. Register 5, *Le Cinquieme Registre des Baptimes et Mariages des Blancs et des Personnes de Couler libre et esclaves,* 6, SLC.

7. Jean Ursin Durel, called Ursin

Born August 5, 1764, in New Orleans. Berardinis, "Pre-Revolutionary," 106, 73n.

Married Marie Françoise Dejan on July 1, 1789. Notarial Records of Pedro Pedesclaux, 1789, vol. 7, Act 667, NONA.

Died May 4, 1817. Berardinis, "Pre-Revolutionary," 106, 75n. Tombstone, St. Louis Cemetery #1, New Orleans.

8. Félicité Victoire, called **Victoire (2)** in the text

Born June 8, 1766, in New Orleans. Book of Baptisms and Marriages, 1763–1766, 135, SLC.

Married Marie Louis Florent Basile, called Florent, November 29, 1781. Book of Marriages 1777–1784, 161, SLC.

Died after 1818. She is mentioned in her husband's last will and testament, dated June 8, 1816, and probated in September 1818. Succession and Probate Records, Some Early Years Are Loose Papers Dec 10, 1781, 1806–1899, Louisiana. District Court (St. Charles Parish), St. Charles, Louisiana, 1811–1818, September 9, 1818.

9. Aimée Marie Victoire, called Aimée

Born November 17, 1768, in New Orleans. Register of Baptisms, Marriages, Funerals 1764–1774, 36, SLC.

Married Jacques Fortier, October 1787. NONA: F. Rodriguez, 13:905.

Died November 27, 1843. Succession and Probate Records, 1805–1849, Louisiana. Probate Court (Orleans Parish), Successions Probate F, 1843–1844, September 24, 1844.

10. François Honoré

Born March 5, 1771; died young. Book of Baptisms, Marriages, Funerals, 1764–1774, 103, SLC.

III. Third Generation: Grandchildren of Jean Baptiste Durel and Cécile LeBrun

Children of Rose Durel and Michel Fortier

1. Jean Michel

Born November 24, 1774. Baptismal Register for Whites and Colored, 1772–1776, 114 back, SLC.

Life partner c. 1810–1836, Henriette Milon, free woman of color.

Died April 13, 1836. Louisiana Probate Court, Orleans Parish Estate Files; Jean Michel Fortier, May 5, 1736.

2. **Félicité Julie,** called Julie

   Born 1777. Inferred from Estate Inventory of Rose Durel, Louisiana State Historical Museum, Spanish Judicial Records, File 1790.01.05.01, January 1790.

   Married c. 1795 to François Aime, who died September 9, 1799. Fourth Book of Funerals for Whites, from September 3, 1793 to December 24, 1803, 75, SLC.

   Second marriage to Firmin Adelard Fortier. Cochran, *The Fortier Family*, 52.

   Died c. 1806. Cochran, *The Fortier Family*, 52.

3. **Zenon**

   Born July 21, 1780. Baptisms Book 1 for Only Whites, 1777–1786, 103. SLC.

   Died October 6, 1799. Fourth Book of Funerals for Whites, from September 3, 1793 to December 24, 1803, 82, SLC.

4. **Victoire**

   Born 1782.

   Died October 9, 1792. Continuation of the Book for Whites from the first of October 1784 to the conclusion of the book, 56, SLC.

5. **Louis Edmond,** called **Edmond** in text

   Baptized September 10, 1785. Baptisms Book 1 for Only Whites, 1777–1786, 383, SLC.

   Married 1805 to Félicité LaBranche. Cochran, *The Fortier Family*, 81.

   Died March 11, 1849. Cochran, *The Fortier Family*, 81.

6. Marie Isabel

Born September 9, 1787. Baptisms, 1786–1796, 41, SLC.

Death date unknown.

Children of François Durel and Manette Dejan

1. Jean Baptiste, referred to as **Jean Baptiste (3)** in the text

Born c. 1785.

Married c. 1718 to Elizabeth de Glapion. Identified in the baptismal record of their only child. Book of baptisms, 1818–1822, 202, SLC.

Died May 25, 1857. Obituary, *Le Courrier de la Louisiane,* May 27, 1857, 2.

2. Jean Firmin

Baptized September 10, 1785. Baptisms Book 1 for Only Whites, 1777–1786, 384, SLC.

Died young, date unknown.

3. Ursin

Born c. 1789.

Died July 21, 1795. The Fourth Book of Funerals for Whites, from September 3, 1793 to December 24, 1803, 25, SLC.

4. Jean Baptiste Neuville, called Neuville

Born January 5, 1792. Second Book of Baptisms for Whites, beginning May 1786, 150, SLC.

Married c. 1820 to Louise Eugenie Dupuy, who died July 22, 1871. Obituary: *Daily Picayune*, July 23, 1871, 6.

Died February 25, 1841. Margin note in baptismal record.

5. Louis

Born January 9, 1795. Second Book of Baptisms for Whites, beginning May 1786, 358, SLC.

Died before adulthood.

6. Apposint

Born c. 1796.

Died September 23, 1802. Book of Funerals for Whites, 1793-1803, 116, SLC.

7. Justine

Born June 6, 1797. Third Book of Baptisms for Whites, from 1 April 1796 to 7 March 1802, 41, SLC.

Married prior to 1815 to Jean Baptiste Perrault. Orleans Parish Estate Files, Wills and Probate Records, 1756–1984, Marie Dejean Durel, 22 August 1833, New Orleans City Archives, NOPL.

Died, date unknown.

8. Justin (twin of Justine)

Born June 6, 1797. Third Book of Baptisms for Whites, from 1 April 1796 to 7 March 1802, 41, SLC.

Died August 1, 1801. Fourth Book of Funerals for Whites, from September 3, 1793 to December 24, 1803, 99, SLC.

9. Aimée

Born August 28, 1799. Third Book of Baptisms for Whites, from 1 April 1796 to 7 March 1802, 110, SLC.

Married c. 1809 to Michel Andry. Probate Cases, 1823–1845, Michel Andry, 13 April 1835, Probate Court (Orleans Parish), Ancestry.com.

Died November 7, 1857. Obituary: *Daily Picayune,* November 8, 1857, 6; *Le Courrier de la Louisiane,* November 8, 1857, 2.

10. Claudio Faustino, called Justin following the death of the eighth child

Born August 24, 1801. Fourth Register of Baptisms for Whites, 3, SLC.

Married Caroline, maiden name unknown. Passenger Lists of Vessels Arriving at New Orleans, Louisiana,1820–1902, M259-10, 3 November 1832, NAID 2824927, Records of the Immigration and Naturalization Service, RG 85, NARA, College Park, MD.

Died February 28, 1871. Obituary Index: *New Orleans Bee,* April 1, 1871, 1.

11. Jean Julio Delphin

Baptized July 27, 1806. Baptismal Register, 1806–1809, 9, SLC.

Died September 28, 1807. Book of Funerals, 1803–1807, 132, SLC.

12. Victoire

Born November 5, 1803. Fourth Baptismal Register for Whites, 51 back, SLC.

Died January 12, 1808. Book of Funerals 1803–1815, 9, SLC.

13. Michel

Baptized September 12, 1808. Baptisms Register, 1806–1809, 58, SLC.

Lived with Juliette Lacroix, a free woman of color. Federal Census, 1850, New Orleans Municipality 1 Ward 5 family 2109.

Died September 22, 1854. Obituary Index: *Le Courrier de la Louisiane*, September 23, 1854, 1; Louisiana Death Index vol. 16, 249.

14. Antonia Victoria

Baptized 1811. Sixth Register of Baptisms for Whites, 1809–1811, 148 back, SLC.

Died April 8, 1812, buried with her father. Book of Funerals, 1803–1815, 197, SLC.

Children of Marie Félicité Durel and Elias Beauregard,
also called Elias Toutant Beauregard

Note: This family lived many years outside of New Orleans, so records for them are not as complete as for other descendant families.

1. Félicité

Born April 8, 1783. Baptisms Book 1 for Only Whites, 1777–1786, 295, SLC.

Married Manuel Perez prior to 1809, when a son was born. Sixth Register of Baptisms for Whites, 1809–1811, 160, SLC.

2. Bartholomew

Baptized April 19, 1784. Baptisms Book 1 for Only Whites, 1777–1786, 322, SLC.

Death date unknown.

3. Marie Rose

Born July 7, 1786. Second Book of Baptisms for Whites, beginning May 1786, 3, SLC.

Married Jacques Guesnon before 1809, when daughter was born. Seventh Register of Marriages for Whites, 1811–1815, 105, SLC.

Died August 5, 1830. Margin note in baptismal record.

4. Manuel

Birth date unknown.

Married Leocadia Leonard prior to 1814, when a daughter was born. Seventh Register of Marriages for Whites, 1811–1815, 117, SLC.

5. Victoire

Born February 15, 1795. Second Book of Baptisms for Whites, beginning May 1786, 393, SLC.

Death date unknown.

6. Maria Elias

Born April 17, 1799. Third Book of Baptisms for Whites, from 1 April 1796 to 7 March 1802, 101, SLC.

Death date unknown.

Children of Jean Baptiste Durel (2) and Suson Santilly

1. Michel

In the 1810 Federal Census for New Orleans, Michel is listed as Merrick Durel; in 1820, he is listed as Michel Durel.

Baptized September 23, 1781. Baptisms for Colored, 1777–1783, 231. SLC

Died c. 1829. Vieux Carré Survey, 1014–1016 St. Phillip Street.

2. Maria Amada, called Aimée

Born July 2, 1783. Baptisms of Negroes and Mulattos, 1783–1786, 53. SLC.

Unmarried.

Died October 11, 1866. Obituary Index *New Orleans Bee,* October 12, 1866, 1.

3. Maria Félicité, called Félicité

Born March 5, 1785. Baptisms of Negroes and Mulattos, 1783–1786, 105, SLC.

Married Luis Villemont, also called Celestin Villemont, free man of color. Book of marriages, 1806–1821, 222, SLC.

Died 1857. Louisiana State Archives, Orleans Parish Death Index, 24 November 1857, vol. 35, 185.

Children of Jean Baptiste Durel (2) and Clarisse Andry

1. Jean Florent

Born March 11, 1786. Second Book of Baptisms for Whites, beginning May 1786, 7, SLC.

Life partner c. 1819, Idalise Manadé, free woman of color.

Died c. 1878. New Orleans City Archives, Orleans Parish Will Books, v. 26 (1893–1895), Case 43192, 10 July 1894.

2. Eloise

Born January 2, 1788. Second Book of Baptisms for Whites, beginning May 1786, 59, SLC.

Married May 30, 1803, to Jean Baptiste Dejan. Book of Marriages from April 1784 onwards, 150, SLC.

Died after 1850.

3. Victoire, called **Victoire (3)** in the text

Born June 20, 1791. Second Book of Baptisms for Whites, beginning May 1786, 150, SLC.

Married Antoine Abat. Antoine Abat family tomb, St. Louis Cemetery No. 2, New Orleans, Louisiana.

Died October 21, 1864. Obituary Index, *New Orleans Bee,* October 22, 1864, 1, 5.

4. **Jean Baptiste Zenon**

Born December 4, 1793. Second Book of Baptisms for Whites, beginning May 1786, 301, SLC.

Died September 17, 1794. The Fourth Book of Funerals for Whites, from September 3, 1793 to December 24, 1803, 15, SLC.

5. **Michel Valcour**

Born September 22, 1795. Second Book of Baptisms for Whites, beginning May 1786, 413, SLC.

Lived with Barbé Thennat, free woman of color. Federal Census 1850 New Orleans, Municipality 1, Ward 4, family 680; Federal Census 1840 New Orleans, Ward 1.

Died February 13, 1851. Obituary Index, *New Orleans Bee,* February 14, 1851, 1. Louisiana Death Index vol. 12, 634.

6. **Justinian**

Born November 8, 1797. Third Book of Baptisms for Whites, from 1 April 1796 to 7 March 1802, p47, SLC.

Died June 26, 1799. Fourth Book of Funerals for Whites, from September 3, 1793 to December 24, 1803, 66, SLC.

7. **Louis Valsin,** called Valsin

Born July 17, 1799. Third Book of Baptisms for Whites, from 1 April 1796 to 7 March 1802, 111, SLC.

Lived with Suzanne Lorenza. Federal Census 1850, New Orleans Municipality 1 Ward 6 family 3432.

Married Tammy T. Southwick prior to February 11, 1863. Vieux Carré Digital Survey, 1028 Burgundy Street, Feb 11, 1863.

Died October 19, 1883, in New York. Obituary Index, *New Orleans Bee,* October 24, 1883, 1.

8. Jean Baptiste Zenon (second child with this name)

Born December 16, 1801. Fourth Register of Baptisms for Whites, 2. SLC.

Died May 14, 1841. Margin note in baptismal record; Obituary Index, *Le Courrier de la Louisiane,* May 15, 1841, 1, 2. Louisiana Death Index vol. 8, 740.

9. Adolph

Born December 15, 1803. Fourth Register of Baptisms for Whites, 1802–1806, 58 back, SLC.

Married Celestine Forstall. Book of Marriages, 1821–1830, 208, SLC.

Died May 15, 1855. Louisiana Death Index vol. 16, 544.

10. Clara

Born December 18, 1805. Fourth Register of Baptisms for Whites, 1802–1806, 135 back, SLC.

Married Edmond J. Forstall. E. J. Family tomb, St. Louis Cemetery No. 2, New Orleans, Louisiana.

Died May 7, 1879. Obituary Index, *New Orleans Bee,* May 8, 1879, 1. *Daily Picayune,* May 8, 4.

11. Jean Baptiste Gustave

Born c. 1809.

Married. Federal Census 1840, New Orleans Ward 1.

Died July 23, 1861. Louisiana Death Index vol. 21, 546.

12. Infant Daughter, Name Unknown

Died March 28, 1810. Book of Funerals, 1803–1815, 117, SLC.

Children of Victoire Durel and Florent Basile

1. **Victoire Cécile**

Born October 19, 1782. Baptisms Book 1 Only for Whites, 1777–1786, 286. SLC

Married c. 1800 to Louis-Hector de Mons D'Orbigny in Saint-Domingue. P. Louis Lainé, *Archives généalogiques et historiques de la noblesse de France* (Paris: n.p., 1839), 14–15.

Died prior to her father's death in 1816. Succession and Probate Records 1806–1899, Louisiana; District Court (St. Charles Parish) Case Number 1, 9 September 1818.

2. **Jean Florent**

Born July 1, 1784. Baptisms Book 1 for Only Whites, 1777–1786, 383, SLC.

Resident of Havana in 1816. Succession and Probate Records 1806–1899, Louisiana, District Court (St. Charles Parish) Case Number 1, 9 September 1818.

Death date unknown.

3. **François Edward**

Baptized September 10, 1785. Baptisms Book 1 for Only Whites, 1777–1786, 384, SLC.

Died without heirs prior to his father's death in 1816. Succession and Probate Records 1806–1899, Louisiana District Court (St. Charles Parish) Case Number 1, 9 September 1818.

Children of Ursin Durel and Françoise Dejan

1. **François**

Born January 1, 1791. Second Book of Baptisms for Whites, beginning May 1786, 125, SLC.

Died November 27, 1796. Fourth Book of Funerals for Whites, from September 3, 1793 to December 24, 1803, 42. SLC.

2. **Ursin,** referred to as **Ursin (2)** in the text

Born c. 1793.

Married Polymnie Rochefort, date unknown. See Probate record cited below.

Died 1845. Obituary Index, *New Orleans Bee*, February 7, 1845, 2. Louisiana Succession and Probate Records 1805–1849, Probate D, 1844–1845, Case 144, Ursin Durel, 10 July 1845, Probate Court (Orleans Parish), Ancestry.com.

3. **Michel**

Born December 9, 1794. Second Book of Baptisms for Whites, beginning May 1786, 354, SLC.

Died October 3, 1796. Fourth Book of Funerals for Whites, from September 3, 1793 to December 24, 1803, 37, SLC.

4. **Edmond Hubert**

Born September 3, 1796. Third Book of Baptisms for Whites, from 1 April 1796 to 7 March 1802, 24, SLC.

Died May 8, 1799. Fourth Book of Funerals for Whites, from September 3, 1793 to December 24, 1803, 65, SLC.

5. **Louise Caroline**, called Caroline

Born September 27, 1798. Third Book of Baptisms for Whites, from 1 April 1796 to 7 March 1802, 77, SLC.

Married Pierre Louis Messant c. 1832. Orleans Parish Estate Files, L. Caroline Durel, 11 March 1834, New Orleans City Archives, NOPL, Ancestry.com.

Died October 23, 1833. Louisiana Death Index vol. 5, 117.

6. Michel Alfred

Born August 15, 1806. Baptismal Register, 1806–1809, 8, SLC.

Died September 1811. Book of Funerals, 1803–1815, 180, SLC.

7. Hortaire (Arthur, baptized Jean Ortero)

Baptized August 1809. Sixth Register of Baptisms for Whites, 1809–1811, 7, SLC.

Died January 14, 1822. Ursin Durel tombstone, St. Louis No. 1 Cemetery, New Orleans.

8. Theodore

Born February 20, 1811. Seventh Register of Baptisms for Whites, 9 back, SLC.

Married Fortuné St. Cyr, date unknown. Federal Census, 1850, First Municipality, Ward 6, 532.

Died April 16, 1886. Obituary Index, *Daily Picayune,* April 16, 1886, 4; *Daily Picayune*, April 18, 1866, 4.

9. Eugène

Born c. 1814.

Died April 30, 1833. Ursin Durel tombstone, St. Louis No. 1 Cemetery, New Orleans.

Children of Aimée Durel and Jacques Fortier

Note: unless otherwise noted, the source for these individuals is Cochran, *The Fortier Family.*

1. Jean Baptiste

Born February 21, 1789. Second Book of Baptisms for Whites, beginning May 1786, 85, SLC.

Died October 2, 1797. Fourth Book of Funerals for Whites, from September 3, 1793 to December 24, 1803, 52.

2. **Michel**

Baptized January 28, 1791. Second Book of Baptisms for Whites, beginning May 1786, 120, SLC.

Died without heirs, date unknown.

3. **Omer**

Birth date unknown.

Married c. 1813 to Charlotte Adele Chauvin de Lery.

Died September 15, 1820. Succession and Probate Records, 1805–1849; Louisiana; Probate Court (Orleans Parish), Successions Probate F, 1843–1844, Sep 24, 1844.

4. **Norbert**

Only mentioned in probate record of his mother.

Birth date unknown.

Married February 8, 1817, to Delphine Sarpy.

Death date unknown.

5. **Honoré Faustus**

Born August 15, 1794. Second Book of Baptisms for Whites, beginning May 1786, 332, SLC.

Died November 29, 1795. Fourth Book of Funerals for Whites, from September 3, 1793 to December 24, 1803, 28, SLC.

6. Pauline

Born 1796.

Married Jean Pierre Sarpy, date unknown. Succession and Probate Records, 1805–1849; Louisiana. Probate Court (Orleans Parish), Successions Probate F, 1843–1844, Sep 24, 1844.

Died December 15, 1862.

7. Aimée

Born December 20, 1797. Third Book of Baptisms for Whites, from 1 April 1796 to 7 March 1802, 53, SLC.

Unmarried. Succession and Probate Records, 1805–1849; Louisiana. Probate Court (Orleans Parish), Successions Probate F, 1843–1844, September 24, 1844.

Died May 29, 1857.

8. Victoire Victorine

Born August 31, 1799. Third Book of Baptisms for Whites, from 1 April 1796 to 7 March 1802, 125, SLC.

Married Fa Noël Destrehan, date unknown.

Died without heirs, May 8, 1825.

9. Edmond

Born April 3, 1801. Third Book of Baptisms for Whites, from 1 April 1796 to 7 March 1802, 151, SLC.

Death date unknown.

10. Adelard

Birth date unknown.

Married April 22, 1824, to Annette Lelande Ferriere.

Died June 16, 1833.

11. Cydalise

Born September 12, 1807. Register of Baptisms, 1806–1809, 56, SLC.

Married Edourd de Boisbane, date unknown. Succession and Probate Records, 1805–1849; Louisiana. Probate Court (Orleans Parish), Successions Probate F, 1843–1844, Sep 24, 1844.

Death date unknown.

12. Edouard

Born March 3, 1812. Seventh Register of Baptisms for Whites, 1811–1815, 35, SLC.

Married May 22, 1837, to Françoise Euphemie LaBranche.

Died May 22, 1837.

Endnotes

Prologue

1. I used three sources to recreate this encounter: Afro-Louisiana History and Genealogy Slave database, record for "Cuspin," www.ibiblio.org/laslave/individ.php?sid=20705; Pedro Pedesclaux, X, 243, NONA; "Petition to prove ownership of Negro slave and to obtain permit to sell same," no. 1790-03-15-01, Spanish Judicial Records, RG 2, LSM Historical Center.

2. Throughout this book I use the adjective *enslaved* rather than the noun *slave* to emphasize that slavery was a condition imposed on Africans and people of African descent. Slavery did not define who they were. It only defined their status within a social and economic system that was imposed on them. Similarly, I use the word *captive* in referring to enslaved people to underscore that they were held against their will.

3. Ned Sublette, *The World That Made New Orleans: From Spanish Silver to Congo Square* (Chicago: Lawrence Hill Books, 2009), 134–50.

4. Lawrence N. Powell, *The Accidental City: Improvising New Orleans* (Cambridge, MA: Harvard University Press, 2012), 210.

5. The Spanish piaster was widely used in French and Spanish colonies. Also known as a "piece of eight," it was worth about 5.25 French livre (5 livre, 5 sous) at the time of the American Revolution. After the revolution, the United States dollar was introduced at par with the Spanish piaster, and a dollar in 1790 would be worth roughly $34.27 in 2024. Robert A. Selig and the State of Delaware, "Notes on Conversion Between Eighteenth Century Currencies," 2003, http://w3r-archive.org/history/library/seligreptde6.pdf; Official Data Foundation, CPI Inflation Calculator, www.officialdata.org, accessed March 15, 2023.

6. Nell Irvin Painter, *The History of White People* (New York: W.W. Norton & Co., 2010), 72–86.

7. Jennifer M. Spear, *Race, Sex, and Social Order in Early New Orleans* (Baltimore: Johns Hopkins University Press, 2009), 129.

8. The 1963 black-and-white movie *Hud* is set on a ranch in west Texas and stars Paul Newman as an arrogant son in conflict with his father.

9. Charles R. Maduell Jr., "The Durel Family History, Part II," *New Orleans Genesis* XXI, no. 81 (January 1982): 53.

10. Robert de Berardinis, "Pre-Revolutionary French Marriage Evidences: A Durel-LeBrun Example," *National Genealogical Society Quarterly* 88, no. 2 (June 2000): 87–110.

11. Justin H. Durel, "The Call of the Sirens" (unpublished poem, 2017).

12. On the controversy among historians about the Thomas Jefferson-Sally Hemings relationship, see: Pearl M. Graham, "Thomas Jefferson and Sally Hemings," *The Journal of Negro History* 46, no. 2 (April 1961), 89–103; Fawn Brodie, *Thomas Jefferson: An Intimate History* (New York: W.W. Norton, 1974); Annette Gordon-Reed, *Thomas Jefferson and Sally Hemings: An American Controversy* (Charlottesville: University of Virginia Press, 1997); Jennifer Jenson Wallach, "The Vindication of Fawn Brodie," *The Massachusetts Review* 43, no. 2 (Summer 2002), 277–95.

Chapter 1

1. de Berardinis, "Pre-Revolutionary," 87–110. De Berardinis uses and cites primary sources for his account of the marriage of Jean Baptiste Durel and Cécile LeBrun.

2. Julie Hardwick, *The Practice of Patriarchy: Gender and the Politics of Household Authority in Early Modern France* (University Park: Pennsylvania State University Press, 1998), 56; Margaret H. Darrow, "Popular Concepts of Marital Choice in Eighteenth Century France," *Journal of Social History* 19, no. 2 (Winter 1985): 261–72.

3. Henri Sée, *Economic and Social Conditions in France During the Eighteenth Century*, Edwin H. Zeydel, trans. (Kitchener, Canada: Batoche Books, 2004), 109.

4. de Berardinis, "Pre-Revolutionary," 104.

5. Éric Saugera, *Bordeaux Port Nègrier, XVIIe – XIXe siècles* (Biarritz, France: J & D Editions, 1995), Chapters III–V, X-XI.

6. "Registers of certificates of identity and catholicity, submissions and passports concerning the passengers embarked in Bordeaux." This information was recorded by the Bordelaise Genealogical Society at the Departmental Archives of Gironde, date of Departure: January 5, 1753, www.filea.com. Filea is a French online genealogy service.

7. Saugera, *Bordeaux Port Negrier*, 291.

8. Powell, *The Accidental City*, 100–102.

9. Embarkations departing from Bordeaux, 1728, www.filea.com. The same ship sailed in 1730 to Guinée and carried 596 Black captives to Martinique. Saugera, *Bordeaux Port Négrier*, 351.

10. Baptisms Register 2, 1753–1759, 25, entry 262, SLC.

11. Shannon Lee Dawdy, *Building the Devil's Empire: French Colonial New Orleans* (Chicago: University of Chicago Press, 2008), 158.

12. Dawdy, *Building the Devil's Empire,* 176.

13. Gwendolyn Midlo Hall, *Africans in Colonial Louisiana: The Development of Afro-Creole Culture in the Eighteenth Century* (Baton Rouge: Louisiana State University Press, 1992), 72–95,162–63, 175; Powell, *The Accidental City*, 60–77, 122; Dawdy, *Building the Devil's Empire*, 86–90, 197–98.

14. Jessica Marie Johnson, *Wicked Flesh: Black Women, Intimacy, and Freedom in the Atlantic World* (Philadelphia: University of Pennsylvania Press, 2020), 143–50.

15. Johnson, *Wicked Flesh,* 150–165; Hall, *Africans in Colonial Louisiana*, 1–155; Powell, *The Accidental City,* 119; Spear, *Race, Sex, and Social Order,* 7, 85–92, 130–31.

16. Dawdy, *Building the Devil's Empire,* 78.

17. Dawdy, *Building the Devil's Empire,* 183–184.

18. Powell, *The Accidental City,* 110–12; Dawdy, *Building the Devil's Empire,* 181–85.

19. Powell, *The Accidental City*, 131; Sublette, *The World That Made New Orleans*, 81–82.

20. Lease of house, Antoine Aufrere to Jean Baptiste Durel, no. 1758-03-30-03, Judicial Records of the French Superior Council, RG 1, LSM Historical Center.

21. Succession De La Pommeraye, no. 1758-06-02-01, Judicial Records of the French Superior Council, RG 1, LSM Historical Center.

22. Succession of François Songy and Anne Marie Paline, no. 1758-11-20-01, Judicial Records of the French Superior Council, RG 1, LSM Historical Center.

23. Contract of Marriage, no. 1758-01-07-01, Judicial Records of the French Superior Council, RG 1, LSM Historical Center, New Orleans.

24. Marriage Contract, no. 1759-01-29-03, Judicial Records of the French Superior Council, RG 1, LSM Historical Center.

25. Succession of Juan Bautista Durel, no. 1790-06-04-01, Spanish Judicial Records, RG 2, LSM Historical Center.

26. Amelia Peck, ed., *Interwoven Globe: The Worldwide Textile Trade, 1500–1800,* Exhibition catalogue (New York: Metropolitan Museum of Art, 2013), 306; Norman Greville Pounds, *An Economic History of Medieval Europe*, 2nd ed (New York: Taylor and Francis, 1994), 308–20.

27. Petition, no. 1768-04-28-01; Call for bids for church renovation, no. 1769-04-03-02; Civil Case, no. 1769-05-05-05, Judicial Records of the French Superior Council, RG 1, LSM Historical Center.

28. Meeting of the Board of Directors of the Almshouse, no. 1769-01-15-01; Civil Case involving Almshouse, no. 1769-05-07-01, Judicial Records of the French Superior Council, RG 1, LSM Historical Center; Meeting of Almshouse Board of Directors, Black Book 111, April 2, 1769, LSM Historical Center.

29. Meeting of the Almshouse Board of Directors, Black Book 112, June 11, 1769, LSM Historical Center.

30. Powell, *The Accidental City*, 132–52.

31. Meeting of the Almshouse Board of Directors, Black Book 113, July 2, 1769, LSM Historical Center.

32. "Digest of Acts and Deliberations of the Cabildo," Book 1, 6, 49, 168, 203, NOPL.

33. Register of Baptisms, 1767 to 1771, 103, SLC.

34. Jean Baptiste Garic, 6, 309, NONA.

35. Register 2, Baptisms 1753–1759, 53 back, SLC. Jacqueline K. Voorhies, transcriber and compiler, *Some Late Eighteenth Century Louisianians: Census Records 1758–1796* (USL History Series. Lafayette: University of Southwestern Louisiana, 1973), 396.

36. SLC, Register of Baptisms 1764–1774, 36.

37. SLC, Register of Baptisms 1764–1774, 103.

38. SLC, Continuation of the Book for Whites from the first of October 1784 to the conclusion of the book, 2.

39. Emily Clark, *Masterless Mistresses: The New Orleans Ursulines and the Development of a New World Society, 1727–1834* (Chapel Hill: University of North Carolina Press, 2007), 92.

40. Clark, *Masterless Mistresses*, 115n55.

41. Clark, *Masterless Mistresses*, 54–57.

42. Clark, *Masterless Mistresses*, 56, 61.

43. Dawdy, *Building the Devil's Empire*, 59.

44. Prior to 1793, the church located at the head of what is now known as Jackson Square functioned as a parish church, named in honor of Saint Louis, King of France. That structure burned on Good Friday in 1788, in a great fire that destroyed more than eight hundred structures in the city. Upon the building of a new and more imposing structure to replace the old parish church, the Spanish crown elevated it to cathedral status.

45. Register 6, Baptisms, Marriages, Funerals, 80–81, SLC.

46. Spanish Census, Braquier's section; Voorhies, *Some Late Eighteenth Century Louisianians.*

47. The fact that the fifth child, Victoire (1), was baptized in February 1763 and is not listed in the census taken that September indicates that she likely died in infancy.

48. Hardwick, *The Practice of Patriarchy,* 91, 104–17.

49. NONA, Leonardo Mazange, v. 7, folio 28 (back), Jan 12, 1783.

50. Cole, Shawn. "Capitalism and Freedom: Manumissions and the Slave Market in Louisiana, 1725-1820." *The Journal of Economic History* 65, no. 4 (2005): 1008–27. http://www.jstor.org/stable/3874912.

51. B.F. French, *Historical Collections of Louisiana,* Black Code of Louisiana, 1724, Art. XXI. Voorhies, "General Census of Braquier's district of New Orleans made by Sieur Braquier, Captain of Militia , during the Month of September, 1763," *Some Late Eighteenth Century Louisianians*, 23.

52. Leonardo Mazange, 1, folio 218, March 16, 1780, NONA.

53. Leonardo Mazange, 5, no. 98, January 26, 1782, NONA.

54. Ester's purchase of the property is mentioned in the subsequent sale she made to Marie Clair Andry in 1810. Pedro Pedesclaux, 60:281, NONA.

55. Fernando Rodriguez, 3, folio 810 (back), November 15, 1784, NONA.

56. Federal Census, 1810, New Orleans, Royale Street; Funerals of Slaves and Free Persons of Color, 1810–1815, 92, SLC.

57. Sublette, *The World That Made New Orleans,* 96–97. For the number of enslaved individuals who purchased freedom, Sublette cites Thomas N. Ingersoll, "Free Blacks in a Slave Society," in *The African American experience in Louisiana: Part A: From Africa to the Civil War*, ed. Charles Vincent, Louisiana Purchase Bicentennial Series in Louisiana History (Lafayette: Center for Louisiana Studies, University of Southwestern Louisiana, 1999).

58. *Acts Passed at the First Session of the First Legislature of the Territory of Orleans* (New Orleans: Printed by Bradford and Anderson, Printers to the Territory, 1807), 150, https://catalog.hathitrust.org/Record/010460241.

59. In the twentieth century much of this property was consolidated by the Monteleone family and now comprises the Monteleone Hotel.

60. Leonardo Mazange, 7, folio 14, January 11, 1783, NONA.

61. Leonardo Mazange, 7, folio 17 (back), January 12, 1783, NONA.

62. Fernando Rodriguez, 1, folio 980, November 18, 1783, NONA.

63. Fernando Rodriguez, 2, folio 2 (back), January 2, 1784, NONA.

64. Fernando Rodriguez, 2, folio 3 (back), January 2, 1784, NONA.

65. Fernando Rodriguez, 2, folio 4 (back), January 2, 1784, NONA.

66. Fernando Rodriguez, 2A, folio 380 (back), May 13, 1784, NONA.

67. Walls around the original city were finally completed in 1760 during the French and Indian War. Powell, *The Accidental City*, 122.

68. "The Collins C. Diboll Vieux Carré Digital Survey," HNOC, https://www.hnoc.org/vcs/index.php.

69. Johnson, *Wicked Flesh*, 133–34.

70. I have pieced together Pierre Claver's story from a number of sources: Emily Clark, *The Strange History of the American Quadroon: Free Women of Color in the Revolutionary Atlantic World* (Chapel Hill: University of North Carolina Press, 2013), 71, 79, 83, 90; Clark, *Masterless Mistresses,* 170; Hall, Gwendolyn Midlo Hall, compiler, "Afro-Louisiana History and Genealogy, Slave Database, 1719–1820," http://www.ibiblio.org/laslave/; Marriages of Slaves and Free People of Color, 1, Part 1, January 1777–June 1821, 13, SLC; Baptisms of Slaves and Free People of Color, 1802–1804, 151 [back], SLC; Baptisms of Slaves and Free People of Color, 1810–1811, 176, SLC; Baptisms of Slaves and Free People of Color, 1814–1816, 136–38, SLC.

71. Padre Pedro Claver y Cobreró boarded ships carrying enslaved Africans and cared for the sick and maimed. He brought food, drink, and medicine to the pens where new arrivals were kept awaiting auction. It is estimated that during his lifetime he baptized around 300,000 people. His fame spread throughout the Spanish colonies, especially among people of African descent. Spanish priests likely brought stories about him to New Orleans. In the nineteenth century, Claver was canonized as the patron saint of missionary work among all African peoples. In the United States, he is known as Saint Peter Claver and has remained an important saint for Black Catholics.

72. "Marechal Durelle" appears in a list of freedmen and free mulattoes settled in the city of New Orleans compiled by Nicolas Bacus, Captain Moraine, undated but appended to a document dated 1770. Voorhies, *Late Eighteenth Century Louisianians,* 256.

73. Clark, *Strange History*, 71–85.

74. Late in life, Pierre made an astute move: he sold the Royal Street property for $5,700—a high price driven by growing demand in that section of the city—and purchased a house on Burgundy Street for about $1,800. He used some of the

profit to invest in a vacant lot on Perdido Street. By this time their older children were grown: a son apprenticed to a blacksmith and a daughter married to a free man of color. Three children remained at home, and the family was supported by the labor of two enslaved women. Pierre died in 1831, Celeste in 1842. Vieux Carré Digital Survey, 212 Royal Street and 522–524 Burgundy Street, HNOC; Louisiana, U.S., Wills and Probate Records, 1756–1984, Jean Pierre Claver probate record, 1831, Ancestry.com.

75. Fernando Rodriguez, 1:980, November 18, 1783; and 1:981, November 18, 1783, NONA.

76. Saidiya Hartman, *Scenes of Subjection: Terror, Slavery, and Self-Making in Nineteenth-Century America* (Oxford University Press, 1997; rev. ed., W.W. Norton & Co., 2022), 55–65.

77. Marisa J. Fuentes, *Dispossessed Lives: Enslaved Women, Violence, and the Archive* (Philadelphia: University of Pennsylvania Press, 2016), 137–40.

78. Hartman, *Scenes of Subjection*, 137, 150–52.

79. Fuentes, *Dispossessed Lives*, 137.

80. Fernando Rodriguez, 8, folio 600, May 11, 1786, NONA.

81. Fernando Rodriguez, 10, folio 1571, December 19, 1786, NONA.

82. Continuation of the Book of Funerals for Whites from the first of October 1784 to the conclusion of the book, 24, SLC.

83. "Proceedings for the Settlement of the Estate of Juan Bautista Durel," File 1802, June 4, 1790, Document 2544, Spanish Judicial Records, RG 2, LSM Historical Center. The file includes an estate inventory in which the enslaved people are described and valued.

84. Second part of Ninth Register of Baptisms for Whites and Colored, 128, SLC.

Chapter 2

1. Clark, *Quadroon*, 100.

2. Clark, *Masterless Mistresses,* 197–98, especially note 3. Powell, *The Accidental City*, 288.

3. I have not found their marriage record. However, their first son, Michel, was born November 11, 1774. Baptismal register of Whites and of color, 1772–1776, 114b, SLC.

4. The plantation was located in what is now Kenner, Louisiana. Rose died in August 1788 while Michel was on a voyage to France and Spain. Upon his return

in December 1789, he arranged for the estate inventory to be taken. Forty percent is the amount of the estate that was put into trust for her children following her death. The value of the two properties, including buildings, contents, farm equipment, livestock, and captives, was 26,187 *pesos* and 2 *reales*. Rose's death is recorded in Continuation of Book of Funerals for Whites from the first of October 1784 to the conclusion of the book, 15, SLC. The estate inventory is catalogued in Estate of Dame Rosa Durel, no. 1790-01-05-01, Spanish Judicial Records, RG 2, LSM Historical Center.

5. The firm of Reaud and Fortier owned two brigantines, *La Thetus* and *El Azard*. In August 1784, probably in order to collect insurance, the firm asked the court to certify the "unavoidable loss" of eight captives who had died during a voyage of *La Thetus* from Saint-Domingue. The ship's captain, doctor, and crew all attested to the loss. Petition to bring a certain vessel with merchandize from France, Black Book 126, September 11, 1783; Petition to obtain authorization to purchase a brigantine, Black Book 126, September 18, 1783; Petition to prove the unavoidable loss of certain Negro slaves, no. 1784-08-26-02; Petition to prove ownership of brigantine named *Thetus,* no. 1787-03-20-01; Request for translation of a document into Spanish, 1790-03-08-01, Spanish Judicial Records, RG 2, LSM Historical Center.

6. Commission to Miguel Fortier by the King of Spain, Black Book 134, September 17, 1787, LSM Historical Center.

7. Cybèle Gontar, ed., *Salazar: Portraits of Influence in Spanish New Orleans, 1785–1802,* (New Orleans: Ogden Museum of Southern Art/University of New Orleans Press, 2018).

8. In an inventory of Rose and Michel's property made in 1790 following her death in 1788, there was a total of fifty-eight enslaved individuals listed. There is a page missing, so the actual number is probably sixty-two or sixty-three. The total value given for the enslaved is 16,792 pesos, out of a total estate value of 26,187. Estate of Dame Rosa Durel, no. 1790-01-05-01, *Spanish Judicial Records,* LSM Historical Center.

9. Book of baptisms, 1786–1796, 41, SLC.

10. Proof of Loss, no. 1790-03-01-01, Spanish Judicial Records, RG 2, LSM Historical Center.

11. Continuation of the Book for Whites from the first of October 1784 to the conclusion of the book, 15, SLC.

12. F. Rodriguez, 13:905, NONA. On the first of October, 1787, Jacques Fortier (son of Michel and namesake of Jacques Beauregard) married Aimée, the youngest

Durel daughter. Jean Baptiste negotiated this marriage not with the elder Michel, who by then had died, but with his son-in-law, Rose's husband. Thus, the eldest and youngest Durel daughters married Fortier brothers.

13. Victoire's death is recorded in Continuation of the Book for Whites from the first of October 1784 to the conclusion of the book, 56, SLC. Zenon's death is in Fourth book of funerals for Whites, from September 3, 1793 to December 24, 1803, 82, SLC.

14. Sublette, *The World That Made New Orleans*, 169–70.

15. Federal Census, 1810, Orleans Parish, Left Shore, 32 (printed page number), 286 (in sequence of handwritten page numbers).

16. Richard Follett, *The Sugar Masters: Planters and Slaves in Louisiana's Cane World, 1820–1860* (Baton Rouge: Louisiana State University Press, 2005), 8–9, 20–21, 23–24.

17. Hartman, *Scenes of Subjection*, 1–3.

18. Louisiana Civil Code, 1825-1853, Art. 167.

19. Louisiana Civil Code, 1825-1853, Art. 173.

20. Acts Passed at the First Session of the First Legislature of the Territory of New Orleans, Black Code, 150–212.

21. Follett, *The Sugar Masters*, 10–12.

22. Follett, *The Sugar Masters,* 126.

23. Follett, *The Sugar Masters*, 197n2.

24. Follett, *The Sugar Masters*, 131–40.

25. Follett, *The Sugar Masters*, 200–10.

26. Follett, *The Sugar Masters*, 220–27.

27. Follett, *The Sugar Masters*, 151–66.

28. Solomon Northup, *Twelve Years A Slave* (Middletown, DE: Classic Edition, 2023), 58.

29. Alcee Fortier Collection, 1983.65.4–.9, RG 65, LSM. These records consist of plantation journals and related documents kept by Valcour Aime, including a "Statistical Record of Valcour Aime Plantation Slaves" (1983.65.7). I have not been able to analyze these items in detail. They merit further research.

30. Federal Census, 1860, St. James Parish, "Slave Inhabitants of the Seventh District, Right Bank," 51–53.

31. Alcée Fortier, "The Louisiana Sugar Planters of the Old Regime," originally published in *The Tulane Graduates' Magazine*, reprinted in *The Louisiana Planter and Sugar Manufacturer* LII, no.1 (January 3, 1914): 76, https://hdl.handle.net/2027/hvd.hb15ls.

32. Marriages 1777–1784, 161, SLC.

33. The first child, Victoire Cecile Basile, was born October 19, 1782, and baptized April 2, 1783; Baptisms 1777–1786, 286, SLC.

34. The law required children under the age of twenty-five to obtain their parents' permission to marry. Clark, *American Quadroon,* 77.

35. Margaret H. Darrow, "Popular Concepts of Marital Choice in Eighteenth Century France," *Journal of Social History* 19, no. 2 (Winter 1985): 261–72.

36. Clark, *Masterless Mistresses,* 148n34.

37. Book of Baptisms for colored people 1777–1783, 326, SLC; Book of Baptisms, Negros and Mulattos, from 17 June 1783, 90, SLC; Fernando Rodriguez 4:353, NONA.

38. Book 1 of Baptisms for only Whites, 1777–1786, 286, SLC.

39. Book 1 of Baptisms for only Whites, 1777–1786, 383, 384, SLC.

40. F. Rodriguez, 6:774, NONA.

41. F. Rodriguez, 7:107, 166, NONA.

42. Third book of baptisms for Whites, from 1 April 1796 to 7 March 1802, 125, SLC.

43. Information on the aristocratic origins of Louis-Hector de Mons d'Orbigny can be found in *Archives généalogiques et historiques de la noblesse de France* (Paris: P. Louis Lainé, 1839), Section on the de Mons family, 15. Available on Google Books.

44. Sublette, *The World that Made New Orleans,* 200, 247–52.

45. The account of their life in St. Charles Parish is gleaned from the probate record created after Florent's death in 1816. Succession and Probate Records 1806–1899, Case Number 1, 9 September 1818, Loose Papers, 1811–1818, Louisiana District Court (St. Charles Parish).

46. Sublette, *The World That Made New Orleans,* 220–27; Ned Sublette and Constance Sublette, *The American Slave Coast: A History of the Slave Breeding Industry* (Chicago: Lawrence Hill Books, 2016), 428–34.

47. Sublette and Sublette, *American Slave Coast,* 429.

48. Northup, *Twelve Years a Slave*, 20–25.

49. Douglass is quoted in Sublette and Sublette, *American Slave Coast,* 434.

50. Northup, *Twelve Years a Slave*, 48–49.

51. Northup, *Twelve Years a Slave*,49.

52. Northup, *Twelve Years a Slave*, 28, 52–54.

53. *Archives généalogiques*, Section on the de Mons family, 15.

54. Notarial Act, no. 1769-07-25-01, Judicial Records of the French Superior Council, RG 1, LSM Historical Center; "Digest of the Acts and Deliberations of the Cabildo," Book 1, 77, NOPL.

55. Marriages 1777–1784, 161, SLC; Pedro Pedesclaux, 7:667, NONA.

56. One episode gives a glimpse of Ursin's life. In August 1785, his ship was anchored at La Balise, some twenty miles downriver from New Orleans, where the Mississippi enters the Gulf of Mexico. This was where ocean-going ships took on pilots to guide the way up the winding river to the city; they knew best how to steer clear of sandbars and make headway against the current. The settlement included the residences of the pilots and their families, housing for the enslaved men kept there to transfer cargo, a small parish church, and a number of taverns and cabarets. It was a classic "sailor town." One hot evening, a sailor named Jean Olivier killed a man named Joseph, a member of Ursin's crew. Ursin sent word to New Orleans and within two days a constable arrived to arrest the accused and take statements from witnesses. Eventually Olivier was found guilty and sentenced to be hanged in Place d'Armes (now Jackson Square). Criminal proceedings instituted against a sailor, Black Book 129, August 26, 1785, Spanish Judicial Records, RG 2, LSM Historical Center.

57. Population estimate taken from Joseph Logsdon and Caryn Cossé Belle, "The Americanization of Black New Orleans," in *Creole New Orleans: Race and Americanization*, eds. Arnold R. Hirsh and Joseph Logsdon (Baton Rouge: Louisiana State University Press, 1992), Table 1, 206.

58. See Appendix for citations of individual baptisms and deaths mentioned in this paragraph.

59. Sublette, *The World That Made New Orleans,* 173.

60. Federal Census, 1810, New Orleans, 227, 253.

61. Baptisms of Slaves and Free People of Color, 1801–02, 63, SLC.

62. Hall, *Afro-Louisiana History.*

63. Book of Funerals, 1803–1815, 196, SLC.

64. Book of Funerals, 1803–1815, 197 (back), SLC.

65. Baptisms of Free People of Color and Slaves, 1811–1812, 149, SLC.

66. Book of Funerals, 1803–1815, 44, SLC.

67. Passenger Lists of Vessels Arriving at New Orleans, Louisiana,1820–1902, M259-10, 7 November 1831, NAID 2824927, Records of the Immigration and Naturalization Service, RG 85, NARA, College Park, MD.

68. Orleans Parish Estate Files, Wills and Probate Records, 1756–1984, Marie Dejean Durel, 22 August 1833, New Orleans City Archives, NOPL.

69. The property is currently owned by the Historic New Orleans Collection. During the summer of 1991, an archaeological excavation indicated that the existing double cottage was built around 1830, replacing an earlier building constructed after the 1788 New Orleans fire. The original structure on the site appears to have been an outbuilding associated with the French army barracks dating from the 1720s.

70. Federal Census, 1820, New Orleans City, Toulouse Street, 61.

71. Ursin Durel tomb, St. Louis No. 1 Cemetery, New Orleans.

72. Orleans Parish Estate Files, L. Caroline Durel, 11 March 1834, New Orleans City Archives, NOPL, Ancestry.com; Passenger Lists of Vessels Arriving at New Orleans, Louisiana, 1820–1902, M259-12, 13 May 1833, NAID 2824927, Records of the Immigration and Naturalization Service, RG 85, NARA, College Park, MD.

73. Orleans Parish Estate files, Wills and Probate Records, 1756–1984, Françoise Dejan Durel 14 August 1844 New Orleans City Archives, NOPL, Ancestry.com.

74. Register of Marriages from April 1784 onward, 36, SLC.

75. Adjudication of Bids, no. 1769-04-03-02, Judicial Records of the French Superior Council, RG 2, LSM Historical Center.

76. Louisiana Historical Association, "Louise Antoine Andry," *Dictionary of Louisiana Biography,* https://www.lahistory.org/resources/dictionary-louisiana-biography/dictionary-of-louisiana-biography-a/.

77. Orleans Parish Estate Files, 1804–1846, Jean Baptiste Durel, December, 1809, New Orleans City Archives, NOPL, Ancestry.com.

78. St. John the Baptiste Parish was the next upriver from St. Charles Parish. The area was called the German Coast because the original European settlers were German, having been invited to help populate the colony in the early eighteenth century.

79. Louisiana Historical Association, "Manuel Andry," *Dictionary of Louisiana Biography,* https://www.lahistory.org/resources/dictionary-louisiana-biography/dictionary-of-louisiana-biography-a/.

80. Federal Census, 1810, St. John the Baptiste Parish, 354.

81. Second Book of Baptisms for Whites, beginning May 1786, 339, SLC; Probate Cases, 1823–1845, Michel Andry, 13 April 1835, Probate Court (Orleans Parish), Ancestry.com.

82. Underlying Cause of Death 1999–2020, CDC WONDER Online Database, Centers for Disease Control and Prevention, National Center for Health Statistics, https://wonder.cdc.gov/; "Total Deaths Due to Firearms by Race/Ethnicity, 2020," Kaiser Family Foundation, https://www.kff.org/state-category/health-status/deaths-due-to-firearms/.

Chapter 3

1. The Data Center, *The New Orleans Prosperity Index* (April 2018): 6, 58. https://www.datacenterresearch.org/topic/new-orleans-prosperity-index/.

2. An Act to prevent the introduction of Free People of Color from Hispaniola, and other French Islands of America into the Territory of Orleans, June 7, 1806, Acts Passed at the First Session of the First Legislature of the Territory of Orleans, 126. Statute, March 16, 1842, cited in Civil Code of the State of Louisiana with the Statutory Amendments from 1825 to 1852, 52.

3. Civil Code of the State of Louisiana with the Statutory Amendments from 1825 to 1852, Article 95, 14.

4. Gustave de Beaumont, *Marie, or Slavery in the United States: A Novel of Jacksonian America*, trans. Barbara Chapman (Johns Hopkins University Press, 1999), 5.

5. *Acts Passed at the First Session of the First Legislature of Orleans* (New Orleans: Bradford & Anderson, Printers, 1807), 188.

6. Joseph G. Tregle Jr., "Creoles and Americans," in *Creole New Orleans: Race and Americanization*, eds. Arnold R. Hirsh and Joseph Logsdon (Baton Rouge: Louisiana State University Press, 1992), 154.

7. Judy Riffel, ed., *New Orleans Register of Free People of Color, 1840–1864* (Baton Rouge: Le Comite des Archives de la Louisiane, Inc., 2008), 49, NOPL; Federal Census, 1840, New Orleans, Faubourg Tremé, 216; Federal Census, 1850, New Orleans, Fifth Ward, First Municipality, 214; CD: 1841, 66 (Sophie died in 1866, at age seventy-six); Orleans Parish Death Index, NOPL.

8. *New Orleans Register of Free People of Color, 1840–1864*, 14; Federal Census 1840, New Orleans, Municipality 3, District 1, 202; CD:1851, 51.

9. Federal Census, 1830, New Orleans, 205.

10. CD: 1834, 71.

11. Federal Census, 1850, New Orleans, Ward 2, Municipality 1, 136 (207), and Ward 6, Municipality 1, 417.

12. Federal Census, 1860, New Orleans, Ward 4, 144, and Ward 6, 195.

13. Federal Census, 1830, New Orleans, Bourbon Street, 194 (upper left); Federal Census, 1840, New Orleans, Ward 1, 120 (upper right); Federal Census, 1850, New Orleans, Municipality 1, Ward 4, 308, dwelling 426, family 680.

14. CD: 1838, 66; CD: 1841, 66.

15. *Le Courrier de la Louisiane*, August 25, 1841; CD: 1842, 131.

16. Federal Census, 1840, New Orleans, Tremé, 217; 1850 New Orleans, Municipality 1, Ward 5, family 2109.

17. *Le Courrier de la Louisiane,* Obituary, September 23, 1854, 1; St. Ann Baptisms, Free People of Color, 2:38, Act 172, SLC.

18. Baptismal register for Whites and people of color, 1772–1776, 114b, SLC.

19. Property Title Chain for 819, 823–825 Burgundy Street, from 1809 to 1838, Vieux Carré Digital Survey, HNOC; Federal Census, 1820, New Orleans, Burgundy Street, 51; Federal Census, 1830, New Orleans, 175.

20. Clark, *Strange History*, 103.

21. Baptisms Book One for only Whites, 1777–1786, 322, SLC.

22. For extensive studies of women like Henriette Milon, see Johnson, *Wicked Flesh*, and Lisa Ze Winters, *The Mulatta Concubine, Terror, Intimacy, Freedom and Desire in the Black Transatlantic* (Athens: University of Georgia Press, 2016).

23. Clark, *Strange History*, 38.

24. Quoted in Powell, *The Accidental City*, 287.

25. Quoted in Clark, *Strange History*, 150.

26. Affidavit of Edmond Durel, Succession of Fortier (No. 13,094, Supreme Court of Louisiana, April 3, 1899).

27. Notarial act of Marc. Lafitte, notary public, May 11, 1814, transcribed in "Succession of Angela Fortier," Civil District Court of Orleans Parish, Docket 56263, filed January 27, 1899.

28. Louisiana Probate Court, Orleans Parish Estate Files, F Surnames, Fatio–Fusillier: Jean Michel Fortier, May 5, 1736.

29. Property title chain for 819-825 Burgundy Street, Vieux Carré Digital Survey, HNOC.

30. Marguerite Marie Fortier (1881–1950) donated the Hudson portrait to the Louisiana State Museum in 1934. She descended in the Edmond Fortier line. Her great-grandfather was Septime Fortier, and her grandfather was Jean Michel Fortier, who is referenced in the text as being named after the first Jean Michel, the subject of this story. Accession 11321, LSM.

31. Book of Baptisms 1777–1783, 231, entry 832; Book of Baptisms, Negroes and Mulattos, 1783–1786, 53, 115, SLC.

32. Juan B. Garic, 4:333, November 29, 1773, NONA.

33. Spear, *Race, Sex, and Social Order*, 155, 163–65, 172–77.

34. Virginia R. Dominguez, *White by Definition: Social Classification in Creole Louisiana* (New Brunswick, NJ: Rutgers University Press, 1994), 34.

35. Property title chain for 1014–1016 St. Philip Street, Vieux Carré Digital Survey, HNOC; Federal Census, 1820, 68; Michel Durel, cabinetmaker, City Directory, 1822, NOPL.

36. Louis Villemont is later called Celestin Villemont. Book of marriages, 1806–1821, 222, SLC; Celestin Villemont, cabinetmaker, City Directory, 1811, NOPL.

37. Baptisms of slaves and free people of color, 1801–1804, 197 (back), SLC.

38. Federal Census, 1810, Orleans, 253.

39. Federal Census, 1830, New Orleans, 215; Federal Census, 1840, New Orleans, Ward 1, 154.

40. Funerals, 1824–1828, 284, SLC; Property title chain for 1014–1016 St. Philip Street, Vieux Carré Digital Survey, HNOC.

41. Property title chain for 1212–1214½ Bourbon Street, Vieux Carré Digital Survey, HNOC.

42. Orleans Parish Death Index, 24 November 1857, vol. 35, 185, Louisiana State Archives.

43. Orleans Parish Will Books, vol. 14 (1865–1867), Case 27385, October 17, 1866, New Orleans City Archives, NOPL.

44. *New Orleans Republican*, Saturday, January 27, 1872.

45. This account of Jean Florent's life is based on the following sources: Orleans Parish Will Books, vol. 26 (1893–1895), Case 43192, 10 July 1894, New Orleans City Archives, NOPL; CD: 1822, 1824, 1832, 1841, 1851, all found in alphabetical listing for "Durel"; Property title chains: 807 Bourbon, 801–805 Bourbon, 826 Bourbon, 828 Bourbon, 830 Bourbon, 801–803 Royal, 805–808 Royal, 809–811 Royal, 823–825 Decatur, Vieux Carré Digital Survey, HNOC;

Federal Census, 1820, New Orleans, Bourbon Street, Idalise Manadé, 40; Federal Census, 1830, New Orleans, A Durel, (A for the French *aine*, meaning elder, because at the time Jean Florent was the oldest male Durel), 195; Federal Census, 1840, New Orleans, Ward 1, J. F. Durel, 104; Federal Census, 1850, Municipality 1, Ward 4, 452.

46. Book of baptisms, 1822–1825, 7, SLC; Book of funerals, 1820–1824, 108, SLC. The priest wrote in the margin of the baptismal record that he had mistakenly entered it in the book for Whites rather than the one for people of color where it belonged because the mother was a person of color.

47. Book of baptisms of slaves and free persons of color, 1826–1827, 56, SLC.

48. Succession Records 1846–1880, Case Number 4888, 22 December 1851 (Succession of Marie Idalise Durel), Louisiana District Court (Orleans Parish), Ancestry.com.

49. Roger A. Fischer, "Racial Segregation in Ante Bellum New Orleans," *The American Historical Review* 74, no. 3 (1969): 926–37. doi:10.2307/1873129.

50. Tregle, "Creoles and Americans," 160–66.

51. Tregle, "Creoles and Americans," 164.

52. Ryan M. Hall, "A Glorious Assemblage: The Rise of the Know-Nothing Party in Louisiana" (PhD diss., Louisiana State University, 2015).

53. Logsdon and Bell, "The Americanization of Black New Orleans," 208.

54. Louisiana Civil Code, 1825–1853, Act 184.

55. Census figures taken from Logsdon and Bell, "The Americanization of Black New Orleans," 206, Table 1.

56. Logsdon and Bell, "The Americanization of Black New Orleans," 208.

57. Orleans Parish Will Books, vol. 26 (1893–1895), Case 43192, 10 July 1894, New Orleans City Archives, NOPL.

58. Louisiana Probate Court (Orleans Parish), Succession and Probate Records, 1805–1849, April 19, 1837, Jean Baptiste Durel, free man of color, no case number given.

59. SLC, Book of baptisms of people of color, 1818–1820, 112.

60. Obituary, *Le Courrier de la Louisiane*, May 27, 1857, 2; Federal Census, 1850, New Orleans, Ward 4, Municipality 1, 166 (298).

61. Book of baptisms, 1818–1822, 202, SLC.

Chapter 4

1. Federal Census, 1860, New Orleans, Schedule 2–Slave Inhabitants, Fourth Ward, 8.

2. *New Orleans Crescent*, September 5, 1860, 1.

3. *New Orleans Daily Picayune*, April 21, 1861 and November 24, 1861. CD: 1866, iv.

4. US Civil War Soldiers, 1861–1865, National Park Service, https://www.nps.gov/civilwar/search-soldiers.htm. Original record: NARA microfilm M378, roll 9. In the searchable database, there are two Henry Durels from New Orleans who served in the Confederate army, one listed as "Hy Durel" and the other as "H. Durel." The former was the Durel descendant, the latter was one of the foreign French who arrived in the city in the 1840s. He served in the Seventh Cavalry. His record quotes a letter saying that on May 27, 1862, he crossed the enemy line and surrendered himself to the Union captain in charge, stating that he wanted to return home and was willing to take the oath of allegiance to the United States. As many as one in ten Confederate soldiers deserted. Some soldiers fought to defend their families and friends, not the Confederacy as a whole, nor the interests of the wealthy planters. H. Durel was not a native of Louisiana and evidently decided the war was not his to fight. To distinguish between the two men, see Federal Census, 1850, New Orleans, Municipality 1, Ward 3, 181 for Hy. Durel, born in France, and Ward 4, 288 for Henry Durel, born in Louisiana.

5. The earliest evidence I have found of Henry being back in New Orleans after the war is the *New Orleans Crescent,* Thursday April 5, 1866, 1. His name appears in a list of tax collectors. His name is in the list of clerks in the treasurer's office in CD: 1867 and CD: 1868. His residence in the City Hotel is recorded in CD: 1867–1869.

6. *Times-Picayune* (New Orleans), Tuesday, October 5, 1869, 2.

7. *New Orleans Crescent* on Sunday, October 13, 1867, 1.

8. The birth date of Beauregard Charles (Carlos) Durel appears in his death certificate: Texas State Board of Health, Bureau of Vital Statistics, September 3, 1923. General P. G. T. Beauregard was a nephew of Elias Beauregard, who had married Félicité Durel (Chapter 2).

9. CD: 1865 to 1880, alphabetical listing for "Durel"; Federal Census, 1870, New Orleans, Ward 8, 73. Federal Census, 1880, New Orleans, Enumeration District 48, 8 (Henry) and Enumeration District 35, 44 (Félicité).

10. Brian K. Mitchell, S. Edwards Barrington, and Nick Weldon, *Monumental: Oscar Dunn and His Radical Fight in Reconstruction Louisiana* (New Orleans: The Historic New Orleans Collection, 2021), 226n42.

11. The proclamation of the mayor, printed in newspapers on July 30, quoted in Gilles Vandal, *The New Orleans Riot of 1866: Anatomy of a Tragedy* (Lafayette: The Center for Louisiana Studies, University of Southwestern Louisiana, 1983), 167.

12. Nystrom, *New Orleans After the Civil War*, 66.

13. "Congressional Report, Testimony," 78, 87, quoted in Vandal, *The New Orleans Riot,*176.

14. *Times-Picayune* (New Orleans), November 10, 1870, 1.

15. *New Orleans Republican*, Nov 10, 1870, 1.

16. *New Orleans Republican*, November 11, 1870, 1.

17. *New Orleans Republican*, November 12, 1870, 4.

18. *Times-Picayune* (New Orleans), November 11, 1870, 1; *New Orleans Republican*, November 11, 1870, 1, 4.

19. *Times-Picayune* (New Orleans), November 12, 1870, 2; *New Orleans Republican*, November 12, 1870, 4; *Times-Picayune* (New Orleans), November 12, 1870, 1.

20. In various records Numa's name appears as "J. B. Numa Durel," "Numa J. B. Durel," "J.B.N. Durel," and "Jean B. Numa Durel." In daily life he went by Numa, which is an old French name taken from Numa Pompilius, the legendary second king of Rome, who succeeded Romulus and reigned from 715 to 673 BC. The identification of his parents appears in his marriage record: Marriage License book 2, 131, State of Louisiana, Parish of New Orleans, Office of the Recorder of Births, Marriages and Death, NOPL.

21. Federal Census, 1850, New Orleans, Ward 6, First Municipality, 117, dwelling 2492; Federal Census, 1850, New Orleans, Ward 4, First Municipality, dwelling 261, family 464, Widow Abat, head of household; Tax Assessment, 1863, New Orleans, Division 5, 45; Federal Census, 1870, New York City, Election District 7, Ward 16, 30; Federal Census, 1880, New York City, Supv. Dist. 1, Enumeration Dist. 339, 3; City Directories for New York City, 1875 to 1883, Ancestry.com; *L'Abeille de la Nouvelle Orleans,* October 24, Death Notice, 183.

22. Birth Records Index, 1790–1899, 4: 44, State of Louisiana, Division of Archives, Baton Rouge, LA.

23. Book of marriages, 1821–1830, 208, SLC.

24. Federal Census, 1850, Plaquemines Parish, 547; Federal Census, 1860, Plaquemines Parish, 23.

25. Federal Census, 1860, New Orleans, Ward 8, 346. The record indicates he was forty years old at the time, but other records clearly show that he was thirty-four or thirty-five. Also, the name of his youngest son is incorrect, and should be Numa Jr.

26. James G. Hollandsworth Jr., *The Louisiana Native Guards* (Baton Rouge: Louisiana State University Press, 1995). My account of the experience of Black men serving in Louisiana during the Civil War is based on this work.

27. Military Service Record of Numa J B Durel, 74th US Colored Infantry, NAID 84429009, Records of the Adjutant General's Office, 1762–1984, Carded Records Showing Military Service of Soldiers Who Fought in Volunteer Organizations During the American Civil War, 1890–1912, RG 94, NARA, College Park, MD.

28. "Petition of the Free Colored Citizens of Louisiana," *The Liberator* (Boston), April 1, 1864, 3. The article in the paper includes the text of the petition, the names of prominent men who signed it and ends with, "Followed by one thousand signatures of the free colored citizens of Louisiana." Although I have not seen an archival list of the thousand, I have seen a reproduction on which the name "Numa Durel" appears.

29. *New Orleans Republican*, April 12, 1868, 8.

30. Nystrom, *New Orleans After the Civil War*, 77.

31. Federal Census, 1880, New Orleans, Supervisor's District 1, Enumeration District 59, 15. The figures on the number of cigar makers in New Orleans are taken from Melissa Daggett, *Spiritualism in Nineteenth-Century New Orleans: The Life and Times of Henry Louis Rey* (Jackson: University Press of Mississippi, 2017), 106.

32. *Le Carillon* (New Orleans), July 13, 1873. *Le Carillon* is widely quoted by historians. I have used two sources, Tusa, "Le Carillon: An English Translation of Selected Satires," and Dominguez, *White by Definition*, 137–141.

33. Nystrom, *New Orleans After the Civil War*, 151–53; Williams, T. Harry, "The Louisiana Unification Movement of 1873," *The Journal of Southern History* 11, no. 3 (1945), 349–69, https://doi.org/10.2307/2197812.

34. Federal Census, 1820, New Orleans, 47.

35. John Hurley Warner, "The Selective Transport Of Medical Knowledge: Antebellum American Physicians And Parisian Medical Therapeutics," *Bulletin of the History of Medicine* 59, no. 2 (1985), 213–31, www.jstor.org/stable/44441832.

36. "Bernard Duchamp, April 15, 1833," Succession and Probate Records, 1805–1849, Louisiana Probate Court (Orleans Parish), Ancestry.com.

37. Ship *Mozart*, arrival in New Orleans, January 19, 1841, Passenger Lists of Vessels Arriving at New Orleans, Louisiana, 1820–1902, NAID 2824927, Records of the Immigration and Naturalization Service, RG 85, Roll 21, NARA, Ancestry.com.

38. Marriage of Irene Caroline Duchamp and Pierre J. B. Marie Durel at St. Thomas Aquinas Church. Maurice Coutot, comp. *Etat civil reconstitué 1798–1860: Mariages, naissances, décès* (Paris: ARFIDO S.A., 2006), Ancestry.com.

39. Ship *Faglioni*, arrival in New Orleans, March 25, 1845, Quarterly Abstracts of Passenger Lists of Vessels Arriving at New Orleans, Louisiana, 1820–1875, Microfilm M272, ID 2824931, Records of the US Customs Service, RG 36, NARA, Ancestry.com.

40. CD: 1832, 64; CD: 1849, 59.

41. 911 Dauphine Street, Friday, August 14, 1849, Vieux Carré Digital Survey, HNOC.

42. Federal Census, 1850, New Orleans, Fourth Ward, First Municipality, 166 (298).

43. *New Orleans Crescent*, February 2, 1854, 2; *New Orleans Daily Delta,* February 17, 1854, 1.

44. 911 Dauphine Street, April 1, 1854, Vieux Carré Digital Survey, HNOC; Federal Census, 1860, St. James Parish, Sixth District, 597, 598.

45. 619-621 Toulouse St., title chain entries from 1822 to 1826, Vieux Carré Digital Survey, HNOC.

46. Pierre Durel, Surgeon, General and Staff Officers, Non-Regimental Enlisted Men, CSA, Civil War Soldiers and Sailors Database, National Park Service; Index to Compiled Service Records of Confederate Soldiers Who Served in Organizations Raised Directly by the Confederate Government and of Confederate General and Staff Officers and Nonregimental Enlisted Men. Microfilm M818, Roll 7, RG 109, NARA, College Park, MD.

47. He is listed in city directories as either P. Durel or P. F. Durel, residing at 41 Toulouse Street, from 1866 to 1869, CD: 1866, 1868, 1869. In CD: 1870 he is at 213 Bourbon. In CD: 1875 he is no longer listed as a physician, but rather as manager of *Le Carillon*, residing at 173 St. Ann.

48. Tusa, "Le Carillon: An English Translation of Selected Satires."

49. Painter, *The History of White People,* 86–90, 151–83.

50. Painter, *The History of White People,* 64–71, 195–99.

51. This is the last stanza in a poem called "Francoése and the Races," translation taken from Virginia R. Dominguez, *White by Definition: Social Classification in Creole Louisiana* (New Brunswick, NJ: Rutgers University Press, 1986), 292n6.

52. Painter, *The History of White People,* 59–63, 93–94.

53. Nystrom, *New Orleans After the Civil War,* 74.

54. "Monsieur Kellogg and His Orangutan," *Le Carillon*, November 9, 1873. Translated in Tusa, "Le Carillon: An English Translation of Selected Satires."

55. CD: 1861, 36.

56. The White League in Louisiana started in St. Landry Parish in April 1874, and spread rapidly across the state, reaching New Orleans that summer. Nystrom, *New Orleans After the Civil War,* 160–85.

57. Nystrom, *New Orleans After the Civil War,* 164 and 294n5. The italicized emphasis on the abduction of women is in the original newspaper article.

58. Stuart Omer Landry, *The Battle of Liberty Place* (New Orleans: Pelican Publishing, 1955), 236.

59. Tivoli Circle was subsequently named Lee Circle in honor of the Confederate General Robert E. Lee. Lee's statue on the column in the center of the circle was removed in 2017.

60. Nystrom, *New Orleans after the Civil War,* 171–76.

61. Louisiana Biography and Obituary Index, NOPL; Edward Larocque Tinker, *Les écrits de langue française en Louisiane au XIXe siècle: Essais biographiques et bibliographiques* (Geneva: Slatkine Reprints, 1975), 177.

Chapter 5

1. Rodolphe Lucien Desdunes, *Our People and Our History,* Sister Dorothea Olga McCants, trans. and ed. (Baton Rouge: Louisiana State University Press, 1973), 141; originally published as *Nos Hommes et Notre Histoire* (Montreal: Arbour & Dupont, 1911).

2. Estelle M. Fortier Cochran, *The Fortier Family and Allied Families* (n.p., 1963), 55–58.

3. Alcée Fortier, "A Few Words About the Creoles of Louisiana: An Address Delivered at the Ninth Annual Convention of the Louisiana Educational Association" (Baton Rouge: Truth Books, 1892), 6–7.

4. Alcée Fortier, *A History of Louisiana,* vol. IV, part II (Paris: Goupil & Co., 1904), 153. Stuart Omer Landry, *The Battle of Liberty Place* (Gretna, LA: Pelican Publishing Company, 1955): 236.

5. "The Creoles of history and the Creoles of romance. A lecture delivered in the hall of the Tulane University, New Orleans, by Hon. Charles Gayarré, on the 25th of April, 1885" (New Orleans: C.E. Hopkins, 1885).

6. Arlin Turner, *George W. Cable: A Biography* (Baton Rouge: Louisiana State University Press, 1966).

7. The use of dialect was a common feature of the local color genre, in which this novel fell.

8. George Washington Cable, *The Grandissimes* (New York: Charles Scribner's Sons, 1885), 215.

9. Cochran, *The Fortier Family,* 49.

10. It is one of the laments of my life that I did not learn it when I was young. Ironically, my language requirement in high school was French, but it was poorly taught and had little impact. What little I know I learned as an adult.

11. Alcée Fortier, *Louisiana Studies: Literature, Customs and Dialects, History and Education,* (New Orleans: F.F. Hansell & Bro, 1894); Alcée Fortier, collector and editor, *Louisiana Folktales,* 2011 Edition (Lafayette: University of Louisiana at Lafayette Press, 2011); originally published as *Louisiana Folk-tales* in three parts by the American Folk-lore Society (Boston: Houghton Mifflin, 1895).

12. Fortier, *Louisiana Studies,* 43.

13. Fortier, *Louisiana Folktales,* xvii.

14. Fortier, "A Few Words About the Creoles of Louisiana."

15. Fortier, *A History of Louisiana,* vol. IV, part II, 87–88.

16. *New York Times,* March 26, 1904.

17. James B. Bennett, *Religion and the Rise of Jim Crow in New Orleans* (Princeton, NJ: Princeton University Press, 2005), 136

18. Bennett, *Religion and the Rise,* 136, 144, 153–54, 168.

19. CD: 1927, Introduction.

20. An advertisement for Creole toothpaste is in the *Herald* (New Orleans), March 16, 1922, 14.

21. Alice Moore Dunbar-Nelson, "People of Color in Louisiana," *Journal of Negro History* 2 (1916), 367, reprinted in Sybil Kein, *Creole: The History and Legacy of Louisiana's Free People of Color* (Baton Rouge: Louisiana State University Press, 2000), 9.

22. Desdunes, *Our People and Our History,* 141–48; Louisiana Historical Association, "Homer Adolphe Plessy," Dictionary of Louisiana Biography, https://www.lahistory.org/resources/dictionary-louisiana-biography/dictionary-of-louisiana-biography-p/.

23. Desdunes, *Our People and Our History,* 142–44.

24. Fortier, *A History of Louisiana,* vol. IV, Part II, 234–35.

25. Louisiana, Wills and Probate Records, 1756–1984, Ancestry.com; Will Book, vol. 7, 1842–1844, Succession of Henriette Milon, fcw, 29 March 1844.

26. Federal Census, 1850, New Orleans, Municipality 1, Ward 4, 118 and Municipality 1, Ward 5, 230.

27. Federal Census, 1860, New Orleans, Ward 5, 240. CD 1861, 176.

28. I have used three sources to reconstruct Delphine Fortier's attempts to inherit property: Orleans Parish Civil District Court, No. 56263, "Succession of Angela Fortier," April 1888; Supreme Court of Louisiana, Docket No. 13094, "Succession of Fortier," 3 April 1899; and a transcription of the Supreme Court case in *The Southern Reporter* vol. 26 (St. Paul, MN: West Publishing Company, 1900): 565. All these sources reference an earlier case that now appears to be missing or misfiled: Orleans Parish Second District Court, No. 18976, "Succession of Edmond Gustave Fortier," 23 September 1862. Reference to the deathbed marriage of Delphine's parents first appeared in the missing record and is repeated in the others.

29. *The Southern Reporter*, "Succession of Fortier," 565.

30. Federal Census, 1850, New Orleans, Municipality 1, Ward 4, 118, and Municipality 1, Ward 5, 230; Clark, *Strange History*, 88–89.

31. Federal Census, 1870, New Orleans, Ward 5, 195; Federal Census, 1880, New Orleans, Supv. Dist. 1, Enumeration Dist. 35, Sheet 13.

32. Federal Census, 1880, New Orleans, Supv. Dist. 1, Enumeration Dist. 57, Sheet 9870; CD, 1877: 281.

33. Orleans Parish Civil District Court, No. 56263, "Succession of Angela Fortier," April 1888.

34. Orleans Parish, "Succession of Fortier," 554–68.

35. Birth Records Index, 1790–1899, 6: 477, State of Louisiana, Division of Archives, Baton Rouge, LA. The record was discovered by Benji Castrillo when doing research on the Delzé family. Note that the recorder made an error when he wrote out the date of her birth but corrected it when he wrote it numerically.

36. Delphine had five children. The first was Eugenie Jourdain, who married Alphonse Pellebon, a cigarmaker, and after they separated, she worked as a seamstress. Second was John Jourdain, who was a cigarmaker, and his wife worked as a maid. Third was Adorelia Jourdain, a presser in a pants factory who married Joseph Blache, a driver for a hardware store. Fourth was a daughter named Elmire Jourdain, who apparently died young, for she is only mentioned in the 1880 census. Fifth was Emile Jourdain, who was a laborer. Federal Census, 1900, New Orleans, Ward 5, Precinct 7, District 2, Supv. Dist. 1, Enumeration Dist. 49, Sheet 11B; Federal Census, 1910, New Orleans, Ward 7, Precinct 10, Supv. Dist. 1, Enumeration Dist. 119, Sheet 2A; Ward 5, Precinct 6, Supv. Dist. 1, Enumeration Dist. 78, Sheet 10B; Federal Census, 1920, New Orleans, Ward 5, Precinct 8, Supv. Dist. 1, Enumeration Dist. 88, Sheet 13B; Ward 6, Precinct 4, Supv. Dist. 1, Enumeration Dist. 101, Sheet 1B; Ward 6, Precinct 5, Supv. Dist. 1, Enumeration Dist. 102, Sheet 6A; Benji Castrillo graciously provided information on Adorelia Jourdain and Emile Jourdain.

37. Death Records, 170: 348, State of Louisiana, Division of Archives, Baton Rouge, LA. Delphine's death record gives her age at death as seventy-two. However, her birth record indicates that she was actually seventy-eight.

Chapter 6

1. Military Registration Card, September 12, 1918, Local Board Div. 7, 2501 Urquhart Street, New Orleans, Louisiana. Edward was described as mulatto in the federal censuses for 1900, 1910, and 1920.

2. Donald E. DeVore and Joseph Logsdon, *Crescent City Schools: Public Education in New Orleans, 1841–1991* (Lafayette: Center for Louisiana Studies, University of Southwestern Louisiana, 1991), Chapter 5.

3. Bennett, *Religion and the Rise*, 158–59.

4. Devore and Logsdon, *Crescent City Schools,* Chapter 2.

5. Devore and Logsdon, *Crescent City Schools*, 76–77.

6. CD: 1874, 907, 934; CD: 1889, 1064, 1095.

7. Devore and Logsdon, *Crescent City Schools*, 88–98.

8. Devore and Logsdon, *Crescent City Schools,*116.

9. *Times-Democrat* (New Orleans), July 17, 1898, 12.

10. *Times-Democrat* (New Orleans), May 5, 1900, 3.

11. Devore and Logsdon, *Crescent City Schools*, 119.

12. Bennett, *Religion and the Rise*, 162–92.

13. *Daily Picayune* (New Orleans), October 4, 1891, 7.

14. *Times-Picayune* (New Orleans), April 9, 1898, 6; *Times-Picayune,* (New Orleans), October 7, 1900, 14; *Times-Democrat* (New Orleans), August 17, 1903, 5; *Times-Picayune* (New Orleans), September 23, 1906, 7.

15. Bennett, *Religion and the Rise*, 217; Arthé A. Anthony, "'Lost Boundaries': Racial Passing and Poverty in Segregated New Orleans." *Louisiana History* 36, no. 3 (1995): 306, http://www.jstor.org/stable/4233208.

16. Bennett, *Religion and the Rise*, 193.

17. *Times-Picayune* (New Orleans), July 29, 1917, 94.

18. Bennett, *Religion and the Rise,* 220–21.

19. WWII Draft Registration Cards for Louisiana, 10/16/1940 - 03/31/1947, Records of the Selective Service System, RG 147, NARA, St. Louis, MO. Physical characteristics are taken from their WWII draft cards.

20. CD: 1894, 309; CD: 1898, 275; Federal Census, 1900, New Orleans, Louisiana, Fifth Precinct, Supv. Dist. 1, Enumeration Dist. 79, sheet 5; U.S. Civil War Pension Index: 1861–1934, Records of the Department of Veterans Affairs, 1773–2007, RG 15, Series T288, Roll 134, NARA, College Park, MD.

21. CD: 1879, 748–50; CD: 1920, 1890.

22. Federal Census, 1900, New Orleans, Sixth Precinct, Supv. Dist. 1, Enumerator Dist. 67, 4; Federal Census, 1900, New Orleans, Fifth Precinct, Supv. Dist. 1, Enumerator Dist. 79, 5; Federal Census, 1910, Sixth Precinct, Supv. Dist. 1, Enumerator Dist. 130, 19B-20A.

23. Marriage Records Index, 1831–1964, State of Louisiana, Division of Archives, Baton Rouge, LA, Ancestry.com.

24. CD: 1903, 187, 296, 1031.

25. Lawrence J. McCaffrey, "Irish America," *The Wilson Quarterly* 9, no. 2 (1985): 78–93, www.jstor.org/stable/40468527.

26. CD: 1892, 68, 991; CD 1893, 72, 1043; CD 1894, 1035; CD 1895, 78, 1137. Frank Thriffiley's political activities are documented in numerous articles in the *Times-Picayune* from 1892 to 1900. His resignation was reported on August 8, 1894. See also Brian Gary Ettinger, "John Fitzpatrick and the Limits of Working-Class Politics in New Orleans, 1892–1896," *Louisiana History* 26, no. 4 (1985): 341–67, www.jstor.org/stable/4232448.

27. Federal Census, 1910, New Orleans, Ward 8, Precinct 3, Supv. Dist. 1, Enumeration Dist. 126, sheet 6B; CD: 1880, 497; CD: 1887, 1018; CD: 1900, 564; CD: 1901, 560; CD: 1902, 543; CD: 1903, 580; CD: 1904, 580; CD: 1905, 612, 1208.

28. *Times-Picayune,* September 23, 1906, 7; Marriage Register, State of Alabama, Mobile County, October 23, 1906; 1907 Mobile City Directory, R.L. Polk and Company, 249.

29. By May 1907, they were back in New Orleans and Walter was again playing on the usher's baseball team. *Daily Picayune* (New Orleans), May 26, 1907, 30; *Daily Picayune* (New Orleans), June 16, 1907, 30.

30. *Times-Democrat* (New Orleans), December 1, 1913, 1–2.

31. *Times-Democrat* (New Orleans), February 1, 1916, 10; Matthew J. Schott, "The New Orleans Machine and Progressivism," *Louisiana History* 24, no. 2 (1983): 141–53, www.jstor.org/stable/4232262.

32. Federal Census, 1900, New Orleans, Ward 8, Precinct 5, Supv. Dist. 1, Enumeration Dist. 128, sheet 5B; CD: 1910, 367; *Lumber World Review* XXIII, no. 3 (August 10, 1912): 45, 54; *Lumber World Review* XXIII, no. 5 (September 10, 1912): 43; *The Southern Lumberman* 105 (April-June 1922): 41.

33. CD: 1917, 394; CD: 1920, 503; CD: 1921, 562; CD: 1922, 5701; CD 925, 589, 1805; Federal Census, 1920, New Orleans, Ward 8, Precinct 3, Supv. Dist. 1, Enumeration Dist. 132, sheet 1b.

34. Draft Registration Card, Joseph Numa Durel, Allensworth Precinct, Tulare California, June 5, 1917, Ancestry.com; Federal Census, 1820, Allensworth Township, Tulare, California, Supv. Dist. 6, Enumeration Dist. 192, Sheet 1B.

35. *Item Tribune* (New Orleans), May 13, 1928, 24; Federal Census, 1930, Los Angeles, California, Ward AD 62, Block 184-203, Supv. Dist. 17, Enumeration Dist. 297, Sheet 16A.

36. CD: 1925, 588; Federal Census, 1930, New Orleans, Ward 4, Enumeration District 36-52, Supervisor District 11, Sheet 52A.

37. CD: 1926, 544, 1592; CD 1927, 587; CD: 1928, 587; CD: 1929, 537, 1581.

38. Federal Census, 1930, New Orleans, Ward 4, Block 490, Supv. Dist 11, Enumeration District 36-52, sheet 52A; Daphne Spain, "Race Relations and Residential Segregation in New Orleans: Two Centuries of Paradox," *The Annals of the American Academy of Political and Social Science* 441 (1979): 82–96, www.jstor.org/stable/1043295.

39. CD: 1930, 520; CD: 1931, 520. Note that city directories came out early in the year and really reflect the situation as it was toward the end of the previous year. In the 1930 directory (reflecting late 1929), all three companies, Hillcoat-Durel, Southland, and John W. Durel & Son, are listed in the business section. Walter is listed at John W. Durel & Son, 703 Canal Bank Building, and living at 5202 Conti. In the next directory (1931) none of the companies are listed, and Walter's name does not appear in the alphabetical listing of residents. He described himself as a building contractor in the 1930 Census, taken in April. For background on the lumber industry during this period, see James E. Fickle, "'Comfortable and Happy'? Louisiana and Mississippi Lumber Workers, 1900–1950," *Louisiana History* 40, no. 4 (1999): 407–32, www.jstor.org/stable/4233613.

40. Federal Census, 1940, New Orleans, Catherine Durel, Ward 4, Block 57, Supv. Dist. 1, Enumerator Dist 36-90, sheet 19B.

41. Memorial page for Edward Durel, Memorial No. 140557751, Find a Grave online database, https://www.findagrave.com/memorial/140557751/edward-joseph-durel.

42. CD: 1924, 559; CD: 1925, 588; CD: 1926, 544; CD: 1928, 547: CD: 1930, 520. Milton's first name was Emile, and he appears as Emile in city directories during the 1920s. (He starts to appear as Milton in the 1930s.) He is not

listed in the directories for 1921, 1922, 1923, 1927, and 1929 and presumably was unemployed those years. There is another Milton Durel listed in the twenties, who was White.

43. Puerto Rico, U.S., Arriving Passenger and Crew Lists, 1923, Records of the Immigration and Naturalization Service, 1787–2004, RG 85, NARA, Washington, DC; New York, U.S., Arriving Passenger and Crew Lists, August 19, 1923, Records of the Immigration and Naturalization Service, 1787–2004, RG 85, NARA, College Park, MD, Ancestry.com.

44. Stanley Lebergott, Bureau of Labor Statistics, "Labor Force, Employment, and Unemployment, 1929–39. Estimating Methods," *Monthly Labor Review* 67, no. 1 (July 1948): 51, http://www.jstor.org/stable/41831550.

45. William A. Sundstrom, "Last Hired, First Fired? Unemployment and Urban Black Workers During the Great Depression," *Journal of Economic History* 52, no. 2 (1992): 415–29, http://www.jstor.org/stable/2123118.

46. Federal Census, 1930, New Orleans, Ward 8, Block 47, Enumeration Dist. 36-127, Supv. Dist. 11, Sheets 18A and B; CD: 1931, 520; CD :1932, 493; CD: 1933, 470, 471; CD: 1935, 481; CD: 1938, 1859; CD: 1940, 387.

47. Federal Census, 1940, New Orleans, Ward 8, Block 16, Supv. Dist. 1, Enumeration Dist. 36-207, Sheets 1B, 2A.

48. CD: 1931, 520, 1620; CD: 1932, 493; CD: 1933, 470, 471; CD: 1935, 481, 1541; CD 1940, 387.

49. Federal Census, 1940, New Orleans, Catherine Durel, Ward 4, Block 57, Supv. Dist. 1, Enumerator Dist. 36-90, sheet 19B; Mary Durel, Ward 8, Block 16, Supv. Dist. 1, Enumerator Dist. 36-207, sheet 1B and 2A.

50. Ernest M. Culligan, "The Procurement of Man Power," *The Annals of the American Academy of Political and Social Science* 220 (1942): 8–17, www.jstor.org/stable/1022695.

51. The Selective Service registration cards for Mederic, Milton, Milton's brother Arnold, and Arnold's son (Arnold Jr.) are located in WWII Draft Registration Cards for Louisiana, 10/16/1940–03/31/1947, Records of the Selective Service System, NARA, St. Louis, MO, Ancestry.com.

52. Historical Section, Bureau of Naval Personnel, *The Negro in the Navy*, United States Naval Administrative History of World War II, no. 84 (1947).

53. CD: 1949, 446; Electronic Army Serial Number Merged File, 1938–1946, NAID 1263923, RG 64, Box 13026, Reel 68, Records of the National Archives and Records Administration, 1789–ca. 2007, NARA, College Park, MD; Hospital

Admission Card Files, ca. 1970–ca. 1970 NAID 570973, RG 112, Records of the Office of the Surgeon, General (Army), 1775–1994, NARA, College Park, MD; New Orleans, Louisiana, Marriage Records Index, 1831–1964, State of Louisiana, Division of Archives, Baton Rouge, LA. Ancestry.com.

54. WWII Draft Registration Cards for Louisiana, 10/16/1940–03/31/1947, RG 147, Records of the Selective Service System, NARA, St. Louis, MO; "Report of Changes of USS George O. Squires," March 15, 1944, and "Muster List for Draft Number 1624," March 13, 1944, Muster Rolls of U.S. Navy Ships, Stations, and Other Naval Activities, 01/01/1939–01/01/1949, NAID 594996, Records of the Bureau of Naval Personnel, 1798–2007, RG 24, NARA, College Park, MD.

55. *US Naval Hospital Aiea Heights, T.H., Christmas, 1944* (Falls Church, VA: Department of the Navy Bureau of Medicine and Surgery, December 1944), US Militaria Forum, December 2, 2018, https://www.usmilitariaforum.com/forums/index.php?/topic/320026-us-naval-hospital-aiea-heights-th-1944-photos-roster/. Arnold Jr.'s name appears in the list Pharmacist Mates, Third Class. In a group photo of the PHMC3s, taken from a distance, there are about a dozen Black faces among a sea of White ones.

56. "Certification of Military Service: Durel, Milton Emile," National Personnel Records Center, NARA, College Park, MD; BIRLS Death File, 1850-2010, US Department of Veterans Affairs, Ancestry.com.

57. Federal Census, 1950, New Orleans, Louisiana, Enumeration District 36-379, 1-2. CD 1945, 369; CD: 1947, 389: CD: 1949, 446; CD: 1952, 335: CD: 1954, 320–21; CD: 1956, 312; CD:1958, 324; CD 1960, 325.

58. Letter from Francis Mederic Durel to Antoinette Caillouet Durel, August 25, 1944, in possession of the author.

59. Letter from Francis Mederic Durel to Antoinette Caillouet Durel, June 26, 1944, in possession of the author.

60. "Archbishop Joseph Rummel Dies; New Orleans Foe of Segregation; Prelate, 88, Excommunicated 3 Who Resisted Command to Integrate Schools," *New York Times*, November 9, 1964, 33.

Chapter 7

1. After Stafford's parents separated, his mother and siblings moved in with a Black man named Rodney Richardson, a taxi driver and musician. She kept the Durel name. Federal Census, 1940, Ward 4, Block 27, Supv. Dist. 1, Enumerator Dist. 36-79, sheet 14A, Rodney Richardson.

2. Federal Census, 1940, New Orleans, Ward 4, Supervisor District 1, Enumeration District 36-82, sheets 8A, 9A, 9A, 10A, 10B, 13B. *Sanborn Fire Insurance Map from New Orleans, Orleans Parish, Louisiana*. Sanborn Map Company, Jul. 1950, vol. 2, 1951, Library of Congress, www.loc.gov/item/sanborn03376_026/.

3. Rebecca J. Scott, "Defining the Boundaries of Freedom in the World of Cane: Cuba, Brazil, and Louisiana after Emancipation," American Historical Review 99, no. 1 (February 1994): 78–80, https://www.jstor.org/stable/2166163; Follett, *The Sugar Masters*, 234.

4. Katherine, van Wormer, David W. Jackson III, and Charletta Sudduth, *The Maid Narratives: Black Domestics and White Families in the Jim Crow South* (Baton Rouge: Louisiana State University Press, 2012), 15–16.

5. Susan Tucker, *Telling Memories Among Southern Women: Domestic Workers and Their Employers in the Segregated South* (Baton Rouge: Louisiana State University Press, 1988), 3, 192.

6. DeVore and Logsdon, *Crescent City Schools,* 200–201.

7. DeVore and Logsdon, *Crescent City Schools,* 235–50.

8. Diane T. Manning and Perry Rogers, "Desegregation of the New Orleans Parochial Schools," *The Journal of Negro Education* 71, no. 1/2 (2002): 31–42, http://www.jstor.org/stable/3211223; "Older Generation Called 'Lost Cause' in Racial Integration Field at College Students Meet," National Catholic Welfare Council (NCWC) News Feed (Domestic) (Washington, DC), March 22, 1954, 12; "Archbishop Rummel Reiterates No Definite Plan Fixed for Integration of Catholic Schools," NCWC News Feed (Domestic), March 5, 1956, 15; "'In and When' Restriction is Placed on Integration for Catholic Schools," *Catholic Standard and Times* (Archdiocese of Philadelphia, PA) November 18, 1960, 11; "Catholic School Integration Awaits Orleans Progress," *Advocate* (Archdiocese of Newark, NJ), November 17, 1960, 4; "New Orleans Story Behind Excommunications Issued by Archbishop Rummel," and "Desegrated Schools Are Ninety Per Cent Enrolled," *Monitor* (Archdiocese of San Francisco, CA), April 20, 1962, 3. All news articles accessed through the online Catholic News Archive of the Catholic Research Resources Alliance, thecatholicnewsarchive.org.

9. Devore and Logsdon, *Crescent City Schools,* 251–66.

10. Michelle Alexander, *The New Jim Crow: Mass Incarceration in the Age of Colorblindness*, tenth anniversary edition (New York: The New Press, 2020), 26-27. Richard Lowy, "Yuppie Racism: Race Relations in the 1980s," *Journal of Black Studies* 21, no. 4 (1991): 445–64, http://www.jstor.org/stable/2784688.

11. US Bureau of Labor Statistics, "Unemployment Rate - 20 Yrs. & Over, Black or African American Men [LNS14000031]," Federal Reserve Bank of St. Louis, https://fred.stlouisfed.org/series/LNS14000031.

12. Alexander, *The New Jim Crow*, 65–68, 123–24.

13. Alexander, *The New Jim Crow*, 122–23; Allen J. Beck, Ph.D. and Paige M. Harrison, "Prisoners in 2000," *Bureau of Justice Statistics Bulletin* (August 2001): 5, 11.

14. Ta-Nehisi Coates, *Between the World and Me* (New York: Spiegel and Grau, 2015), 14–16.

15. Obituary for Latisha Shantell 'Tisha' Brown, *Times Picayune* (New Orleans), February 16, 1995, B4.

16. Sarah Carr, "Long-Troubled Douglass High Could Lose Its Identity," *Times-Picayune* (New Orleans), September 21, 2008, https://www.nola.com/news/article_2783c413-8608-5c13-80e0-478c11d06a11.html.

17. "The Murders of 1994: Lessons from New Orleans' Deadliest Year," *Times-Picayune* (New Orleans), June 16, 2016, https://www.nola.com/news/article_a31d9d4d-1015-5502-b8ea-6c6c5a74f524.html?mode=comments.

18. Patrick Pearse, "The Mother," in *The Penguin Book of Irish Verse,* edited by Brendan Kennelly (Baltimore: Penguin Books, 1970), 296.

Bibliography

Alexander, Michelle. *The New Jim Crow: Mass Incarceration in the Age of Colorblindness.* Tenth anniversary edition. New York: The New Press, 2020.

Anthony, Arthé A. "'Lost Boundaries': Racial Passing and Poverty in Segregated New Orleans." *Louisiana History* 36, no. 3 (1995): 291–312, http://www.jstor.org/stable/4233208.

de Berardinis, Robert. "Pre-Revolutionary French Marriage Evidences: A Durel-LeBrun Example." *National Genealogical Society Quarterly* 88, no. 2 (June 2000): 87–110.

Bennett, James B. *Religion and the Rise of Jim Crow in New Orleans.* Princeton, NJ: Princeton University Press, 2005.

Clark, Emily. *Masterless Mistresses: The New Orleans Ursulines and the Development of a New World Society, 1727–1834.* Chapel Hill: University of North Carolina Press, 2007.

Clark, Emily. *The Strange History of the American Quadroon: Free Women of Color in the Revolutionary Atlantic World.* Chapel Hill: University of North Carolina Press, 2013.

Coates, Ta-Nehisi. *Between the World and Me.* New York: Spiegel and Grau, 2015.

Dawdy, Shannon Lee. *Building the Devil's Empire: French Colonial New Orleans.* Chicago: University of Chicago Press, 2008.

DeVore, Donald E. and Joseph Logsdon. *Crescent City Schools: Public Education in New Orleans, 1841–1991.* Lafayette: Center for Louisiana Studies, University of Southwestern Louisiana, 1991.

Dominguez, Virginia R. *White by Definition: Social Classification in Creole Louisiana.* New Brunswick, NJ: Rutgers University Press, 1994.

Follett, Richard. *The Sugar Masters: Planters and Slaves in Louisiana's Cane World, 1820–1860*. Baton Rouge: Louisiana State University Press, 2005.

Fuentes, Marisa J. *Dispossessed Lives: Enslaved Women, Violence, and the Archive*. Philadelphia: University of Pennsylvania Press, 2016.

Hall, Gwendolyn Midlo. *Africans in Colonial Louisiana: The Development of Afro-Creole Culture in the Eighteenth Century*. Baton Rouge: Louisiana State University Press, 1992.

Hardwick, Julie. *The Practice of Patriarchy: Gender and the Politics of Household Authority in Early Modern France*. University Park: Pennsylvania State University Press, 1998.

Hartman, Saidiya. *Scenes of Subjection: Terror, Slavery, and Self-Making in Nineteenth-Century America*. Oxford University Press, 1997. Revised edition, W.W. Norton & Co., 2022.

Hirsh, Arnold R. and Joseph Logsdon, ed. *Creole New Orleans: Race and Americanization*. Baton Rouge: Louisiana State University Press, 1992.

Johnson, Jessica Marie. *Wicked Flesh: Black Women, Intimacy, and Freedom in the Atlantic World*. Philadelphia: University of Pennsylvania Press, 2020.

Johnson, Rashauna. *Unfree Labor in New Orleans during the Age of Revolutions*. Cambridge, UK: Cambridge University Press, 2016.

Kein, Sybil. *Creole: The History and Legacy of Louisiana's Free People of Color*. Baton Rouge: Louisiana State University Press, 2000.

Kendi, Ibram X. *Stamped from the Beginning: The Definitive History of Racist Ideas in America*. New York: Nation Books, 2016.

Logsdon, Joseph, and Belle, Caryn Cossé. "The Americanization of Black New Orleans." In *Creole New Orleans: Race and Americanization*, edited by Arnold R. Hirsh and Joseph Logsdon. Baton Rouge: Louisiana State University Press, 1992.

Maduell, Charles R., Jr. "The Durel Family History, Part II." *New Orleans Genesis* XXI, no. 81 (January 1982): 53.

Mitchell, Brian K., S. Edwards Barrington, and Nick Weldon. *Monumental: Oscar Dunn and His Radical Fight in Reconstruction Louisiana*. New Orleans: The Historic New Orleans Collection, 2021.

Northup, Solomon. *Twelve Years A Slave*. Middletown, DE: Classic Edition, 2023.

Nystrom, Justin A. *New Orleans After the Civil War*. Baltimore, MD: Johns Hopkins University Press, 2010.

Painter, Nell Irvin. *The History of White People*. New York: W.W. Norton & Co., 2010.

Peck, Amelia, ed. *Interwoven Globe: The Worldwide Textile Trade, 1500–1800*. New York: Metropolitan Museum of Art, 2013. Exhibition catalogue.

Pfeffer, Miki. *Southern Ladies and Suffragists: Julia Ward Howe and Women's Rights at the 1884 New Orleans World's Fair*. Jackson: University Press of Mississippi, 2014.

Pounds, Norman Greville. *An Economic History of Medieval Europe*. 2nd ed. New York: Taylor and Francis, 1994.

Powell, Lawrence N. *The Accidental City: Improvising New Orleans*. Cambridge, MA: Harvard University Press, 2012.

Saugera, Éric. *Bordeaux Port Nègrier, XVIIe – XIXe siècles*. Biarritz, France: J & D Editions, 1995.

Scott, Rebecca J. "Defining the Boundaries of Freedom in the World of Cane: Cuba, Brazil, and Louisiana after Emancipation." *The American Historical Review* 99, no. 1 (1994): 70–102. https://doi.org/10.2307/2166163.

Sée, Henri. *Economic and Social Conditions in France During the Eighteenth Century*. Translated by Edwin H. Zeydel. Kitchener, Canada: Batoche Books, 2004.

Spear, Jennifer M. *Race, Sex, and Social Order in Early New Orleans*. Baltimore: Johns Hopkins University Press, 2009.

Sublette, Ned. *The World That Made New Orleans: From Spanish Silver to Congo Square*. Chicago: Lawrence Hill Books, 2009.

Sublette, Ned and Constance Sublette. *The American Slave Coast: A History of the Slave Breeding Industry*. Chicago: Lawrence Hill Books, 2016.

Tregle, Joseph G., Jr. "Creoles and Americans." In *Creole New Orleans: Race and Americanization*, edited by Arnold R. Hirsh and Joseph Logsdon. Baton Rouge: Louisiana State University Press, 1992.

Tucker, Susan. *Telling Memories Among Southern Women: Domestic Workers and Their Employers in the Segregated South*. Baton Rouge: Louisiana State University Press, 1988.

Turner, Arlin. *George W. Cable: A Biography*. Baton Rouge: Louisiana State University Press, 1966.

Tusa, Bobs M. "Le Carillon: An English Translation of Selected Satires." *Louisiana History* 35, no. 1 (Winter, 1994): 67–84.

van Wormer, Katherine, David W. Jackson, III, and Charletta Sudduth. *The Maid Narratives: Black Domestics and White Families in the Jim Crow South*. Baton Rouge: Louisiana State University Press, 2012.

Vandal, Gilles. *The New Orleans Riot of 1866: Anatomy of a Tragedy*. Lafayette: The Center for Louisiana Studies, University of Southwestern Louisiana, 1983.

Winters, Lisa Ze. *The Mulatta Concubine, Terror, Intimacy, Freedom and Desire in the Black Transatlantic*. Athens: University of Georgia Press, 2016.

Published Primary Sources

Acts Passed at the First Session of the First Legislature of the Territory of Orleans. New Orleans: Printed by Bradford and Anderson, Printers to the Territory, 1807. https://dp.la/item/6246429ddf8a51820f0ebb21bf8a43a0.

French, B. F. *Historical Collections of Louisiana: Embracing Translations of Many Rare and Valuable Documents Relating to the Natural, Civil, and Political History of that State*. New York: D. Appleton, 1851.

Voorhies, Jacqueline K., transcriber and compiler. *Some Late Eighteenth Century Louisianians: Census Records 1758–1796*. USL History Series. Lafayette: University of Southwestern Louisiana, 1973.

Secondary Sources Available Online

Hall, Gwendolyn Midlo. Compiler. "Afro-Louisiana History and Genealogy, Slave Database, 1719–1820." http://www.ibiblio.org/laslave/.

HNOC: "The Collins C. Diboll Vieux Carré Digital Survey," The Historic New Orleans Collection. https://www.hnoc.org/vcs/. This is an electronic version of the Vieux Carré Survey, housed at the Historic New Orleans Collection.

Index

A

Abat, Antoine, 76, 82
Abat, Paul Emile, 76
Agassiz, Louis, 109
Aime, Edwidge, 114–16
Aime, François-Gabriel, 39, 65, 114
Aime, Michel, 68, 72, 116
Aime, Valcour, 39–40, 69, 72, 114, 116
Alexander, Mary (Babelle), 134, 142, 147, 149–50, 152
Amarante, enslaved by Jean Baptiste Durel, 14, 22–23, 26
Ana, enslaved by François Durel, 49–50
Andry, Gilbert, 55–56
Andry, Louis, 54
Andry, Manuel, 54–57
Andry, Marie Claire (Clarisse) (Durel), 18–19, 28, 54–57, 74, 82, 86, 134
Andry, Michel, 55
Angelica, enslaved by Florent Basile, 42
Antoine, Caesar, 110
Antonia, enslaved by François Durel, 49
Antonio, enslaved by Rose Durel, 32
Arabella, enslaved by Françoise Dejan, 53–54, 88–89
Aubry, Charles Philippe, 8–9.
August, enslaved by Ursin Durel (2), 88
Augustin, enslaved by Rose Durel, 33

B

Babet, enslaved by Florent Basile, 44–45
Banks, Nathaniel, 100
Barthelemie, boy enslaved by Jean Baptiste Durel, 12, 15, 17
Basile, François Edward, 42
Basile, Jean Florent, 42–43
Basile, Louis Florent, 28, 41–47, 78
Basile, Victoire Cécile, 42–43
de Beaumont, Gustave, 60
de Beaumarchais, Pierre-Augustin Caron, 41–42
Beauregard, Bartholomew, 78
Beauregard, Bartholomew Toutant, 65
Beauregard, Elias Toutant, 28, 65
Beauregard, Madame, 11
Beauregard, P.G.T., General, 94
Bell, John, 92
Beloxine, enslaved by Ursin Durel (2), 88
de Berardinis, Robert, xii
Bernard, Patricia Durel, 173
Betsy, enslaved by Florent Basile, 44–45
Betsy, enslaved by Ursin Durel (2), 88, 170
Bill, enslaved by Florent Basile, 44–46
Le Blanc de la Combe, Louis-Felix, 47
Blumenbach, Johann Friedrich, ix, 84, 107
de Boré, Étienne, 35
Breckenridge, John C, 92

Brown, Catherine Durel, 157, 173
Brown, Linda Durel, 160, 165, 169
Brown, Tisha, 169, 174
Brulard, Louise, 86, 99, 134, 136, 141–42, 146
Brulard, Sebastian, 99
Butler, Benjamin, 99–100

C
Cable, George Washington, 118–19
Carlos, enslaved by Rose Durel, 32, 34
Carlyle, Thomas, 108
Carrick, Annie, 134, 138
Celie, enslaved by Ursin Durel (2), 88, 170
Célistin, Joseph Henry, 76
Célistin, Louise, 76
Charvenet, Marie Louise, 69
Christoval, enslaved by Rose Durel, 33
Claver (Clavert), Pierre, 20–22
Claver y Cobreró, Pedro, Padre, 21
Coates, Ta-Nehisi, 168–69
Cochran, Estelle Fortier, 120
Congo, Louis, 5
Couvent, Marie, 137
Cress, enslaved by Rose Durel, 33
Cueré, enslaved by Rose Durel, 32
Cuspin, enslaved personal servant, vii–viii, 170

D
Davis, Marguerite, 63
DeBlanc, Alcibiades, 110
Decou, Blanche, 134, 149–50, 152, 174
Dejan, Antoine, 47
Dejan, Clara Abat, 76, 81–82
Dejan, Eugène, 81
Dejan, Françoise, 28, 47–54, 86
Dejan, Jean Baptiste, 72
Dejan, Manette, 28, 47–55, 62–63, 68, 83, 86, 104
Delery, Carlotta Chauvin, 69
Delphine, enslaved by Françoise Dejan, 53
Delzé, Camille, 128
Delzé, Caroline, 114, 126–29, 131
Desdunes, Rodolphe, 125
Deslonde, Charles, 55–57
Deslonde, Jacques, 55
Deslonde, Margarite, 55
Deslonde, Maria, 55
Destrehan, Jean-Nöel, 57
Dominica, enslaved by Rose Durel, 33
Douglass, Frederick, 45
Duchamp, Caroline, 86, 102–7
Duchamp, Clarisse, 105–6
Dufaut, Theresa, 20, 22
Dunbar-Nelson, Alice Moore, 125
Dunn, Oscar, 101–2
Durel, Adelaide, 62
Durel, Adolph, 78, 99
Durel, Aimée, xvi, 9, 25, 28, 35, 43, 68
Durel, Aimée, *mestiza*, 74–76, 79, 81–82
Durel, Anastasie, 62
Durel, Antoinette Caillouet, 134, 150
Durel, Arnold, 134, 147, 149, 151, 157–58, 160
Durel, Arnold, Jr., 147, 152, 158
Durel, Beauregard, 94
Durel, Carmelite, 62
Durel, Caroline, 52–53
Durel, Cécile, free child of color, 84
Durel, Clarisse. *See* Andry, Marie Claire

Durel, Deseada, 68
Durel, Edmond, 48
Durel, Edward, 134–38, 140–42, 145–48, 154, 173–74
Durel, Edward, 170
Durel, Ester, 13, 18–23, 27
Durel, Eugène, 53
Durel, Ferdinand, 149–50, 152
Durel, Gustave, 93
Durel, Félicité, daughter of Jean Baptiste Durel, xvi, 9, 28, 65
Durel, Félicité, daughter of François Durel, 55
Durel, Félicité, *mestiza*, 74–76
Durel, Forester (Pierre Joseph Marie), 84, 86, 102–12
Durel, François, xvi, 28, 42, 47–50, 54–55, 74, 83
Durel, François Honoré, xvi, 9–10, 28
Durel, Françoise. *See* Dejan, Françoise
Durel, Hattie, 145–46
Durel, Henry, 86–87, 89–98, 134–35
Durel, Henry Bernard, 89, 94
Durel, Hortaire (Arthur), 53
Durel, J.B. (Jean Baptiste) Numa, 86, 98–102, 134–36
Durel, Jean, free man of color, 62
Durel, Jean-Antoine, 1
Durel, Jean Baptiste, xi, xvi, 1–27, 29–30, 42, 47–48, 54, 62, 64, 86, 114, 134
Durel, Jean Baptiste (2), 9, 15, 19, 28, 54, 62, 74, 78, 82, 86, 134
Durel, Jean Baptiste (3), 50–52, 59, 83–84, 104
Durel, Jean Baptiste (4), 83–84, 104
Durel, Jean Baptiste, free child of color, 84
Durel, Jean Florent, 78–82, 85, 98, 104, 113, 119
Durel, Jean Victor, 78–79, 81
Durel, Jeanne, 62
Durel, Joseph, 145–46
Durel, Justin, 51–52
Durel, Justine, 62
Durel, Kate (Thriffiley), 134–35, 142–43, 150, 157
Durel, Lena, 147, 149
Durel, Louis Florent, 81
Durel, Madere, 62
Durel, Manette. *See* Dejan, Manette
Durel, Marechal, 13, 21
Durel, Marie, free child of color, 83
Durel, Marie, free child of color, 84
Durel, Marie Idalise, 78–79
Durel, Marie Odile, 78
Durel, Mathurin, xvi, 9, 15, 28
Durel, Mederic, 134–35, 141, 147–48, 150–51, 153–54
Durel, Michel, son of Ursin (1), 48
Durel, Michel, son of François Durel, 50, 62–63, 85, 104
Durel, Michel, *mestizo*, 74–76
Durel, Milton, 134, 141, 148–54, 157, 165, 169, 174
Durel, Milton (son of Stafford), 165
Durel, Nezida, 94
Durel, Octave, 62
Durel, Patrice, 62
Durel, Rose (Marie), called Rose, xvi, 9, 15, 24, 28, 29–36, 39, 42, 64–65, 69, 114, 116
Durel, Rose, daughter of Numa Durel, 149–50
Durel, Sophie, 62
Durel, Stafford, 134, 147, 157–61, 165, 167–70
Durel, Stafford, Jr., 157, 165, 173
Durel, Theodore, 53
Durel, Terrence, 170–71

Durel, Ursin, vii–viii, xvi, 9, 25, 28, 47–49, 52, 74, 86, 134, 173–74
Durel, Ursin (2), 48, 52–54, 75, 86, 88–89, 112, 134
Durel, Ursin (3), 134, 138
Durel, Valcour, 62
Durel, Valsin, 86, 98
Durel, Victoire (1), xvi, 9–10, 28
Durel, Victoire (2), xvi, 9–10, 28, 41–47, 74
Durel, Victoire (3), 76, 79, 81–82
Durel, Walter, 134–36, 138–47, 150, 174
Durell, Edward, 103

E

Ector, enslaved by Rose Durel, 33
Edouard, enslaved by Françoise Dejan, 53
Emerson, Ralph Waldo, 108

F

de Fauquier, Monsieur, 2
Félicité, enslaved by Jean Baptiste Durel, 12, 15, 17
Félicité, enslaved by François Durel, 49
Felix, enslaved wigmaker, vii–viii, 170
Figuero, enslaved by Rose Durel, 33
Fitzpatrick, John, 142
Flor, enslaved by Rose Durel, 33
Forstall, Celestine, 99
Fortier, Adelard, 57, 65, 68, 72
Fortier, Aimée, 68
Fortier, Alcée, 111, 114, 116–18, 120–23, 126, 132, 164
Fortier, Alexander Septime, 69
Fortier, Delphine, 114, 116, 126–32
Fortier, Edmond, 35, 44, 57, 65, 67–68, 72, 78, 114, 116, 120
Fortier, Edmond (son), 67, 69
Fortier, Edmond Gustave, called Gustave, 67, 69, 114, 126–28, 130–31
Fortier, Estelle, 130
Fortier, Félicité, 69
Fortier, Félicité Angela, 69, 126, 129
Fortier, Félicité Rosella, 69, 126, 130
Fortier, Felix, 67–68
Fortier, Florent, 114
Fortier, François Omer, 69
Fortier, Gabriel, 69
Fortier, James, 164
Fortier, Jean Michel, 30, 35, 64–73, 78, 85, 104, 116, 119–20, 126–27, 130
Fortier, Jean Michel, son of Septime Fortier, 72
Fortier, Jacques, 25, 28, 35, 56–57, 68
Fortier, Julie, 31, 35, 39, 65, 114
Fortier, Lucien Armand, 69
Fortier, Louise Gabriella, 68
Fortier, Louise Matilde, 68.
Fortier, Marie Henriette, 68, 126
Fortier, Marie Isabel, 34
Fortier, Michel, 28–36, 39–40, 42, 44, 55, 57, 64, 68, 116
Fortier, Natalie, 69
Fortier, Norbert, 130
Fortier, Septime, 72
Fortier, Victoire, 35
Fortier, Victorine, 68
Fortier, Zenon, 35
Foucault, Denis-Nicolas, 8–9
Fourneau, 7
Francisca, enslaved by Rose Durel, 32
François, enslaved by Madame Beauregard, 11

Françoise, enslaved by Theresa Dufaut, 22
Frederic, Margarite, 76
Frederic (or Frederick), Ursin, 75–76
Frederic, Madame Ursin, 76
de La Frénière, Nicholas Chauvin, 6
de La Frénière, Nicholas Chauvin (son), 8–9

G
Gayarré, Charles, 118–19, 121, 124
Genie, enslaved by Ursin Durel (2), 88
de Glapion, Elizabeth, 83, 86
Guime, enslaved by Rose Durel, 32
Guyol, Armand, 92

H
Hanzy, Shirleyrine, 134, 160–61, 165, 167–70, 173
Hayes, Rutherford B., 111
Henritte, enslaved by Ursin Durel (2), 88
Hillcoat, Robert, 145
Honoré, enslaved by François Durel, 49
Hudson, Julien, 72

I
Issabel, enslaved by Jean Baptiste Durel, 13, 24
Issodoro, enslaved by Rose Durel, 32

J
Jean, enslaved by Florent Basile, 44–45
Jean, child enslaved by Jean Baptiste Durel, 12, 15, 24–25
Jean, man enslaved by Jean Baptiste Durel, 12
Jefferson, Thomas, xiii, 44, 59, 87
Jocobo, enslaved by Rose Durel, 33
Johnson, Andrew, 95
Josef, enslaved by Rose Durel, 33
Joseph (Josef), enslaved by Jean Baptiste Durel, 14, 25
Joublanc, Adolphe, 131
Joublanc, Delphine, 131
Jourdain, John, 129
Juan, enslaved by Rose Durel, 33
Juan Bautista, enslaved by Rose Durel, 32 (2 entries)
Juan Luis, enslaved by Rose Durel, 33
Juan Pedro, enslaved by Rose Durel, 33
Jautare, Vanetin, 7

K
Karo, Phillippe, 68
de Kerlérec, Louis Billouart, Chevalier, 7
King, Martin Luther, Jr., 163, 175
Knoll, Félicité, 86–87, 89–91, 94, 134
Kook, enslaved Akan warrior, 56

L
Lacroix, Julliette, 63
LaBranche, Félicité, 65, 67–68, 114
LaBranche, Maltilda Fortier, 69
LaBranche, Michel Lucien, 69
Lafite, Célma, 91
LaJonchère, C., 98
LaJonchère, Celestine, 86, 99, 134
LaJonchère, Joseph, 99
LaJonchère d'Aunoy, Marie Celeste, 99
Lanu, enslaved by Forester Durel, 106
Lapierre, Marianne, 54
LeBrun, Cécile, xi–xiv, xvi, 1–30, 42–43, 47, 86, 134

Lebelle, enslaved by Rose Durel, 32
Lendos, enslaved by Rose Durel, 32
Lincoln, Abraham, 92, 95, 101
Logis, Nicholas, 7
Loiseau, Barbé Aimée, 83
Lormoir, Marie Louise, 7
Louis, enslaved by Madame Durel, 11–13, 24
Lubin, enslaved by Jean Michel Fortier, 72
Lucien, Mary, 134–35, 142, 148
Luis, enslaved by Rose Durel, 32–33 (3 entries)

M

Maduell, Charles R. Jr., xii
Magdalena, enslaved by Jean Baptiste Durel, 14, 23
Manadé, Idalise, 78–79, 81–82, 85, 98, 104, 113
Manadé, Marie Rose, 78
Mandeville, Elisabet, 20
Mann, Horace, 137
Manuel, enslaved by Rose Durel, 33
Marcello, Benny, 166
Margarita, free woman of color, 20
Margarita, enslaved by Rose Durel, 32–33 (two entries)
Maria, enslaved by Rose Durel, 32
Maria, enslaved by Florent Basile, 42
Maria Louisa, enslaved by Rose Durel, 32–33 (two entries)
Marianna, enslaved by Rose Durel, 32
Marie, girl enslaved by Jean Baptiste Durel, 12, 15–16, 24–25, 49
Marie, woman enslaved by Jean Baptiste Durel, 13, 16-18
Marie Jeanne, woman enslaved by Jean Baptiste Durel, 12, 15–16, 24, 170
Martin, Mathilde, 83
Martonne, free woman of color, 20
McCue, Billy, 143
McDonogh, John, 139
Meiners, Christoph, 108
Melice, enslaved by Ursin Durel (2), 88
Messant, Pierre, 53
Messant, Sophie, 53
Milon, Henriette, 64–69, 72, 79, 85, 104, 114, 116, 126
Monget, Angelique, 47
de Mons d'Orbigny, Louis-Hector, 43
de Mons d'Orbigny, Mathilde, 43
Monvoisin, Raymond, 106
Morin, Marie Adele, 81

N

Nancy, free Black woman, 63
Neptuno, enslaved by Rose Durel, 33
Nicholls, Francis T., 169
Noël, enslaved by Ursin Durel (2), 88
Northup, Solomon, 39, 45–46
Nott, Josiah, 107–9

O

Obama, Barak, 110
Octave, enslaved by Ursin Durel (2), 88
Octavie, enslaved by Ursin Durel (2), 88
O'Reilly, Alejandro, 9, 74

P

Pearse, Pádraic, 170
Pedro, enslaved by Rose Durel, 32–33 (2 entries)
Plantevigne, John, 140
Plessy, Homer, 125

Petre, enslaved by Jean Baptiste Durel, 13, 24
Philipe, enslaved by Florent Basile, 42
Pierre, enslaved by Florent Basile, 44–45
Pierre, enslaved by Ursin Durel (2), 88
de Pomarède, Jean Borie, 2
Principe, enslaved by Rose Durel, 33

Q
Quamana, enslaved Akan warrior, 56
Quays, William, 20

R
Ramon, enslaved by Rose Durel, 33
Reaud, Alex, 30
Reed, Theresa Durel, 157, 165, 170–71, 173
Richardson, Rodney, 158
Riché, Françoise, 20
Robinet, Marie Françoise, 51
Rochefort, Polymnie, 86, 134
Roman, Josephine, 40, 114
Romia, enslaved by Rose Durel, 32
Roosevelt, Franklin D., 151
Rosa, enslaved by Rose Durel, 32–33 (3 entries)
Rose, enslaved by Jean Baptiste Durel, 14, 24
Ruiz, Nellie, 160
Ruiz, Thelma (Durel), 134, 147, 158, 160
Rummel, Joseph F., 154, 164

S
de Salazar y Mendoza, Josef Francisco Xavier, 30
Same, enslaved by Rose Durel, 33
Santilly, Pierre François, 74
Scott, Jean, 174
Séjour, Victor, 120
Shaler, Nathaniel Southgate, 109
Songy family, 7
Soniat, Gustave, 129
Stowe, Harriet Beecher, 92
Suson, enslaved by Santilly, 74–75, 82

T
Telemac, enslaved by Rose Durel, 33
Thennat, Barbé, 62
Therese, enslaved by Jean Baptiste Durel, 13, 24
Thierry, Camile, 120
Thomas, Eva, ix, 162
Thompson, enslaved by Rose Durel, 33
Thriffiley, Frank, 142–43
Thriffiley, Bernadette, 143
Thriffiley, Loretta, 143
Thriffiley, Kate. *See* Durel, Kate
Thriffiley, Thomas, 143
Toussaint, enslaved by Françoise Dejan, 53
Truman, Harry, 154

U
de Ulloa, Don Antonio, 8

V
Valentino, enslaved by Rose Durel, 33
de Vaudreuil, Pierre de Rigaud, Marquis, 6
Victor, enslaved by Ursin Durel (2), 88
Villemont, Louis, 75
Voye, Madame, 11

W
Warmoth, Henry, 102
Washington, George, 7

www.ingramcontent.com/pod-product-compliance
Lightning Source LLC
LaVergne TN
LVHW090152201225
827871LV00004B/20
9781959569213